The Myth of Masculinity

The Myth of Masculinity

Joseph H. Pleck

The MIT Press
Cambridge, Massachusetts
London, England

This book was set in VIP Baskerville and VIP Gill Sans by DEKR Corp.
and printed and bound by Halliday Lithograph in the United States of
America.

Library of Congress Cataloging in Publication Data

Pleck, Joseph H.
  The myth of masculinity.

  Bibliography: p.
  Includes index.
  1. Men—United States.   2. Masculinity (Psychology)
3. Sex role—United States.   I. Title.
HQ1090.3.P57   305.3   81-6058
ISBN 0-262-16081-1   AACR2

Contents

Acknowledgments

The support of many colleagues and friends over the last ten years has been essential to the development of this book and to the earlier work that prepared me to write it. These include Elizabeth Pleck, Jack Sawyer, Robert Fein, Mary Rowe, Anne Peplau, Zick Rubin, Pauline Bart, James Harrison, Robert Brannon, Elizabeth Douvan, Robert Lewis, Joyce Lazar, Graham Staines, Alan Gross, Linda Garnets, and Jane Hood. Particular thanks are due to Robert Fein, who started me writing this book; Jim Harrison, with whom I first comprehensively explored the male sex role identity paradigm; Linda Garnets, with whom I further studied both the identity and strain paradigms; Alan Gross and Anne Peplau for their comments on an earlier draft; and Robert Brannon, who provided particularly detailed comments and warm support. I thank them all. I would also like to acknowledge with gratitude the moral support for the completion of the manuscript provided during 1978–1980 by the Wellesley College Center for Research on Women; its former Director, Carolyn M. Elliott; and its current Director, Laura Lein. In addition, I would like to thank Rebecca Fisher, Judy Paquette, Marguerite Rupp, and Tracy Sluicer for their valiant assistance in the preparation of the final manuscript.

Finally, I dedicate this book to my mother, Katherine F. Pleck, and to my father, Joseph H. Pleck.

Permissions

I gratefully acknowledge permission to quote excerpts from the following:

by Consulting Psychologists Press, Inc., Palo Alto, CA 94306. Reprinted by special permission of publisher.

David Abrahamsen, *The Psychology of Crime.* Copyright © 1965 by Columbia University Press. Reprinted by permission of publisher.

Theodor Adorno et al., *The Authoritarian Personality.* Copyright © 1950 by Harper and Row, Inc. Reprinted by permission of publisher.

David Matteson, *Adolescence Today: Sex Roles and the Search for Identity.* Copyright © 1975 by Dorsey Press. Reprinted by permission of publisher.

Joel Milgram and Dorothy Sciarra, "Male preschool teacher: The realities of acceptance," *Educational Forum* (1974) 38(2):245–247. Copyright © 1974 by Kappa Delta Pi Honor Society in Education. Reprinted by permission of publisher.

Talcott Parsons, "The social structure of the family," in Ruth N. Anshen (ed.), *The Family: Its Function and Destiny.* Copyright © 1959 by Harper and Row, Inc. Reprinted by permission of publisher.

Donald J. West et al., *Understanding Sexual Attacks.* Copyright © 1978 by Heineman Educational Books, Ltd. Reprinted by permission of publisher.

1

Psychology Constructs Masculinity

It is an unfortunate truth that a great many people in our culture do entertain feelings of incompetence about fulfilling their sex role as they define it for themselves. . . . One of the difficulties in helping people with this type of problem is that they are rarely aware of their inner sense of weakness. Furthermore, the whole matter of sex identity is such a sensitive issue that people become sharply defensive when you raise questions in that area. (Fisher and Fisher, 1976, p. 119)

This book critically analyzes the male sex role identity (MSRI) paradigm, a set of ideas about sex roles, especially the male role, that has dominated the academic social sciences since the 1930s and more generally has shaped our culture's view of the male role. In essence, this paradigm represents the way that our society has constructed a psychology of masculinity. Yet the MSRI paradigm heretofore has not received adequate critical attention; it has not been clearly identified as a general theoretical perspective, nor have its individual components been subjected to rigorous analysis.

A Quiz on Sex Roles

	True	False
1. Developing a secure sense of one's masculinity (for males) or femininity (for females) is one of the most important tasks in personality development.	——	——

2. A secure sense of masculinity or femininity comes primarily from one's relationship with the

parent of the same sex in childhood and
adolescence.   ____ ____

3. Excessive masculinity on the outside often
indicates that a man is unsure about his
masculinity on the inside.   ____ ____

4. Growing up in a household without a father is
likely to cause serious sex role identity problems
for boys.   ____ ____

5. Many things can go wrong in personality
development to cause people to be insecure in
their sex roles. As a result, a relatively large
proportion of people, especially males, have sex
role identity problems.   ____ ____

6. Homosexuality reflects a profoundly disturbed
sense of one's masculinity or femininity.   ____ ____

7. Two problems faced by men today compared
to a hundred years ago that make it hard for
them to feel really masculine are that their jobs
are more passive and sedentary and their
authority over their wives is diminished.   ____ ____

8. Having a secure sex role identity, as shown by
sex-appropriate traits and characteristics, is one
of the most important contributors to good
psychological adjustment.   ____ ____

9. One of the main sources of male violence,
crime, and delinquency is that many men need to
compensate for their insecure sense of
masculinity.   ____ ____

10. The reason for the initiation ceremonies for
the male adolescent in many cultures is that they
serve to help the boy develop a secure sex role
identity, especially in societies where the boy has
lived or associated primarily with women earlier
in life.   ____ ____

11. Because of his intense early identification
with his mother, a boy develops an early

feminine sex role identity, which later he must
overcome to have a secure masculine identity.   ———   ———

12. Black males are especially vulnerable to sex
role identity problems because of the high rate of
paternal absence and the lack of good male role
models among blacks.   ———   ———

13. Many men participate in bodybuilding and
sports to compensate for an inner insecurity in
their masculinity.   ———   ———

14. We need more men in daycare centers and
elementary schools to provide boys with male sex
role identity models.   ———   ———

15. The reason for the hostility and violence that
some men show toward women is men's fear of
the psychological femininity in themselves
deriving from their early relationships with their
mothers.   ———   ———

16. The current blurring of women's and men's
sex roles is making it hard for children to
develop healthy sex role identities.   ———   ———

The more statements you checked as true, the more your own
personal interpretation of the male role (and of sex roles in
general) has been influenced by the MSRI paradigm. Those to
whom I have administered this quiz on the average check half of
these sixteen items as true. It is not surprising that so many
endorse these statements; the ideas that they express have been
taught by psychologists and sociologists as the correct way of
understanding the psychology of masculinity.

In essence, the MSRI paradigm holds that the fundamental
problem of individual psychological development is establishing
a sex role identity. Sex role identity is the extremely fragile outcome of a highly risky developmental process, especially so for
the male. An individual's sex role identity ideally derives from
his or her relationship with the same-sex parent. A man's efforts
to attain a healthy sex role identity in this way are thwarted by
such factors as paternal absence, maternal overprotectiveness, the

feminizing influence of the schools, and the general blurring of male and female roles that is occurring now in society.

According to the MSRI paradigm, the failure of men to achieve masculine sex role identity is a major problem in our culture, one obvious expression of which is male homosexuality. A man also reveals his insecurity in his sex role identity by phenomena such as delinquency, violence, and hostility toward women. If we understand the factors that cause sex role identity problems in men, then we can prevent or reduce these problems in the future and perhaps even provide help now.

The distinctive feature of the MSRI paradigm is its view that sex roles develop from within, rather than being arbitrarily imposed from without: Because of an innate psychological need to develop sex role identity, the individual is preprogrammed to learn a traditional sex role as part of normal psychological development; thus culturally defined sex roles do not arbitrarily restrict individuals' potential—on the contrary, they are necessary external structures without which individuals could not develop normally. From this perspective, individuals must be fitted to traditional roles, and the problem of traditional sex roles is only that so many people fail to fit them, not the nature of the roles themselves.

Summary of Propositions

The MSRI paradigm can be formulated more systematically in eleven propositions, each of which represents a particular line of research on sex roles conducted by social scientists, particularly personality and social psychologists.

1. Sex role identity is operationally defined by measures of psychological sex typing, conceptualized in terms of psychological masculinity and/or femininity dimensions.
2. Sex role identity derives from identification-modeling and, to a lesser extent, reinforcement and cognitive learning of sex-typed traits, especially among males.
3. The development of appropriate sex role identity is a risky, failure-prone process, especially for males.
4. Homosexuality reflects a disturbance of sex role identity.
5. Appropriate sex role identity is necessary for good psychological adjustment because of an inner psychological need for it.

6. Hypermasculinity in males (exaggerated masculinity, often with negative social consequences) indicates insecurity in their sex role identities.

7. Problems of sex role identity account for men's negative attitudes and behaviors toward women.

8. Problems of sex role identity account for boys' difficulties in school performance and adjustment.

9. Black males are particularly vulnerable to sex role identity problems.

10. Male adolescent initiation rites are a response to problems of sex role identity.

11. Historical changes in the character of work and the organization of the family have made it more difficult for men to develop and maintain their sex role identities.

Propositions 1 and 2 concern the structure and developmental origins of sex role identity. Propositions 3–6 focus on the results of failure in sex role identity development. Propositions 7–11 interpret various problems faced by males in terms of sex role identity issues. Taken together, these eleven propositions constitute a comprehensive and consistent analysis—indeed, a world view—of sex roles.

I must acknowledge that the way I integrate these specific propositions about sex roles into the MSRI paradigm is an act of interpretation. This is unavoidable: identifying the theoretical perspective underlying research necessarily involves theoretical inference and speculation. A particular researcher may subscribe to some propositions while rejecting others. Still, the ideas of the identity paradigm form an internally consistent and comprehensive theory about sex roles that should be analyzed as a whole.

Although applicable in theory to both sexes, in practice these propositions predominantly concern males. Most of these propositions either specify ways that the development of sex role identity is more difficult for males than females or apply only to males. The key features of the MSRI paradigm were first developed and empirically tested in all-male samples. Further, I believe, these ideas developed in response to, and as part of, general cultural concerns about the male role. Therefore, although theoretically the paradigm is sufficiently general to describe the male or female sex role, I label it the *male* sex role identity paradigm to emphasize and make explicit its history and social function.

Cultural Importance of the MSRI Paradigm

When, ten years ago, I began studying the male role as a psychologist, I reviewed the discipline's standard arguments. Gradually, I came to see them as parts of the MSRI paradigm, a theoretical analysis of the sex roles I had been taught as an undergraduate and graduate student in psychology. Indeed, I came to realize, since this view dominates our culture more generally, I had been absorbing it since childhood.

It is difficult to convey the full historical and social significance of the MSRI paradigm in our culture. Since the 1930s, it has overwhelmingly dominated both scientific and popular conceptions of sex roles and their inherent problems. Many talented and creative American psychologists participated in its development; indeed, it may be said without exaggeration that the history of the lines of research that went into its formation is practically a history of American psychology related to sex roles between 1936 and the late 1970s. This underlying theoretical perspective has been so pervasive and so taken for granted that, until the present, both professionals and the public have accepted it uncritically, without being aware that it is only one possible way of understanding sex roles.

Because the MSRI paradigm generally is taken for granted, intellectual effort is required to look at it critically. Thus, although new ideas about the proper roles of men and women have swept through our society since the 1960s, the MSRI paradigm has not been called into question. A few examples will make the point. Ann Oakley's *Sex, Gender, and Society* (1974) perceptively countered many traditional arguments about the nature and sources of sex differences and sex roles but simply restates the traditional argument that a man's feminine psychological identification with his mother in infancy and early childhood is the major source of his sex role problems. Marshall Segall's *Human Behavior and Public Policy: Political Psychology* (1977) includes a chapter on sex roles providing a good review of recent feminist-oriented research on the problems of the female role, yet the short section on the male role in this chapter simply summarizes the traditional argument that violent male behavior results from insecurity in sex role identity due to such factors as paternal absence and unconscious feminine identification with the mother.

The MSRI paradigm may be found also in many recent books about the need for men's liberation. A frequent argument is that fathers should spend more time with their children, certainly a good recommendation. One of the most well-known recent books on men's liberation argues for it, however, on the basis of research allegedly showing that a son whose father is absent from the household is more likely to become a homosexual than a son whose father is present (Farrell, 1974, p. 116). Several other recent statements of the case for men's liberation (for example, Rudy and Peller, 1972; H. Goldberg, 1973, p. 73, and 1976, pp. 50, 180) exphasize that insecurity in sex role identity is a major problem of the male role.

An easy and usually accurate way of telling whether a particular argument derives from the MSRI paradigm is simply to note whether it has one or more of the following characteristics: (1) it uses terms like *insecure* or *inadequate;* (2) it emphasizes the potential psychologically harmful consequences of a man's relationship with his mother; and (3) it views homosexuality as the worst misfortune that can befall a man.

The MSRI paradigm is, ultimately, a product of its culture. It gives intellectual shape and scientific legitimacy to deep-seated cultural concerns about masculinity and its definition. Two nagging questions underlie the more than four decades of social scientific research rooted in the MSRI paradigm: What makes men less masculine than they should be? and, What can we do about it? Through the MSRI paradigm our society constructed a psychology of masculinity to answer these questions.

Evolution of the MSRI Paradigm

The MSRI paradigm has not remained static over time, but rather has evolved in response to trends in the social sciences and in the society at large. It originally grew out of the mental testing tradition in early American psychology. The successful development of standardized intelligence tests in the early twentieth century represented a milestone in the emergence of psychology as a modern science and provided the model that the first sex role identity researchers followed in the 1930s. Using the techniques pioneered in the study of intelligence, they created the first masculinity-femininity scales, tests designed to assess how individuals rank on a hypothetical continuum ranging from masculine to feminine. In this early phase, researchers conceptualized sex role identity as single, overall dimension in the personality (termed here the *simple* conception of sex role identity).

Beginning in the 1940s, the rising influence of psychoanalytic theory on academic psychology led to a second major phase of MSRI research. Based on the psychoanalytic concept of the unconscious, the paradigm now distinguished sex role identity at the conscious and unconscious levels. This *multileveled* conception led to the view that apparently masculine behavior in men might indicate overcompensation for an unconscious feminine identity. The multileveled conception of sex role identity generated many new lines of research, and dominated the field for two decades.

In the late 1960s, MSRI theorists began conceiving of masculinity and femininity as two independent psychological dimensions, rather than as opposite ends of the same dimension. In this conception, an individual's sex role identity can be *androgynous,* that is, both masculine *and* feminine at the same time; indeed, androgynous identity is viewed as the ideal. This development corresponded to the social critique of traditional sex roles emerging during this period.

The paradigm's evolution from the simple to the multileveled conception to the androgynous conception has been stimulated not only by larger trends in the social sciences and society but also by empirical problems internal to the paradigm. Research based on the simple concept of sex role identity did not yield the expected results. For example, groups of males predicted to have feminine identities (such as boys with absent fathers and homosexuals) often had *more,* not less, masculine scores than other males. The various masculinity-femininity tests proved to be less strongly related to each other than they should have been if they all assessed a single, global dimension of sex role identity in the personality.

Such findings could be explained by using the multileveled conception. Studies based on the multileveled conception, however, led to new problems. Researchers then searched for an alternative model of sex role identity that might resolve these problems and proposed, among others, the androgynous conception. In turn, research on androgyny has generated certain puzzling results.

Androgyny, however, has proved to be an important transitional concept to a whole new way of viewing sex roles that has emerged both in the social sciences and in society. Instead of seeing traditional sex roles as desirable and their internalization via sex role identity as the goal of psychological development, this new interpretation views these roles as limiting and constricting. I call this new interpretation of sex roles the sex role strain (SRS) paradigm, and it can be summed up in the following propositions (distinguished from MSRI propositions by stars).

1.* Sex roles are operationally defined by sex role stereotypes and norms.
2.* Sex roles are contradictory and inconsistent.
3.* The proportion of individuals who violate sex roles is high.
4.* Violating sex roles leads to social condemnation.
5.* Violating sex roles leads to negative psychological consequences.
6.* Actual or imagined violation of sex roles leads individuals to overconform to them.
7.* Violating sex roles has more severe consequences for males than females.
8.* Certain characteristics prescribed by sex roles are psychologically dysfunctional.
9.* Each sex experiences sex role strain in its paid work and family roles.
10.* Historical change causes sex role strain.

The brief history of sex role research just recounted fits the hypothetical pattern of scientific progress Thomas Kuhn describes in *The Structure of Scientific Revolutions* (1962). Kuhn argues that, contrary to the usual view, the most important scientific progress does not occur through the orderly accumulation of small increments of knowledge but rather through a discontinuous, sometimes quite abrupt, shift in the fundamental theoretical paradigm underlying research. Generalizing from analyses of the transitions from Ptolemaic to Copernican astronomy and from Newtonian to Einsteinian physics, Kuhn holds that, in any area of scientific inquiry at any given time, a dominant paradigm determines the lines of research conducted and provides the conceptual context for interpreting their results. If the paradigm is not valid, then its various lines of research begin to generate anomalous results—that is, findings inconsistent with, and unexplainable by, the paradigm. Investigators committed to the dominant paradigm at first make efforts to explain away or discount these anomalous results. As anomalous results accumulate, the paradigm is reformulated in an increasingly complicated fashion, in an effort to incorporate them. Numerous variant versions of the paradigm appear. Eventually, however, these reformulations are recognized as theoretically cumbersome and unpersuasive. The old paradigm is abandoned, and a new and fundamentally different paradigm emerges. According to Kuhn, it is precisely this shift in paradigms that constitutes scientific progress.

The identity paradigm has indeed dominated research on sex roles for four decades, and its anomalous results have caused it to evolve through three major stages (as well as a host of minor reformulations). And in fact a new and radically different paradigm is taking shape.

This book is a systematic critique of the MSRI paradigm and offers the SRS paradigm as an alternative. It discusses the key references in the primary research literature relevant to these paradigms, identifying, interpreting, and evaluating their meaning and implications. It thus aims to make the primary literature accessible to the thoughtful general reader. While the book attempts to be nontechnical, it is clearly analytical in nature. The sex role field is now in fact in a critical transitional stage in which the elements of the emerging new paradigm have become visible, but many elements of the old still persist. By analyzing the old paradigm and systematically formulating the new, this book aims to foster this transition.

Definitions

Sex Role

The term *sex role* refers to the set of behaviors and characteristics widely viewed as (1) typical of women or men (*sex role stereotypes*), and (2) desirable for women or men (*sex role norms*). The behaviors and characteristics comprising sex roles include aspects of personality (traits, dispositions) and social roles (especially activities performed at the job and in the family). In personality, the male role may be characterized as aggressive, achievement oriented, and emotionally inexpressive. In specific social roles, it may be characterized by such terms as breadwinner, husband, and father.

This definition of sex role differs from that of the more general concept of social role in that most definitions of the latter are concerned only with desirable behaviors and characteristics (Thomas and Biddle, 1966, p. 29; R. Brown, 1965, pp. 154–155), while those of the former consider both desirable *and* typical behaviors and characteristics (see also Brannon and David, 1976,

p. 5). In more abstract language, other social roles are usually defined only in prescriptive terms, whereas sex role is defined in both prescriptive and descriptive terms. A sex role is a special type of social role—special in both the kind of social group to which it refers and its descriptive element.

Sex Role Stereotypes

Sex role stereotypes are widely shared descriptive beliefs about what the sexes actually *are*. Thus they constitute the first of the two components of the definition of sex role. Sex role stereotypes can be assessed by asking individuals to rate each sex as a group (for example, "men," "the typical man") according to a standardized list of adjectives. They are assessed also by the items in sex role attitude scales concerning the actual characteristics of the sexes today.

Sex Role Norms

Sex role norms are widely shared prescriptive beliefs about what the sexes ideally *should be*. Thus they constitute the second component of the definition of sex role. Sex role norms can be assessed by asking individuals to rate the characteristics that are prescriptively expected for each sex (for example, rating "the ideal man"), again using a standardized list of adjectives. They are assessed also by items in sex role attitude scales concerning the characteristics that are desired and valued in each sex.

Both sex role stereotypes and norms are defined as widely shared beliefs. If only one individual is firmly convinced that all women are mathematical geniuses, we would not conclude that mathematical genius is part of the female stereotype. Stereotypes and norms are group, not individual, phenomena. Nonetheless, it is common and convenient to refer to a single individual's descriptive or prescriptive beliefs about the sexes as that individual's sex role stereotypes or sex role norms.

Sex Typing

Sex role stereotypes and norms are beliefs held about men and women as social groups. *Sex typing,* by contrast, refers to the actual characteristics of a particular individual along sex role related dimensions. From the point of view of an individual, sex role stereotypes and norms are third-person characteristics ("Men are..."), while sex typing is a first-person characteristic ("I am. . .."). Unlike stereotypes and norms, sex typing is not a component of the definition of sex role.

Sex typing can be considered in two related but different contexts. The first is differences *between* the sexes; here, the development of sex typing refers to the processes whereby males and females come to have different characteristics on the average. The second, more usual context concerns differences *within* each of the sexes; here, the development of sex typing refers, for example, to the process whereby one boy develops more "masculine" behaviors and characteristics than does another boy.

Sex typing is assessed by scales in which individuals rate themselves (or are rated by others) along sex role-related dimensions. Traditional masculinity-femininity tests and certain toy-preference tests for children are examples of sex typing measures. Newer scales, such as the Bem Sex Role Inventory (Bem, 1974) and the Personal Attributes Questionnaire (Spence, Helmreich, and Stapp, 1974) are also sex typing measures. These newer scales are based on a different theory of the psychometric structure of sex typing than are older measures, but they are sex typing measures nonetheless.

Sex Role Identity

Sex role identity is a hypothetical psychological structure by which, it is thought, an individual psychologically "validates" or "affirms" his or her sex group. By developing sex role identity, an individual goes beyond the simple cognitive awareness of his or her biological sex to psychologically identifying with it. Sex role identity is manifested in sex-appropriate traits, attitudes, and interests. It is assessed by measures of sex typing. In effect, sex role identity is a particular theoretical interpretation of the nature and meaning of sex typing.

Several related terms have been used in the literature to describe what is referred to here as sex role identity: sex identity, sexual identity, and sex role identification. I prefer *sex role identity* to these other terms. *Sex identity* and *sexual identity* often connote or suggest specifically *sexual* behavior, especially sexual perference (that is, heterosexual, bisexual, or homosexual choice of sexual partners). By its fourth proposition, the MSRI paradigm does in fact assume that sexual preference is a manifestation—perhaps the central manifestation—of sex role identity. I believe, though, that it is confusing to name the concept in a way that ties it to this one specific consequence. *Sex role identification* suffers by being too closely related to another particular proposition of the paradigm, namely, the second. *Identification* properly describes the major psychological process by which sex role identity is thought to be acquired, though it is often used to describe the hypothetical outcome of this process. To avoid confusion, in this work *identification* will describe only the hypothetical psychological process of modeling after same-sex models, while identity will refer to the outcome of this as well as other hypothetical processes in the acquisition of sex role identity.

In some recent literature, the term *gender role* is preferred to sex role (for example, Stoller, 1968; Money and Ehrhardt, 1972). The more familiar and widely used term sex role will be employed here, however.

The Male Sex Role Identity (MSRI) Paradigm: A Propositional Summary

Since the gender identity and its accompanying roles are so dependent upon the ways which parents relate to the child, interact with one another, and regard themselves, it becomes apparent that all sorts of variations in gender identity and in the security and stability of the gender identity can develop. Because the entire pattern of a person's relationships will be carried out in accord with his sex, the gender identity will have far-reaching repercussions. (Lidz, 1968, pp. 217–218)

It is a surprising fact that the theorists and researchers who, in my view, have been the major intellectual architects of the MSRI paradigm (Parsons, 1947, 1954, 1959; D. Brown, 1956, 1957a; Colley, 1959; Miller and Swanson, 1960; Slater, 1963; Johnson, 1963; Lynn, 1969; Biller, 1972, 1974) nowhere have presented a systematic formulation of it.[1] Perhaps no one has felt the need to present it systematically precisely because, as the adage puts it, the fish will be the last to discover the ocean. It becomes possible to describe a paradigm systematically only when alternatives are recognized. In any event, I find myself in the ironic position of presenting the MSRI paradigm more comprehensively than have its supporters.

But there is another reason that the MSRI paradigm has not yet received definitive expression: Far from being monolithic and static, it has evolved, and some of its key propositions have two or more alternative forms. These alternatives developed in response to the failure of earlier formulations. This is exactly the process described by Kuhn.

Proposition 1. *Sex role identity is operationally defined by measures of psychological sex typing, conceptualized in terms of psychological masculinity and/or femininity dimensions.*

Masculinity and femininity are important aspects of human personality. They are not to be thought of as lending to it merely a superficial coloring and flavor; rather they are one of a small number of cores around which the structure of personality gradually takes shape.... The M-F dichotomy, in various patterns, has existed throughout history, and is still firmly established in our mores. In a considerable fraction of the population it is the source of many acute difficulties in the individual's social and sexual adjustment. (Terman and Miles, 1936, p. 451)

Part of everyone's total identity is the pattern of sex-linked characteristics, both learned and unlearned, that mark him as masculine or feminine. American women and men, for example, differ in physical strength, gait, vocal inflection, posture, initiative taken in courtship, types of interest, and the like. Depending on a particular man's characteristics in each of these areas, he may be classified as being predominantly masculine, or predominantly feminine, or in some intermediate group. (Miller and Swanson, 1960, p. 88)

In many ways, the first proposition is the most difficult and abstract. Males vary among themselves, females vary among themselves, and the two sexes vary between themselves, on a wide variety of specific traits, attitudes, and interests that are related to sex roles, that is, that are culturally interpreted as being more typical and appropriate for one sex or the other. In the literature of developmental psychology, *sex typing* is the term used for this variation in sex role-relevant characteristics, which occurs both within and between the sexes. As used here, sex typing does not carry with it any assumptions about the relationships among specific sex-typed characteristics or its psychological sources and consequences. At the broadest level, the MSRI paradigm is a general interpretation of the nature, sources, and consequences of sex typing.

Psychological Sex Typing: Three Conceptions

The MSRI paradigm views sex typing as internally organized along psychological masculinity and/or femininity dimensions, but the paradigms' conceptualization of its exact structure has varied. It is easiest to describe the different conceptions of sex typing in the MSRI paradigm in terms of their historical development.

The Simple Conception

At first it was held that sex-typed characteristics do not vary randomly or haphazardly within each sex, so that not all random combinations of sex-typed characteristics are equally possible. On the contrary, if a man is strong in one sex-appropriate trait (for example, aggressiveness), hypothetically he will tend to be strong in other sex-appropriate traits (for example, interest in sports) and weak in sex-inappropriate traits (for example, emotional sensitivity). In other words, in this earliest stage the MSRI paradigm conceptualized sex typing as a single bipolar continuum ranging from masculinity at one pole to femininity at the other. Technically, this is known as the *unitary-bipolar* conception of sex typing; it is also referred to here as the *simple* conception. Along this dimension individuals of the same sex or different sexes may be compared; any individual's place on this masculinity-femininity continuum may be determined by testing for any set of specific sex-typed characteristics. For example, a researcher might create a questionnaire that asks whether a person likes physical contact sports, competing with people, reading mechanics magazines, and so forth—this is what most so-called masculinity-femininity (m-f) tests do. The researcher then adds the number of masculine things the person likes and subtracts the number of feminine things the person likes to yield a single, overall m-f score, according to which the individual's degree of sex typing is either high, low, or in between. In corresponding fashion, the individual's sex role identity would be rated adequate, inadequate, or in between.

The Multileveled Conception

In the second stage of theoretical development, a more complex and sophisticated *multileveled* conception of both sex typing and sex role identity emerged, according to which there are several levels of sex role identity in the individual. This notion is well established in everyday discourse, as when we speak of someone being "sure" of his masculinity or her femininity "on the surface" or "outside," but being insecure "deep down" or "on the inside." Miller and Swanson's (1960) distinction between conscious and unconscious levels of sex role identity, and their argument that individuals "compensate for" or "defend against" cross-sex identity at the unconscious level by developing appropriate sex role identity at the more superficial, conscious level, is the most important theoretical formulation of this idea. Various m-f tests have been developed to assess sex role identity at the unconscious level (for example, by assessing preferences for different kinds of shapes and figures). The multileveled conception necessarily requires a more complex classification of the types of sex role identity than does the simple; men characterized by conscious masculine identity and unconscious feminine identity are of particular theoretical interest.

The Androgynous Conception

In the third and most recent stage of development, the notion of different levels of sex role identity is dropped, but a new distinction is introduced in its place: Psychological masculinity and femininity are treated as two distinct, independent dimensions rather than as opposite poles of the same dimension. This conception of the internal structure of sex typing, and thus of sex role identity, is referred to technically as the *dual-unipolar* conception; it may also be called the *androgynous* conception. Interpreting androgyny as a recent phase in the evolution of the MSRI paradigm will be justified later when it is argued that certain aspects of recent research on androgyny clearly fit within, and extend, this paradigm; other aspects are clearly innovative, however, and contribute significantly to the emerging new paradigm.

All three stages of the conceptualization of the internal structure of sex-typed traits, attitudes, and interests see these sex-typed characteristics as organized along dimensions of psychological masculinity and/or femininity. The exact nature of the one or more dimensions has been formulated in three different general ways, but all these formulations assume dimensions of the personality experienced by the individual as masculine and/or feminine.

Sex Typing as the Operationalization of Sex Role Identity

In science, concepts are given operational definitions so that they may be studied quantitatively. Sex typing is the operational definition of sex role identity, which is to say that the latter is studied by measuring the former. For example, according to the simple conception of sex role identity, a male who scores as highly masculine in his sex typing (that is, has various masculine-typed traits, attitudes, and interests) is described as having an "adequate," "secure," or "appropriate" sex role identity, while a male at the other end of the sex typing continuum (that is, has few masculine and many feminine preferences) is described as having an "inadequate," "insecure," "inappropriate," "cross-sex," or "disturbed" sex role identity. As another example, a researcher will study the hypothesis that paternal absence causes sex role identity problems among boys by comparing scores on sex typing measures of boys with fathers to boys without fathers.

Proposition 2. *Sex role identity derives from identification-modeling and, to a lesser extent, reinforcement and cognitive learning of sex-typed traits, especially among males.*

An identification is a belief that some of the attributes of a model (parents, siblings, relatives, peers, and so on) belong to the self. If a six-year-old boy is identified with his father, he necessarily regards himself as possessing some of his father's characteristics, one of which is maleness or masculinity. . . . One of the important consequences of the boy's desire for a strong identification with his father is his attempt to take on the father's characteristics. For each time he successfully imitates a behavior or adopts an attitude of the father, he perceives an increased similarity to the latter. This perception of increased similarity strengthens his belief that he possesses some of the father's covert characteristics. One of these covert attributes is the self-label of masculinity. (Kagan, 1964a, pp. 146–147)

Demands for masculine sex-role behavior are often made by women in the absence of readily available male models to demonstrate typical sex-role behavior. Such demands are often presented in the form of punishing, *negative* admonishments, i.e., telling the boy what not to do rather than what to do and backing up the demands with punishment. . . . Such methods of demanding typical sex-role behavior of boys are very poor methods of inducing learning. . . . Negative admonishments given at an age when the child is least able to understand them and supported by punishment are thought to produce anxiety concerning sex-role behavior. (Lynn, 1966, pp. 468–469)

Males tend to identify with a culturally defined masculine role, whereas females tend to identify with their mothers. (Lynn, 1969, p. 97)

The MSRI paradigm views the acquisition of sex role identity as occurring primarily through psychological processes during socialization—through *learning* in the broadest sense of the term. In the simple and multileveled conceptions of sex role identity, the foremost of these processes is *identification* with or *modeling* after the parent of the same sex; there is a theoretical difference between the two terms, important in another context, but they may be combined here into the single term *identification-modeling*. To a lesser extent, individuals may also identify with other same-sex adults. (According to the androgynous conception of sex role identity, the child identifies with both parents.) At the same time, two other processes are also important: reinforcement for sex-appropriate behavior and cognitive learning of the cultural norms and stereotypes for one's own sex. (According to the androgynous conception, there are reinforcement and cognitive learning of both masculine and feminine characteristics for both sexes.) For several reasons discussed in the next proposition, it is argued that adult same-sex models are less available to males than to females. As a result, reinforcement and cognitive learning are more important contributors to sex role identity in males than in females.

Proposition 3. *The development of appropriate sex role identity is a risky, failure-prone process, especially for males.*

Males tend to have greater difficulty than females in achieving same-sex identification. . . . More males than females fail more or less completely in achieving same-sex identification, making instead an opposite-sex identification. (Lynn, 1969, p. 103)

If the emergence of the sex role-typed traits used as indicators of sex role identity depended only on the unfolding of some inner biological programming, then sex role identity development could never fail. But the acquisition of sex role identity is thought to depend critically on psychological learning processes requiring facilitative environmental conditions (in particular, the presence of same-sex parental identification models). Thus the development of sex role identity is a risky undertaking.

It is considered an especially risky undertaking for males because in their case several factors hamper identification-modeling, the primary process for acquiring sex role identity. First, every child's earliest strong attachment is to its mother, who for the male child is of course the opposite-sex parent. According to the MSRI paradigm, this attachment leads to a feminine, cross-sex identity that has to be overcome if a boy is to develop his male sex role identity, and even so it may present an enduring problem for the male. Second, fathers (and other adult males) are considerably less available .to sons than mothers (and other adult males) are to daughters—certainly less available in terms of the time they spend with boys, and perhaps as well in terms of other characteristics such as warmth. Third, fathers are more likely than mothers to be entirely absent during some significant period during child rearing.

For these reasons males must rely more on the two other hypothesized processes for acquiring sex role identity: reinforcement and cognitive learning. According to the identity paradigm, however, these processes do not lead to a sex role identity as secure as that rooted primarily in identification: In the view of the simple and the androgynous conceptions, reinforcement and cognitive learning are not as efficient in producing sex role identity as identification; in the view of the multileveled conception, reinforcement and cognitive learning produce sex role identity only at the more superficial, conscious levels of personality.

Proposition 4. *Homosexuality reflects a disturbance of sex role identity.*

The passive male homosexual and the active female homosexual are individuals whose sexual behavior is to be understood as an outgrowth or expression of their overall inversion; the male invert psychologically perceives himself as a female, and accordingly looks to the "opposite" sex for sexual gratification. . . . Inversion has its roots in the earliest years of life when the child forms, at first involuntarily and later consciously, an identification-attachment to the parent of the opposite sex and thereby introjects the sex role of the opposite sex. The invert, then, is a psychosomatic misfit, having the body of one sex and the personality of the other sex. (Brown, 1975b, pp. 615, 618)

A central component of healthy sex role identity, according to this proposition, is sexual attraction to members of the other sex. Thus homosexuality is a principal manifestation of disturbed sex role identity; if a person sexually prefers members of the same sex, this indicates that the individual identifies with the other sex. For example, if a man is sexually attracted to other men, this must mean that at some deep level he experiences himself to be a woman and has a feminine sex role identity.

Proposition 5. *Appropriate sex role identity is necessary for good psychological adjustment because of an inner psychological need for it.*

Personal normality presupposes that an individual has assimilated not only those values and ideals which are regarded as necessary and proper for all persons, but also those which are uniquely appropriate to one's sex role, as a man or as a woman. When identification has occurred predominantly with the opposite-sexed parent rather than the parent of the same sex, the individual is predisposed to homosexuality. Where there is a divided sexual identification, the resulting personality is likely to be neurotic. (Mowrer, 1950, p. 15)

Some children either resent or experience anxiety over the behaviors that are assigned to their biological sex. This assumption is not inconsistent with the fact that some adolescents and adults strive to avoid adoption of sex-typed responses because of anxiety over the behaviors that are prescribed for their sex role. These individuals are typically in conflict and are likely to manifest a variety of psychopathological symptoms. (Kagan, 1964a, pp. 145–146)

The father is an important model for his child. The father's positive involvement facilitates the development of the boy's cognitive functioning, self-concept, his ability to control his impulses and to function independently and responsibly, and his overall interpersonal competence. Much of the father's influence is related to his impact on the boy's sex role development. (Biller, 1974, p. 84)

This is perhaps the most fundamental proposition in the MSRI paradigm. It implies that the males with the most stereotypically masculine psychological characteristics should show the most favorable scores on measures of psychological adjustment.

Interestingly, even the most systematic formulations of the MSRI paradigm do not address directly the reason for this conjectured relationship. There are, however, three logically distinct hypotheses to account for it: *innate psychological need, situational adaptation,* and *social approval.* Of these, the identity paradigm adheres to the first (the latter two will be discussed fully later).

According to the first hypothesis, it is not psychologically sufficient for individuals simply to be cognitively aware that they are males or females; they have an innate psychological need to "validate" or "affirm" their biological sex by having sex role identities (which are measured by sex typing tests). If this innate need is not satisfied, then the individual will be psychologically maladjusted.

In conjunction with the simple conception of sex role identity, the fifth proposition leads to the specific expectation that among males masculinity should be positively related to good psychological adjustment. The multileveled conception leads to a more complex set of predictions: Masculine conscious sex role identity leads to good adjustment if the unconscious identity is also masculine; if conscious masculine identity is combined with unconscious feminine identity (that is, hypermasculinity), then certain distinctive forms of maladjustment will be evident; and if sex role identity at both levels is feminine, then the male generally will be maladjusted. According to the androgynous conception, good psychological adjustment goes along with having both traditionally masculine and feminine characteristics.

Proposition 6. *Hypermasculinity in males (exaggerated masculinity, often with negative social consequences) indicates insecurity in their sex role identities.*

Regardless of his actual identity, each male who is at all sensitive to the values of his peers is inclined to view himself in as masculine a light as possible; this identity is most rewarded. If he is actually feminine, he may repress the signs of this identity, or he may acknowledge them but misinterpret their significance. (Miller and Swanson, 1960, p. 88)

Structural features of contemporary societies create a problem of masculine identification. Boys initially identify with and depend on their mothers, but they realize that they must, when they grow up, become men and not women. Much of the exaggerated roughness and toughness of preadolescent and adolescent boys should be understood . . . as the result of unconscious needs to repudiate a natural identification with their mothers. (Toby, 1966, p. 20)

One might expect high-scoring [that is, authoritarian] men to think of themselves as very masculine, and that this claim would be the more insistent the greater the underlying feelings of weakness. Low-scoring men, on the other hand, having actually more personal and masculine identity—perhaps by virtue of having had less threatening parental figures—can afford to admit failures and doubts along these lines. In fact, there seems to be, in the high-scoring men, more of what may be called *pseudo-masculinity*—as defined by boastfulness about such traits as determination, energy, industry, independence, decisiveness, and will power—and less admission of passivity. . . . The typical low-scoring man more readily accepts his own femininity than the high scorer. (Adorno et al., 1950, pp. 428, 405)

This proposition can be viewed as an elaboration of part of the fifth proposition. Following the multileveled conception of sex role identity (specifically, Miller and Swanson's formulation of it), the MSRI paradigm distinguishes two kinds of men with conscious masculine sex role identities: those with and those without *unconscious* masculine sex role identities. The MSRI paradigm describes the latter category of men as *hypermasculine*. That is, these men show extreme, exaggerated masculine behaviors at the conscious level in order to "compensate for" or "defend against" their insecure male identities at the unconscious level.

The hypermasculine behaviors most often studied include crime and violence, repressive social attitudes, and bodybuilding. Hypermasculinity is seen also as one source of men's negative attitudes and behaviors toward women (see the next proposition). Hereafter the term *hypermasculinity hypothesis* describes the argument that exaggerated, negative male behaviors result from insecurity in male sex role identity.

Proposition 7. *Problems of sex role identity account for men's negative attitudes and behaviors toward women.*

A boy, in his attempt to gain an elusive masculine identification, often comes to define his masculinity largely in negative terms, as that which is not feminine or involved with women. There is an internal and external aspect to this. Internally, the boy tries to reject his mother and deny his attachment to her and the strong dependence on her that he still feels. He also tries to deny the deep personal identification with her that has developed during his early years. He does this by repressing whatever he takes to be feminine inside himself, and, importantly, by denigrating whatever he considers to be feminine in the outside world. (Chodorow, 1974, p. 50)

Since it is "girl-like" activities that provoked the punishment administered in an effort to induce sex-typical behavior in boys, in developing dislike for the activity which led to such punishment the boys should develop hostility toward "girl-like" activities. Also, boys should be expected to generalize and consequently develop hostility toward all females as representatives of this disliked role. (Lynn, 1966, p. 469)

The MSRI paradigm distinguishes three different (and somewhat inconsistent) processes whereby failures in the development of sex role identity in males produce negative attitudes toward (and in extreme cases sexual and physical violence against) women. First, all children early in life experience the mother as a powerful, dominating, overwhelming figure. The female child, by virtue of being the same sex as the mother, is able to deal with and overcome this perception of the mother by identifying with her. The male child, however, is not able to solve the problem in this simple way, and instead responds to this perception by hating and fearing his mother. Males ultimately generalize these feelings to all women.

Second, the boy's early relationship with his mother results in an unconscious feminine identification with her. The boy defends against this unconscious feminine part of himself by developing negative attitudes and behaviors toward those who actually *are* feminine. This argument is, thus, a specific application of the hypermasculinity hypothesis.

Third, the development of male sex role identity depends in large part on being punished by the mother (and by other women) for feminine behavior. Thus the boy comes to associate women with being punished, and therefore develops hostility to women.

Proposition 8.   *Problems of sex role identity account for boys' difficulties in school performance and adjustment.*

Though run at the top by men, schools are essentially feminine institutions, from nursery school through graduate school. In the school, women set the standards for adult behavior, and many favor students, male and female, who most conform to their own behavior norms— polite, clean, obedient, neat and nice ones. (Sexton, 1970, p. 25)

This proposition (see particularly Sexton, 1970; Biller, 1973, 1974) holds that the educational system, especially elementary education, exacerbates boys' sex role identity difficulties. In the schools, most teachers are female, and male sex role models are lacking. Also, it is argued, teachers punish masculinity and reward femininity in boys. As a result of these and other factors, boys perceive schools as feminized environments and show poor school performance as well as other problems. Theorists call for increasing the proportion of male teachers, especially at the elementary level, and masculinizing the schools more generally to overcome these problems. I shall refer to this general argument as the *school feminization hypothesis.*

Proposition 9.   *Black males are particularly vulnerable to sex role identity problems.*

For the black man in this country, it is not so much a matter of acquiring manhood as it is a struggle to feel it his own. Whereas the white man regards his manhood as an ordained right, the black man is engaged in a never-ending battle for its possession. For the black man, attaining any portion of manhood is an active process. He must penetrate barriers and overcome opposition in order to assume a masculine posture. For the inner psychological obstacles to manhood are never so formidable as the impediments woven into American society. (Grier and Cobbs, 1966, p. 59)

According to this proposition, the black male has been psychologically emasculated by slavery. Moreover, the acquisition of appropriate male identity is more difficult for blacks because of the higher rate of paternal absence among them. Further, when they are present, many black fathers are poor role models for their sons. Sex role identity problems among black males are then reinforced by high rates of unemployment as well as overrepresentation in low-paying, low-prestige jobs. The problem is particularly severe for black males in low-paying service jobs that carry the connotations of servility or women's work.

Proposition 10. *Male adolescent initiation rites are a response to problems of sex role identity.*

We . . . present the cross-sex identity and initiation hypothesis explicitly as follows: In societies with maximum conflict in sex identity, e.g., where a boy initially sleeps exclusively with his mother and where the domestic unit is patrilocal and hence controlled by men, there will be initiation rites at puberty which function to resolve this conflict in identity. This hypothesis suggests that the initiation rites serve psychologically to brainwash the primary feminine identity and to establish firmly the secondary male identity. (Burton and Whiting, 1961, p. 90)

This proposition holds that male initiation rites serve to build or consolidate male sex role identity and are especially necessary in societies in which childrearing arrangements make it difficult for boys to identify with their fathers and other adult males. Foremost among these childrearing arrangements is a pattern called *exclusive mother-child sleeping arrangements,* that is, the child sleeps in its mother's room until a quite late age, and often the father does not live in the same household—a pattern in some primitive societies. The argument is that in such societies, initiation rites serve to counteract the sex role identity problems this and other childrearing arrangements cause males.

Proposition 11. *Historical changes in the character of work and the organization of the family have made it more difficult for men to maintain their sex role identities.*

The average American man may not yet be aware that he is in crisis. He believes that as a male his position—social, economic, and sexual—

makes him superior to the female. Nevertheless, all through American society, the male's behavior shows that he actually is experiencing a change which affects his traditional roles as father, lover, and provider. This change may be summed up in a single word: emasculation. The American male is being operated on by a force other than the castrating female, however; he is being shaped by a technologically oriented culture. (Ruitenbeek, 1967, p. 17)

This is the one proposition in the MSRI paradigm pertaining specifically to men's adult social roles at the job and in the family. It sees a threat to the traditional ways in which men have validated their sex role identities from two developments: the dominance men traditionally had in relation to women and in the family is being replaced by more egalitarian relationships; the man's work role is undergoing change, becoming less physical and independent, and more sedentary and passive. The solution to these problems, from the perspective of the MSRI paradigm, is to restore men's traditional social roles with women, in the family, and at the job.

Masculinity and femininity are important aspects of human personality. They are not to be thought of as lending to it merely a superficial coloring and flavor; rather they are one of a small number of cores around which the structure of personality gradually takes shape.... The M-F dichotomy, in various patterns, has existed throughout history, and is still firmly established in our mores. In a considerable fraction of the population it is the source of many acute difficulties in the individual's social and sexual adjustment. (Terman and Miles, 1936, p. 451)

Part of everyone's total identity is the pattern of sex-linked characteristics, both learned and unlearned, that mark him as masculine or feminine. American women and men, for example, differ in physical strength, gait, vocal inflection, posture, initiative taken in courtship, types of interest, and the like. Depending on a particular man's characteristics in each of these areas, he may be classified as being predominantly masculine, or predominantly feminine, or in some intermediate group. (Miller and Swanson, 1960, p. 88)

Proposition 1. *Sex role identity is operationally defined by measures of psychological sex typing, conceptualized in terms of psychological masculinity and/or femininity dimensions.*

Sex Typing in Males: Two Case Studies

There is nothing abstract about the concept of sex typing. Consider Kagan and Moss's (1962) well-known longitudinal study of personality development, *Birth to Maturity: A Study in Psychological Development*, which examines the development of personality characteristics over the life cycle by comparing the personality ratings and evaluations given a group of males and females at various times during their childhood, adolescence, and adulthood. Sex typing is one of the work's key variables of interest. To show how this rating is made, as well as to illustrate the meaning of the concept, Kagan and Moss reproduce excerpts from the case records of one boy rated masculine and another boy classified nonmasculine.

These case records describe males who were young boys in the 1940s; *S* is an abbreviation used in psychological research for *the subject* (that is, the person being observed or described).

Excerpts from the case study of the masculine boy include the following:

(Age 3) In nursery school *S* was extremely energetic. Even when pushing small cars around the floor he seemed to be putting the greatest possible force into it.

(Age 6) With adults he usually tried to get his own way, and he required supervision when some desire was inconsistent with the requirements of adults. . . . He was impetuous and unrestrained in his vocalizations, interrupting others and arguing right through a peer's explanation. He indulged in a lot of competitive word-games in which he compared ability, possessions, hurled insults, challenges, experiences, and stories. . . .

(Age 7) *S* is a well-built, attractive looking youngster; a real little boy. When I saw him, he was building a barracks with blocks. There was a good deal of give and take between the children. *S* had built the barracks, and another boy built a torpedo boat. This quite naturally led to war-play. In a very short time all the children in the room were machine-gunning each other. *S* yelled to another boy, "I'm the Japs and you're the Germans. No, what I mean is him and me are the Japs and you're the Americans. All guns turn this way. . . ."

(Age 7½) He loves to play and exert himself physically but does ·not like to lose. His honesty in competitive situations is sketchy, not listening to the directions and seeing how much he can get away with. There is much compensatory clowning and bravado, and *S* might say, "I let him beat me because I thought there would be more races and I could have beat him in there if I had wanted to." While *S* is a terrific *alibi Ike,* he would argue over every score he received. *S* would be a much better athlete if he did not try so very hard to win. (Pp. 161–162)

By contrast, Kagan and Moss describe the nonmasculine boy as follows:

(Age 3) *S* is a pale, bleached-out looking child with blond hair, light blue eyes, and very little color in his face. He is tall, thin, and stoop-shouldered. He lacks compactness and sturdiness of muscle or body build. He gave the general impression of being gangling, and this was accentuated by the fact that he did not have good control over his body.

(Age 4) He was an overly dressed boy, always very trim, and never approaching the usual group dishevelment at the end of the day. S was also able to sustain a thoroughly fatuous smile for long periods of time. S seemed to be on the sedentary side, and in most activities he showed no vigor. . . .

(Age 6) Pasty-skinned, skinny, a loiterer, a slumper, and given either to frozen periods or taking queer gangling or stiff poses. He seemed less like a nursery-school child than a miniature caricature of an adolescent with self-consciousness and emotional difficulties getting in the way of whatever motor controls he might have. S was picked on a good deal, and much of his behavior invited teasing. When someone turned on him, he became helpless, cried, ran to an adult, or sat with a mute grin. He seemed to have no resistance against verbal attacks. S often commented that there was no reason for him to make anything because the other kids would break it. S did not seem to quite fit into the group. He was much like a 2-year-old in his reaction to pain and was helpless when someone else was hurt. In contrast to the interest of most boys in athletics or construction, S became interested in flowers. He was very careful as he picked them so that the stems wouldn't be hurt, sorting out a bunch of beautifully contrasting colors and making up names for the flowers. Hyacinths, for example, were "those sparkly purple flowers." He quickly caught on to the use of the magnifying glass and eagerly brought in specimens of flowers to examine. Occasionally he took delight in the dolls or tiny dishes when he thought no one was looking at him. . . .

(Age 11) S does not participate at all on the playground with the other boys. The teachers often find him in the schoolroom when he should be out on the playground with his peers. He does not seem to care about being active and would rather be by himself. He has become more interested in reading lately, and he likes books. (Pp. 163–165)

These case reports are particularly rich in data about traditional conceptions of masculinity. Most of the time, however, researchers assess sex typing not by such elaborate case studies but by masculinity-femininity (m-f) tests.

Proposition 1 cannot be evaluated in an empirical sense, since it is a definition. Instead, this chapter will consider the issues that have arisen at each of the three successive stages in the identity paradigm's conceptualization of sex typing: simple, multileveled, and androgynous.

The Simple Conception of Sex Typing

Over the past forty years, a great many tests have been devised to assess the simple conception of sex typing, beginning with Terman and Miles's (1936) Attitude-Interest Analysis Test (AIAT). The basic strategy for devising simple sex typing tests is called the *known groups method*. Researchers administer a large pool of potential items to two groups already "known" to differ in the concept being studied—in this case, sex role identity. Samples of men and women are used most often for this purpose, but sometimes samples of male (much less frequently, female) heterosexuals and homosexuals are used in addition. After the items are administered, the responses of the groups are compared to determine to which items the groups respond differently, on the average, at a statistically significant level. The items that meet this criterion are then assembled as a masculinity-femininity scale. If, for example, significantly more men than women respond affirmatively to an item asking whether they read mechanics magazines, then answering yes to this item is scored masculine and answering no is scored feminine. The more such items to which an individual responds positively, the more psychologically masculine the individual is.

The following are important examples of simple sex typing scales: the Terman-Miles AIAT; the Gough Fe scale; and the It Scale for Children (ITSC).

The Terman-Miles Attitude-Interest Test (AIAT)

This scale, published in 1936, is no longer used as a measure of simple sex typing. The Terman-Miles scale does have great historical importance, however, as the forerunner of all subsequent measures of sex typing. Terman and Miles were rooted in the mental testing tradition of early twentieth-century psychology, whose operationalization of human intelligence represented a major methodological breakthrough and, more than anything else, established psychology as a modern science. After intelligence, the next major area of personality that psychology turned to was sex typing.

The opening remarks of Terman and Miles's *Sex and Personality* (1936) set the stage for their analysis of sex typing:

The belief is all but universal that men and women as contrasting groups display characteristic sex differences in their behavior, and that these differences are so deep and pervasive as to

lend distinctive character to the entire personality. That masculine and feminine types are a reality in all our highly developed
cultures can hardly be questioned, although there is much difference of opinion as to the differentiae which mark them off
and the extent to which overlapping of types occurs. . . .

The belief remains that the sexes differ fundamentally in
their instinctive and emotional equipment and in the senti-
ments, interests, attitudes, and modes of behavior which are the
derivatives of such equipment. It will be recognized that these
are important factors in shaping what is known as personality,
hence the general acceptance of the dichotomy of the masculine and feminine personality types. The belief in the actuality
of M-F types remains unshaken by the fact, abundantly at-
tested, that observers do not agree in regard to the multitudi-
nous attributes which are supposed to differentiate them.
Although practically every attribute alleged to be characteristic
of a given sex has been questioned, yet the composite pictures
yielded by majority opinion stand out with considerable clearness.

But along with the acceptance of M-F types of the sort we
have delineated, there is an explicit recognition of the existence
of individual variants from type: the effeminate man and the
masculine woman. Grades of deviates are recognized ranging
from the slightly variant to the genuine invert who is capable of
romantic attachment only to members of his or her own sex,
although, as we shall see later, judges rating their acquaintences
on degree of masculinity and femininity of personality seldom
show very close agreement.

For many reasons, both practical and theoretical, it is highly
desirable that our concepts of the M-F types existing in our
present culture be made more definite and be given a more
factual basis. Alleged differences between the sexes must give
place to experimentally established differences. A measure is
needed which can be applied to the individual and scored so as
to locate the subject, with a fair degree of approximation, in
terms of deviation from the mean of either sex. Range and
overlap of the sexes must be more accurately determined than
is possible by observational and clinical methods. (Pp. 1–2)

Terman and Miles admit repeatedly that "observers do not
agree" about the exact nature of any average psychological differences between the sexes. (The situation is no different today.)
Moreover, they implicitly acknowledge that the construct of sex
typing requires the assumption that psychological differences between the sexes can be determined reliably and replicably, past
confusion and disagreement on this matter being due only to the
unreliability of observational and clinical methods.

Terman and Miles established the pattern that the field of sex role research has followed ever since. They first discuss psychological differences between the sexes, but quickly shift their focus to masculine and feminine types. Once these types are established, they address the issue of within-sex variation in these sex role temperaments. They ground their analysis on *between*-sex differences, but only as a means of providing an assessment procedure for studying *within*-sex differences. In brief, Terman and Miles established sex *typing* as the central concern of sex role research. It is often thought that the central concern of sex role research has been sex differences. But in fact studies of within-sex typing far outnumber studies of between-sex differences.

The AIAT includes seven subscales: word associations, inkblot associations, information, emotional and ethical attitudes, interests, opinions, and introvertive response. Each subscale is constructed by the known groups method; items relevant to the scale are administered to large samples of males and females and those that significantly differentiate the sexes are accepted. Each subscale yields a score ranging from masculine to feminine and an overall m-f score results from summing them.

The Gough Femininity (Fe) Scale

Gough (1952) first developed a 58-item form of the Fe scale, using samples of high school students from Manitowoc, Wisconsin, and college students at the University of California at Berkeley. He wrote that "the goal . . . has been to develop an instrument which is brief, easy to administer, relatively subtle and unthreatening in content, and which will, at the same time, differentiate men from women and sexual deviates from normals" (p. 427). (Note here Gough's linking comparisons between men and women and between heterosexuals and homosexuals.) He included a somewhat briefer 38-item form in the California Personality Inventory (CPI), a well-known general personality questionnaire (see also Gough, 1964, pp. 73–74; Megargee, 1972, pp. 90–93). The following list presents examples of items from the briefer form; the feminine response for each item is indicated by T (true) or F (false) following each item.

I think I would like the work of a building contractor.   (F)
I prefer a shower to a bathtub.   (F)
I get excited very easily.   (T)

In school I was sometimes sent to the principal for cutting up. (F)

I like mechanics magazines. (F)

This scale is typical of many simple sex typing scales based on questionnaire self-reports. It includes emotional traits and reactions, occupational preferences, activity preferences, and general opinions that are interpreted as indicators of psychological masculinity-femininity.

Simple Sex Typing Scales for Children: The It Scale for Children (ITSC)

A third important measure of simple sex typing, and the one most commonly used with children, is D. Brown's (1956) It Scale for Children (ITSC). The experimenter shows the child drawings of a child named It,[1] supposedly drawn to be ambiguous as to sex, and asks the child to indicate It's choices on three different tasks. In the first task, the child is shown a set of 16 pictures of toys or objects, of which 8 are masculine (such as a tractor, dumptruck, toy soldier, and knife) and 8 are feminine (such as a necklace, purse, dishes, and doll buggy), and is asked to pick the ones It likes, until a total of 8 are chosen. In the second task, the child is shown 8 pairs of new pictures, each of which one item is masculine and one feminine, and is asked to choose which item in each that It would rather play with. Examples of these pairs are Indian princess/Indian chief; trouser and shirt/dress; sewing materials/airplane parts; girls playing/boys playing. In the third task, the child is shown pictures—a girl, a boy dressed as a girl, a girl dressed as a boy, and a boy—and is asked which of these It would like to be.

The child's masculinity score on this test is the sum of all the masculine choices in the first two tasks together with a score derived from the third task.[2] Brown's rationale for asking children to report It's choices rather than their own was his belief that the latter would reflect their conformity to social expectations rather than their real preferences, which would be more easily observed as projected on It. A number of other sex-typed toy, game, and activity-preference measures similar to the first and second task of the ITSC also have been developed. These measures, however, typically ask children to report their preferences directly.

The Conceptual Rationale for m-f Scales[3]

The procedures used for creating simple sex typing measures raise several conceptual issues. First, the method of selecting items in effect assumes that the same characteristics that differentiate adequate from inadequate sex role identities within each sex also differentiate men from women and heterosexuals from homosexuals. This assumption has two sources. The mental testing tradition had operationally defined intelligence as the capacity to answer items that older children can and younger children cannot answer. Assessing sex typing as those characteristics that differentiate men from women was a simple extension of this principle. This assumption is given additional credence by the proposition that sex role identity results primarily from psychologically identifying with male or female figures.

But there is a serious logical problem in using men and women as known groups for the construction of m-f tests that becomes apparent when m-f tests are used to compare groups defined by other social characteristics. For example, it has been argued that black males have more sex role identity problems than white males because the former score as more feminine on simple sex typing tests (Pettigrew, 1964, p. 17–24). The logic of the argument is that since black males differ from white males in the same ways that females differ from males, black males are higher in femininity. But another way of describing the same data is that white females differ from white males in the same ways that blacks differ from whites; therefore, white females psychologically are more black than white males and have insecure racial identities. It seems plausible to argue that differences between men and women provide the basis for assessing the hypothetical trait masculinity-femininity until one realizes that individuals can be classified in many different ways that logically provide the basis for many other analogous but quite absurd traits.

Do the Items in Sex Typing Scales Actually Differentiate the Sexes?

To make general use of a sex typing scale derived from a particular sample of men and women, one must assume that the items differentiating men from women in that sample at that particular time will differentiate men from women in other groups and at other times. Many sex typing tests, however, were originally developed on small or oddly selected samples. For example, the

Minnesota Multiphasic Personality Inventory (MMPI) Mf (m-f) scale, the most frequently used test of sex typing, is based on comparisons of 54 male soldiers, 67 women airline employees, and 13 male homosexuals in the early 1940s (Dahlstrom, Welsh, and Dahlstrom, 1972a, pp. 201–202); Manosevitz (1971) also points out that the median education of the sample used for the development of the MMPI was a whole was 8.0 years. Further, even in good samples, sex differences are not particularly consistent either across social groups or time. Vincent (1966), for example, finds that 18 of the 38 items in Gough's Fe scale (nearly half) no longer differentiate males from females in a large sample drawn from a Southern college. Similarly, when LaTorre and Piper (1978) administer the first three of seven subtests of the Terman-Miles AIAT to a sample of 352 men and women, including both students and adults, they find that few of the items in the first two subtests significantly differentiate the sexes, and only about half the items in the third subtest do so.

It might seem unimportant that many individual items in the older m-f tests no longer differentiate the sexes, provided the total scale score still does. For example, LaTorre and Piper (1978) assert that, in spite of the majority of nondifferentiating items in the AIAT, the "measure's validity was reconfirmed in a different subculture some 40 years after its original development" because men and women still have significantly different average scores. This argument, however, misunderstands the rationale for m-f tests. They were not devised to distinguish males from females— obviously, simpler methods exist for making this distinction. Rather, their purpose is to make within-sex differentiations on sex role-related characteristics. To do this as accurately as possible requires that every item in a test significantly differentiate the sexes; any item that fails to do so contributes a component of error to the total scale score. The more nondifferentiating items, the more error.

Actually, the instability of sex differences accounts in part for the plethora of simple sex typing scales. Many researchers concoct new m-f scales by starting with items from previous sex typing scales, removing items that no longer differentiate, and adding some new ones that do. This happened, for example, when the MMPI Mf scale was developed with items from subtests 5, 6, and 7 of the Terman-Miles AIAT (Dahlstrom, Welsh, and Dahlstrom, 1972a, pp. 201–206). Since so many sex typing scales borrow in this fashion, and nearly all borrow directly or indirectly from the Terman-Miles AIAT, in principle a comprehensive review would show the many samples for which a given item no longer differentiates the sexes—which would make a devastating critique of the whole idea of sex typing scales.

Is Sex Typing Organized around a Single Dimension?

Yet another critical question is whether the various traits, preferences, and responses that sex typing measures employ actually measure the same thing. Even if each item in a scale reliably differentiates men from women, this does not guarantee that they assess the same underlying concept. For example, men and women differ in their average height and SAT mathematical aptitude score, but this fact alone would not justify summing the two as a measure of sex role identity. Rather, it is necessary to show that the items in a scale assess the same thing by demonstrating that they are empirically related to each other. In psychometrics—the field of psychology concerned with the construction, reliability, and validity of psychological tests—this scale property is termed its *internal consistency reliability* or *homogeneity reliability.* When one considers the diverse contents of m-f scales (the Gough scale, for example, ranges from "I think I would like the work of a building contractor" to "I prefer a shower to a bathtub"), their internal reliability seems open to question.

Few studies evaluate the internal consistency of currently used m-f scales; the one most exhaustively evaluated remains Terman and Miles's AIAT. Terman and Miles performed their evaluation, however, at a time when the statistical techniques for such evaluation were quite primitive; they assessed the AIAT only by *split-half correlations* (that is, correlations between the score based on one half of the scale's items with the score based on the other half).[4] The only example known to me of a traditional sex typing scale evaluated by a sophisticated measure of internal consistency is a single study showing a K-R 21 value of 0.36 for the MMPI Mf scale (Dahlstrom, Welsh, and Dahlstrom, 1972b, p. 260); for this reliability index, the value is quite low.

Interrelationships among items have been examined also by a statistical procedure called *factor analysis,* which determines the extent to which a set of variables can be grouped together into internally coherent factors. Factor analysis is usually performed in such a way that each factor consists of variables that are related to each other but as unrelated as possible to variables contributing to other factors. Factor analysis should be used on summary scores derived from multi-item tests, not on collections of individual items.[5] Nevertheless, many factor analytic studies have been conducted with pools of items from one or more sex typing scales, and their finding is that there is no single underlying masculinity-femininity factor. Various constituent factors have been found, however (see Constantinople, 1973; Edwards and Abbott, 1973, p. 248). Tyler (1968, p. 211), for example, concludes that sex typing scales are not unidimensional but, rather, include different components—emotional qualities, interests, and abilities—that have little empirical relationship. Unfortunately, different studies do not agree about what these different components are. Projective and children's sex typing measures have not been factor analyzed.

The third way to determine whether sex typing constitutes a single, coherent psychological continuum is to examine the relationships among the summary scores from different sex typing scales. When measures of (supposedly) the same concept have a high degree of relationship to each other, psychometricians say that they have high convergent validity. Evaluating relationships among scales involves exactly the same principle as evaluating relationships among items. Within samples of one sex, the various questionnaire self-report scales tend to correlate positively, but only at moderate levels. The square of the correlation coefficient indicates the *common variance,* that is, the variance held in common by the two variables. The correlations between m-f measures in same-sex samples usually are between 0.3 and 0.5, indicating 9–25% common variance. (Correlations are somewhat higher in mixed-sex samples, but the correlations within each sex are the appropriate ones to examine here; see Constantinople, 1973, and Harrison, 1975, for detailed discussions). These correlations are statistically significant, but whether they should be regarded as demonstrating that these tests measure the same thing is a matter of judgment. Constantinople (1973) concludes that "in summarizing these data, it seems fair to say that although the tests have something in common, a considerable proportion of the variance associated with any two tests is not held in common" (p. 398).

Edwards and Abbott (1973, p. 248) likewise conclude that the convergent validity of masculinity-femininity scales simply has not been demonstrated.

There have been only two studies reporting data about the interrelationships among children's sex typing measures. Biller (1968) found a correlation of 0.75 between the m-f scores derived from two different toy and game preference measures in a sample of 185 5-year-old boys. Sears, Rau, and Alpert (1965, table 26) also report the relationship between two toy and game preference measures in samples of 19 girls and 21 boys 4 and 5 years of age. These two measures are strongly correlated at 0.69 for girls, but only slightly correlated for boys at 0.20. These data are too slight and inconsistent, however, to permit any generalization.

The Multileveled Conception of Sex Typing

The simple conception of sex typing dominated throughout the 1930s and 1940s and then yielded to the multileveled conception during the 1950's. The newer conception had two sources. First was the concept of the unconscious, contributed by psychoanalytic theory. (It is important to note that the earlier, simple conception of sex typing had originated quite independently of psychoanalytic theory, as the product of a marriage between the mental testing movement and early twentieth-century pre-psychoanalytic "sexology." Terman and Miles's intellectual predecessors were Alfred Binet and Havelock Ellis, not Sigmund Freud.) A second source was the development of more subtle sex typing tests. When researchers found that scores on these more subtle tests were only negligibly related to scores on the earlier self-report questionnaire tests, they developed the multileveled conception in order to explain this lack of relationship.

The Franck Drawing Completion Test

The best-known of the subtle sex typing tests is the Franck Drawing Completion Test (FDCT; Franck and Rosen, 1949). The Franck test consists of 36 items, each a simple abstract design that subjects are instructed to complete in any way they like. Based on a comparison of the responses of men and women, Franck and Rosen (1949) formulate the following criteria for distinguishing masculine from feminine performance:

Men characteristically *close off* stimulus areas; they tend to *enlarge, expand* the stimulus, often by means of upward exten-

sions. They tend to emphasize *sharp or angular line*. Where a *single line* will do, they make no attempt to double or support it. Where there is a choice of unifying or separating the parts of a stimulus, they prefer *unity*.
Women leave stimulus areas *open* or elaborate the area *within* the stimulus rather than expand (when they do expand it is usually downward). They tend to *blunt* or *enclose* sharp lines or angles, and to *reinforce* protruding single lines by doubling them. They prefer pairs to unity. (Pp. 251–252)

Franck and Rosen note an overall similarity between these features and Erik Erikson's (1943; see also 1964) well-known account of sex differences in the play constructions of boys and girls. Erikson reports that, when girls and boys are asked to arrange on a table a standard set of toy figures and objects as they saw fit, girls create protected, enclosed spaces more often than boys, who are inclined to construct open spaces, often with projecting figures and towers. Both Erikson and Franck and Rosen interpret the differences they find as reflecting differences in the fundamental self-images of the two sexes rooted in their experiences of their bodies.

Miller and Swanson

The multileveled conception of sex role identity is implied, but not explicitly developed, in *The Authoritarian Personality* (Adorno et al., 1950) one of the most important and influential studies in the history of American psychology. Sanford (1966, p. 196), a member of this study's staff, noted that "the authors of *The Authoritarian Personality* became convinced that one of the main sources of the personality syndrome was ego-alien femininity—that is to say, underlying femininity that had to be countered by whatever defenses the subject had at his disposal." The first formal statement of the multileveled conception was an unpublished lecture given by Sanford in 1950 at the University of Michigan, "Masculinity-Femininity in the Structure of the Personality," which first appeared in print only in 1966. Sanford's lecture nonetheless had a powerful impact through its influence on Daniel Miller and Guy Swanson's (1960) *Inner Conflict and Defense*, whose publication established the dominance of the multileveled conception. Their presentation of the multileveled conception of sex role identity is worth reproducing in full:

One of our primary purposes in the studies to be reported was to compare the reactions to conflict of three different kinds of men. One of our groups of subjects was feminine both unconsciously and consciously (we shall refer to this combination by the letters FF); a second was unconsciously feminine but consciously very masculine (FM); and a third was unconsciously and consciously masculine (MM). [Author's note. This paragraph is footnoted as follows: We are indebted to R. Nevitt Sanford for his suggestions, made in a lecture at the University of Michigan, of techniques for identifying the three types.]. . .

We made two assumptions about the origins of the three patterns in our developmental orientation. First, we assumed that each boy initially identifies with his mother and then transfers to his father. As an infant, he spends most of his time with his mother. He learns about objects, people, time, causality, social rules, and other such properties of his world through constant contact with her. He becomes very dependent on her because she feeds and cleans him, protects him from harm, and prevents him from misbehaving. He consequently comes to expect her to help him to overcome emergencies.

Later, the father usually becomes the more significant person. He become more visible as a source of discipline. He has certain unique abilities which the son admires. His life outside the home piques the child's curiosity. By identifying with his father, a son gradually acquires the expressive gestures, the habits, and the interests that are typical of males rather than females in our society. We thought that these earlier identifications would not be conscious, since they are embedded in a large number of activities and occur before events are labeled verbally.

A second assumption about identity involved fixation. We saw each stage of development as entailing the acquisition of skills that form the building blocks of the next stage. Hence, if some difficulty occurs at one stage, the child may not master all the requisite skills. He then remains more closely identified with the mother—and, therefore, more feminine—than another boy who can forge ahead. And, depending upon the degree of difficulty, he is correspondingly handicapped in learning the more complex skills of the next stage.

Whether he is masculine or feminine in his underlying identity, the average male child, as he matures and develops friendships, feels an increasing social pressure to act in a masculine manner. If his gestures are feminine, or he lacks an interest in machinery, he may become the object of ridicule. If he is proficient in sports played by boys, he gains considerable recognition from his friends.

Frequently, masculine values are acquired by identification with a great football player, a jet pilot, or some mythical hero. By patterning himself after Robin Hood or Tarzan, a young boy comes to idealize physical prowess, fairness, democracy, support of the weak and oppressed, and great courage which may at times verge on needless foolhardiness or cruelty. These values are quite different from the self-sacrifice, gentle sensitivity, and succorance that characterize such feminine ideal prototypes as Juliet or Florence Nightingale. In contrast to the earlier parental identifications, later ones with heroes, real or ideal, are probably matters of conscious concern for every normal boy. They are part of his conscious sex identity.

Some of the principles that we have just outlined cast light on the origins of our three types of sex identity. When both unconscious and conscious identities are predominantly feminine, the boy's identification with his mother cannot have been affected by the norms of his peers. He consciously accepts his feminine characteristics, although he may deny their significance. If the FF does not deny his femininity and accepts his traits as being feminine, he may engage in homosexual activities, or he may express himself in such activities as hair dressing or designing women's clothing.

The unconscious feminine identity may be defended against by a conscious masculine one. While the FM remains identified primarily with his mother, he aspires to be masculine, and consciously considers himself so. To convince himself and others that he is not feminine, a boy may engage in activities that appeal only to masculine men. For example, he may cultivate exceptional skill in weight-lifting or in wrestling. Yet, the unconscious femininity manifests itself too. The usual outlets are expressive styles, particularly those that are not considered meaningful. In special circumstances it is possible, for example, for a man to behave passively with a person in authority and still think the he is being masculine.

In the presumably mature boy, both unconscious and conscious identities are masculine. The MM has identified with his father, and there is no incompatibility between unconscious and conscious reactions. (Miller and Swanson, 1960, pp. 88–90)

By postulating that the Gough scale assesses the conscious level of sex role identity while the Franck test assesses its unconscious level, Miller and Swanson classify males (they did not study females) by these two measures into three sex role identity categories: (1) unconscious masculine and conscious masculine (MM); (2) unconscious feminine and conscious masculine (FM); and (3) unconscious feminine and conscious feminine (FF).

Miller and Swanson do not make use of what is obviously the logically missing category in their typology: unconscious masculine and conscious feminine (MF). They omit this category because their developmental theory does not allow it. But Sanford's

1950 lecture, which they acknowledge as the source of their typology, not only includes MF as a category but in fact considers the MF group to be the most creative and psychologically integrated. Miller and Swanson's deliberate omission of the MF group marks an important event in the history of the MSRI paradigm.

Insofar as the multiple-level conception uses two (or more) simple sex typing measures in combination, it is subject to two of the criticisms of simple sex typing measures (their use of males and females as known groups, and unstable sex differences). Another criticism can be made as well. In Miller and Swanson's (1960) study, Franck and Gough scores are uncorrelated. Miller and Swanson interpret this as supporting their contention that these two measures assess different levels of sex role identity. Actually, Miller and Swanson's own theory implies a positive correlation between measures of the two levels. The categories FF, FM, and MM are held by them to comprise a sequential series of stages for males: In the first stage, a boy completely identifies with his mother (FF); in the second, he shows an overlay of masculine behaviors at the conscious level but remains identified with his mother at the unconscious level (FM); and only at the most advanced stage is his sex role identity masculine at both levels (MM). Thus, if the three groups are of roughly equal size (as they are in Miller and Swanson's and later studies), then the two sex typing measures should be moderately correlated since two thirds of the sample score in the same direction on the two measures (the FFs and the MMs). It follows that Miller and Swanson's own theory of multiple levels of sex role identity implies a moderate positive correlation between the Franck and Gough tests. The reason that the correlation Miller and Swanson actually find is close to zero may well be because a fourth group (MF), about equal in size to the other groups, has been included in the computation of the correlation, though excluded from their theory.

The empirical basis for a multileveled conceptualization of sex role identity is not low correlation among measures of different levels but whether (1) measures of the same hypothetical level are internally reliable and highly related and (2) measures of the two levels, and the typology generated by combining them, have the relationships theoretically expected with other variables. There are too few studies to say whether projective sex typing measures are internally reliable or highly related; the reliability of and the relationships between measures that assess the conscious level are only moderate. The second criterion will be taken up later.

Biller and Lynn

Biller (1968, 1972) and Lynn (1969) have proposed another model of multiple levels of sex role identity that has been applied widely in studies of children in which a distinction is made between sex role *orientation*, sex role *preference*, and sex role *adoption*. Sex role orientation is the deepest level of sex role identity, assessed by projective measures like the It scale. Sex role preference is an intermediate level, reflected by children's self-reports of their game, toy, or activity interests. To assess sex role preference, children may be asked to indicate their personal choices for the toys or activities depicted in the first two parts of the It scale. Sex role adoption is the level of sex role identity closest to the surface, reflected in children's actual activities. This level of sex role identity is assessed by ratings by teachers, parents, or other observers of children's actual participation in sex-typed activities.

It is interesting to recall that D. Brown (1956) originally rejected self-report measures of sex role identity. Further, he considered his It scale to be a measure of a superficial level of identity. Biller and others, however, have interpreted it as assessing the deepest level, presumably because of the projective nature of the task. These contradictory interpretations of the same measure illustrate its essential ambiguity.

Biller and Lynn's formulation of three levels in sex role identity overlaps with Miller and Swanson's formulation of two levels; sex role orientation parallels unconscious sex role identity, while sex role preference and adoption may be viewed as two components of conscious sex role identity in which self-reported preferences are distinguished from actual observed behavior. These two formulations have been applied in quite different contexts, however—Miller and Swanson's in studies with adolescents and adults focusing on the hypothetical consequences of the three types of sex role identity, and Biller and Lynn's in studies with children concerning the sources of the three levels.

Some of the problems raised by Miller and Swanson's two-level hypothesis apply equally to Biller and Lynn's three-level hypothesis. Two studies are relevant on this point. In a study of 5-year-old boys Biller (1968) finds that two measures interpreted as reflecting sex role orientation—a highly modified and shortened version of the It scale and a Draw-a-Person test (scored according to the sex of the first figure drawn and the degree of differentiation between drawings of a male and a female)—are relatively highly correlated (0.58). The two measures interpreted as reflecting sex role preference (a game-choice test and a toy-choice test) are, as noted earlier, highly correlated (0.75). Sex role adoption is assessed by only one measure, a teacher's rating. Biller combines the measures within the orientation and preference categories to create summary measures of these two hypothetical levels. He then reports that the median intercorrelation between these two summary measures and the adoption measure is 0.23. His interpretation of this pattern of correlations—high between measures assessing the same hypothetical level of masculinity and lower between summary measures of different hypothetical levels—supports the hypothesis of multiple levels.

Sears, Rau, and Alpert (1965) find that the median intercorrelation among five masculinity-femininity measures is 0.15 for boys and 0.36 for girls. These measures include the It scale, two tests of toy and activity preferences, and an observational measure of the proportion of time spent in boys' and girls' play areas. The study also employs nursery-school teachers' ratings of the boys on a scale ranging from "sissy" to "entirely masculine, a buck," and ratings of girls on a scale ranging from "tomboy" to "coquette, a clinging vine."[6] Grouping Sears, Rau, and Alpert's correlations according to the hypothetical levels proposed by Biller and Lynn reveals a quite inconsistent pattern in which the measures of the same hypothetical level are not correlated any more strongly than measures of different levels. The Sears, Rau, and Alpert sample departed from Biller's in a number of ways that might account for these differences; the former was slightly younger, from a higher and more restricted range of social classes, and from a different region of the country (namely, southern California, whereas the latter's was drawn from North Carolina).

Again, the criterion for assessing the soundness of conceptualizing different levels of sex role identity is not the correlations between levels but whether (1) the measures within each hypothetical level are highly related and (2) the measures have predictable and meaningful relationships to other variables. Data on the first point are too limited and inconsistent to make a judgment, and data on the second point will be taken up later.

The Androgynous Conception of Sex Typing

In the late 1960s and early 1970s, dissatisfaction with the multi-leveled conception of sex typing and sex role identity began to build. The situation was a perfect illustration of Kuhn's thesis applied to part of a paradigm; disconcerting results concerning the source and consequences of sex typing conceptualized according to the multilevel model had started to appear, and new measures of sex typing, corresponding to alternative theoretical conceptions were proliferating (for example, Rosenberg, Sutton-Smith, and Morgan, 1961; Gonen and Lansky, 1968). Among these alternatives was Biller and Borstelmann's (1967, p. 255) original proposal for androgyny: "Masculinity and femininity should not be conceived as mutually exclusive polar opposites, but rather as two separate, sometimes divergent, sometimes overlapping continuums." Biller (1968, p. 16) explicitly argues that researchers need to assess different levels of sex role identity because of "the problems of measuring sex role as if masculinity and femininty were opposite ends of a continuum," which, he notes, had been discussed in three earlier studies. Gonen and Lansky (1968) were actually the first to assess masculinity and femininity empirically as separate dimensions. But this androgynous conception of sex typing remained unnoticed in the research literature for four years, until Bem (1972) independently proposed it again. Bem and others recognized its potential for interpreting sex role change as desirable. In essence, the proliferation of new conceptions of sex typing due to problems internal to the identity paradigm coincided with a social movement reconsidering the nature of sex roles, with androgyny the beneficiary.

The Bem Sex Role Inventory (BSRI)

Bem (1972, 1974) notes that traditional sex typing scales assume that masculinity and femininity are opposites. That is, these m-f scales are constructed in such a way, that, if individuals score high on masculinity, then by definition they have to score low on femininity, and vice versa. She and others decided to develop sex typing scales based on the alternative assumption that masculinity and femininity are independent, so that masculinity is one psychological dimension (ranging from high to low) and femininity another (ranging from high to low).

An important example of an androgyny scale is the Bem (1974) Sex Role Inventory (BSRI). In the BSRI, subjects are given a list of 60 adjectives, including 20 socially desirable masculine and 20 socially desirable feminine, and asked to describe themselves according to each using a 7-point rating scale going from "Never or almost never true" to "Always or almost always true." Examples of the masculine adjectives are *ambitious, dominant,* and *self-reliant;* feminine adjectives include *affectionate, gentle,* and *understanding.* The scale thus yields a separate score for masculinity and for femininity. The separate masculinity and femininity scores produced by these scales are used in two ways. First, and particularly common in early androgyny studies, these scores can be combined to form four sex typing categories: (1) androgynous (high on both masculinity and femininity); (2) masculine (high on masculinity and low on femininity); (3) feminine (low on masculinity and high on femininity); and (4) undifferentiated. Second, and increasingly common in more recent studies, the two dimensions are simply analyzed separately. Androgyny scales use a criterion for categorizing items as masculine or feminine fundamentally different from one used in traditional m-f scales. In the BSRI, two large samples of subjects (each including both men and women) rated the social desirability of various adjectives as applied to men and to women; adjectives that both samples rated as significantly more desirable for women are categorized as feminine, and those more desirable for men, masculine. Thus, whereas the older sex typing scales were based on actual differences between men and women, the BSRI is based on differences in what is perceived as desirable for men and women. The possible implications of this change in the criterion for selecting items are not clear.

Evaluating Androgyny

There are three kinds of evidence commonly cited in support of the androgynous conception of sex typing. First, the m and f subscales of the BSRI—as well as Spence, Helmreich, and Stapp's (1974) Personal Attributes Questionnaire (PAQ) and Berzins, Welling, and Wetter's (1978) Personality Research Form (PRF) ANDRO—have relatively high internal consistency reliability, as calculated by standard psychometric indices. Second, factor analyses of the BSRI conducted by Gaudreau (1977), Wakefield et al. (1976), and Moreland et al. (1978) produce two factors almost identical to Bem's unipolar m and f subscales. Third, the m and f subscales of various measures of androgyny are uncorrelated in the samples from which these measures were developed.

It is interesting that factor analyses now reveal m and f factors so clearly, since these two dimensions do not appear in any of the many earlier factor analyses of items from simple sex typing scales. The items in most androgyny scales tap a rather limited domain of personality—self-ratings on characteristics described by adjectives—and are all positively valued characteristics. Factor analyses of such a narrow domain of items may not constitute an adequate test of the theory. Indeed, the one currently reported factor analysis of an androgyny scale based on a broader domain of items does not reveal the expected 2-factor structure: a factor analysis of the PRF ANDRO scale, which includes the diverse kinds of items used in traditional m-f scales reveals 18 factors, of which 7 are considered interpretable (Berzins, Welling, and Wetter, 1978). Brannon (1978) points out, however, that findings from factor analyses of individual items cannot be used to prove or disprove a hypothesized factor structure since these findings are so variable and subject to artificial effects such as the wording of the items.

Further, factorial independence or low intercorrelations between the m and f subscales in androgyny measures do not establish that sex typing is best understood as organized around independent masculinity and femininity dimensions; once more the existence of different components of sex role identity neither implies nor is implied by findings that measures of each component are uncorrelated. Some studies in fact do find nonzero correlations between m and f scales. At this point, the safest conclusion is that, while the evidence of independence is consistent with the androgynous conception of sex typing, the former has not established the latter. Better evidence must come from studies finding predictable and meaningful differential antecedents and consequences of masculinity and femininity. Research along these lines will be considered later.

Several studies concern the relationships between various androgyny scales. Spence and Helmreich (1978, pp. 24–25) report an unpublished study by Stapp and Kanner that finds the correlations between the PAQ and BSRI to be 0.75 (for males) and

0.73 (for females) for the m scale and 0.57 and 0.59 for the f scale. Berzins, Welling, and Wetter (1978) find the correlations between parallel scales of the PRF ANDRO and BSRI to be between 0.50 and 0.65. Kelly, Furman, and Young (1978) report equally high correlations among the parallel m and f scales of four currently available androgyny tests. These correlations are higher than those among traditional m-f measures. Kelly, Furman, and Young (1978) also report, however, that, in spite of these high correlations, the proportion of subjects classified differently when these tests are scored by the median-split method (for example, classified as androgynous by one scale, but masculine by another) is very high. Lenney (1979a, p. 709) concludes that "there is no such thing as a single concept of androgyny, independent from either the measuring instrument or the theoretical background underlying the instrument."

The comparability of the various androgyny scales can be assessed on still another important criterion: the relationship between the m and f dimensions. Spence and Helmreich (1978, p. 25) observe that their studies with college students tend to find "uniformly positive" relationships between PAQ m and f scales, while Bem (1974) finds slightly negative correlations between BSRI m and f scales. The Stapp and Kanner study, using both measures in the same sample, finds exactly the same pattern. This evidence suggests that the various androgyny scales may not be measuring the same thing.

Clearly, the time is ripe for an androgynous concept of sex typing, and it has had many positive social implications. In its historical context, however, it is best understood, in terms of Kuhn's thesis, as a stage within the identity paradigm. But, as will be argued later, at the same time it is facilitating a more radical paradigm shift. Some aspects of androgyny research represent a continuation of the MSRI paradigm; others, however, depart from it and contribute to the emerging new paradigm.

An identification is a belief that some of the attributes of a model (parents, siblings, relatives, peers, and so on) belong to the self. If a six-year-old boy is identified with his father, he necessarily regards himself as possessing some of his father's characteristics, one of which is male-ness or masculinity.... One of the important consequences of the boy's desire for a strong identification with his father is his attempt to take on the father's characteristics. For each time he successfully imi-tates a behavior or adopts an attitude of the father, he perceives an increased similarity to the latter. This perception of increased similarity strengthens his belief that he possesses some of the father's covert characteristics. One of these covert attributes is the self-label of mas-culinity. (Kagan, 1964a, pp. 146–147)

Demands for masculine sex-role behavior are often made by women in the absence of readily available male models to demonstrate typical sex-role behavior. Such demands are often presented in the form of punishing, *negative* admonishments, i.e., telling the boy what not to do rather than what to do and backing up the demands with punishment.... Such methods of demanding typical sex-role behavior of boys are very poor methods of inducing learning.... Negative ad-monishments given at an age when the child is least able to understand them and supported by punishment are thought to produce anxiety concerning sex-role behavior. (Lynn, 1966, pp. 468–469)

Males tend to identify with a culturally defined masculine role, whereas females tend to identify with their mothers. (Lynn, 1969, p. 97)

Proposition 2. *Sex role identity derives from identification-modeling and, to a lesser extent, reinforcement and cognitive learning of sex-typed traits, especially among males.*

Originally, the MSRI paradigm postulated only identification-modeling with the same-sex parent as the source of sex role

identity. Later, however, theorists noted that the same-sex parent
and other same-sex adult models are less available to boys than
to girls. Consequently, they argued that identification-modeling
is relatively less important for the development of sex role identity among males than among females, while reinforcement and
cognitive learning of cultural sex role norms and stereotypes are
relatively more important. David Lynn (1966) expresses this view-
point in these words:

The initial parental identification of both male and female infants is with the mother. Boys, but not girls, must shift from
this initial mother identification and establish masculine-role
identification. Typically in this culture the girl has the same-sex
parental model for identification (the mother) with her more
hours per day than the boy has his same-sex model (the father)
with him. Moreover, even when home, the father does not usually participate in as many intimate activities with the child as
does the mother, e.g., preparation for bed, toileting. . . . The
boy is seldom if ever with the father as he engages in his daily
vocational activities, although both boy and girl are often with
the mother as she goes through her household activities. Consequently, the father, as a model for the boy, is analagous to a
map showing the major outline, but lacking most details. . . .
Despite the shortage of male models, a somewhat stereotyped
and conventional masculine role is nonetheless spelled out for
the boy, often by his mother and women teachers in the absence of his father and male models. Through the reinforcement of the culture's highly developed system of rewards for
typical masculine-role behavior and punishment for the signs of
femininity, the boy's early learned identification with the
mother weakens. Upon this weakened mother identification is
welded the later learned identification with a culturally defined,
stereotyped masculine role. (P. 466)

Identification-Modeling

The terms identification and modeling are rooted in two quite
different theoretical traditions, which historically have opposed
each other—the former in psychoanalytic theory and the latter
in social learning theory (Kohlberg, 1966; Mischel, 1966). The
differences between the two, however, are not central to the
discussion here.

While the MSRI paradigm holds that the contribution of identification-modeling to sex role identity is less critical for males
than females, nonetheless the paradigm has sought to establish
its occurrence among males. Identification-modeling theories

usually postulate that other factors in addition to exposure to a same-sex model are needed to produce sex role identity. Mussen classifies these theories into three types, each specifying a particular additional characteristic. According to Mussen, the first is *defensive identification,* deriving from the classical psychoanalytic theory of the male Oedipal crisis: The male child develops a strong emotional attachment to his mother but comes to fear his father's retaliation against him for this attachment. Specifically, the son comes to fear that his father will castrate him (literally or symbolically). According to the theory, the son deals with this fear by becoming like his father through an identification process called identification with the aggressor, and giving up his attachment to his mother.

Mussen calls the second type *developmental identification.* Its intellectual precursor is Freud's theory of anaclitic (literally, leaning on) identification, postulated to account for the female's identification with her mother in the way that the Oedipal complex accounts for the male's identification with his father. The developmental identification theory, however, applies this notion to both sexes. Its premise is that children have dependency needs that cause them to identify with those models from whom they receive gratification. In one way, it is quite problematical to apply this theory to males, for it would seem to predict that children of both sexes will identify with their mothers. But theorists usually postulate that it applies only (or best) to same-sex models.

Mussen's third type is *role theory identification,* by which children are supposed to imitate models whom they perceive as being powerful. Studies have demonstrated the importance of the model's perceived power in facilitating modeling. This formulation suggests, then, that sons will model themselves after their fathers to the extent that they perceive their fathers as powerful and dominant.

These three types of identification postulate three different characteristics of fathers—punitiveness, warmth and nurturance, and power—that facilitate sons' modeling after them. Mussen and his colleagues conducted several studies (summarized in Mussen, 1969) with kindergarten boys to test the relative importance of these three paternal characteristics on a son's masculinity as assessed by the It scale. In most of these studies, the father's warmth and dominance are inferred from doll-play stories the boy is asked to make up. In one study, these variables are assessed by the mother's reports of the father's interaction with the boy. The correlations between scores on the It scale and these indirect and direct measures of paternal punitiveness, warmth, and power tend to confirm that each of these paternal traits plays a role in the son's development of a masculine personality; the developmental identification theory (paternal warmth), however, receives the strongest confirmation. Further, a boy's masculinity appears to be associated with paternal but not maternal warmth.

Mussen (1961) examines the same relationships using different measures in a study with adolescent males. The measure of sex typing is derived from the Strong Vocational Interest Blank (SVIB), a vocational-preference test. The ways adult males are portrayed in the projective stories of the Thematic Apperception Test (TAT) are interpreted as the adolescents' perceptions of their fathers. The result of the study is that more masculine boys portray adult male figures as both warm and powerful but not punitive, lending additional support to the developmental and role theory formulations of identification.

But another major study, Sears, Rau, and Alpert's *Identification and Child Rearing* (1965), does not find these relationships. No relationship was evident between paternal warmth or power, as related by observers, and a wide variety of measures of masculinity of interests in sons (including the It scale). Sears et al. did not find evidence for any general trait of dependency, the presumed motivation for developmental identification. In comparing the study by Sears, Rau, and Alpert with his own, Mussen (1969, p. 723) notes several methodological differences between the two that may account for their divergent results. The subjects in the former study are about one year younger, so that the predicted relationships between paternal behaviors and sons' masculinity might not yet be evident. Further, Sears et al.'s sample came from more highly educated families, perhaps resulting in less sex typing generally and weaker relationships between sons' masculinity and paternal variables.

These studies prompt a number of observations. First, even if a relationship is shown between a father's characteristics and his son's sex typing, this will not demonstrate that the former causes the latter. Quite the reverse may be the case. Or they may only appear to be related because both relate to some confounding third variable. For example, paternal warmth and sons' masculinity may be related because fathers favor masculine sons—a not unlikely possibility in our sex role-oriented culture; then again, paternal power may appear to be related to sons' masculinity only because both are related to lower socioeconomic status.

Second, these studies do not test the identification-modeling theory differentially from the reinforcement theory. That is, they fail to explore the possibility that the same things that make the father more effective as an identification figure may make him more effective as a reinforcer.

Third, the distance between the measures most frequently used in these studies and the concepts that they are thought to assess is considerable. Mussen's conclusion in his studies of kindergarten children that paternal warmth promotes sons' masculinity is based on correlations between, say, (1) boys depicting adult male characters during a doll-play game as being friendly and (2) boys declaring that a stick figure named It likes to play with a dump truck rather than a necklace. Mussen's parallel conclusion in his study of adolescents likewise rests, for example, on the association between, for example, (1) a boy making up a story in which older males are friendly and (2) preferring to be a truck driver rather than an accountant. Accepting the conclusions drawn from such studies requires great faith in the validity of the measures they use—even greater than is usually the case in psychological research.

Similarity between Fathers and Sons

The theory that identification with the father leads to masculinity in the son implicitly assumes that the father himself has a masculine identity. Actually, of course, fathers vary in their masculinity. Mischel (1969, pp. 40–41) is one of the few to point out the problems that this variation causes for identification-modeling theory. Mischel notes, as an extreme case, a study by Greenstein (1966) that finds an association between paternal warmth and sons' homosexuality—the behavior universally considered most incompatible with traditional male sex role identity. Greenstein tries to explain this paradox by suggesting that the fathers rated warmest toward their sons may have been homosexually inclined toward them. But Mischel notes that in this case the sons' homosexuality is evidence of identification. As Mischel (1969, p. 40) notes, "This seemingly paradoxical possibility—in which paternal nurturance enhances the son's identification with his father but also results in a more homosexual son—points up a peculiar feature of identification theory."

Since fathers vary in their masculinity as well as in other traits, perhaps the most obvious way to test the identification theory is to see how much sons resemble their fathers. Similarities between fathers and sons may occur, of course, because of genetic inheritance; but since sons also inherit from their mothers, the genetic factor may be controlled by comparing a sons' similarity with his father to his similarity to his mother. Also, father-son similarity should be less than mother-daughter since the MSRI paradigm postulates that identification-modeling is less important for males than females. Both Lynn (1974, pp. 146–149) and Maccoby and Jacklin (1974, pp. 292–293) conclude that the evidence for father-son similarity is weak. Sons are equally similar to both parents on nonsex-typed traits, and sons appear similar to neither parent on sex-typed ones. Further, sons are not less similar to fathers than daughters are to mothers.[1]

Lynn (1974) distinguishes between studies of sons' *perceived* similarity to their fathers (comparing sons' characteristics with sons' perceptions of their fathers) from studies of *actual* similarity (comparing measures of sons and fathers collected completely independently). There is some tendency for sons to *perceive* themselves and their fathers as similar, but this perceived similarity is not confirmed by studies of actual or tested similarity. The one exception cited by Lynn is similarity between fathers and sons in cigarette smoking.

Maccoby and Jacklin (1974) note that the lack of similarity of sons to *either* parent on sex-typed traits (in contrast to their moderate degree of similarity to both parents on non sex-typed traits) is particularly puzzling. One interpretation may be that children imitate both parents on sex-typed traits but that the effects of imitating these two models cancel each other out when sex typing is assessed by scales that treat masculinity and femininity as opposites. Maccoby and Jacklin note, however, that children do not behave androgynously; actually, they act in sex-typed ways.

Effects of Paternal Absence

A different sort of data often cited in support of the identification-modeling theory of sex role identity is the effect on a son's masculinity of his father's absence during childhood. Herzog and

Sudia's *Boys in Fatherless Families* (1971)[2] presents the most exhaustive examination to date of this question. They note many problems in this research and find that, of the methodologically adequate studies, half show no differences between boys whose fathers are present and boys whose fathers are absent; the other half report weaker or more confused sex typing among boys whose fathers are absent. But the differences in these latter studies, while statistically significant, are small in absolute size and occur for relatively few measures of sex typing.

A number of peculiarities of interpretation are worth noting in the latter studies. First, when results on a particular measure do not conform to the paternal absence hypothesis, that measure is often criticized as inadequate (for example, see Tiller, 1958, on the Draw-a-Family Test); the same measure escapes criticism, however, when it yields results supporting the hypothesis. Perhaps the most striking illustration of this selective criticism is Harrington's (1970) explanation of his study's negative results as due to inaccuracies in his subjects' reports of their fathers' presence or absence—a possibility never raised in studies supporting the hypothesis. Second, these studies infer problems in male sex role identity not only from low masculinity scores but also from high ones, the latter supposedly indicating overcompensation for underlying insecurity. As Herzog and Sudia note, while this interpretation may be true, it makes it impossible to disprove the hypothesis. Herzog and Sudia's (1971) conclusion is compelling:

The evidence here is so fragmentary and so shakily based that it is difficult to achieve or to claim judicious perspective. Taken as a whole, this evidence constitutes almost a projective test. Its ambiguous outlines invite the imposition of a form and a structure dictated by the presuppositions of the analyst rather than by the data.

Our best efforts to analyze the studies and findings reviewed, with allowance for refraction through the lenses of the observers, yield a negative conclusion: that the evidence so far available offers no firm basis for assuming that boys who grow up in fatherless homes are more likely, as men, to suffer from inadequate masculine identity as a result of lacking a resident male model. (P. 62)

Overall, the identification-modeling theory has much less empirical support than is generally believed. I am led to agree with Maccoby and Jacklin's (1974, p. 30) conclusion that "review of the research on selective imitation [has] led us to a conclusion that is very difficult to accept, namely that modeling plays a minor role in the development of sex-typed behavior."

Reinforcement

Reinforcement is the most intuitively obvious of the hypotheses accounting for the development of sex-typed characteristics. Put succinctly, boys become masculine and girls feminine because they are rewarded for sex-appropriate, and punished for sex-inappropriate, behaviors. The MSRI paradigm argues that the reinforcement of sex-typed characteristics by parents and other socializing agents is a more important factor in the development of sex role identity in males than in females.

Reinforcement potentially includes a wide range of phenomena. It may take obvious forms based on cultural views of sex roles, such as encouraging aggression in boys but not girls; but it also may take subtle forms not necessarily rooted in beliefs about sex roles, such as parents talking less to male than female infants. It may be expressed not only in parents' responses to their children's behaviors but also in the chores parents assign or the expectations they hold. It may occur at different stages of the life cycle. There are many different potential reinforcing agents: mother, father, teachers, other adults, peers, and social institutions. Of all these potential forms of reinforcement for sex typing, the MSRI paradigm emphasizes parental reinforcement of clearly sex role-related characteristics early in life.

Do Parents Treat the Sexes Differently?

Maccoby and Jacklin (1974) review research on similarities and differences in the parental treatment of boys and girls in eleven different areas. They note at the outset that the available research pays more attention to mothers than fathers, younger than older children, and middle-class than working-class children. This is their conclusion:

We must summarize our analysis of this reinforcement hypothesis with the conclusion that we have been able to find very little evidence to support it, in relation to behaviors other than sex-typing as very narrowly defined (e.g., toy preference). The reinforcement contingencies for the two sexes appear to be similar. (P. 342)

The specific areas they review, and their conclusions in each, are as follows:

1. *Total parent-child interaction.* Overall, there is no difference in amount of parental interaction by sex of child. Parents do elicit more gross motor behavior in boys.

2. *Verbal interaction.* The results are inconsistent. On balance, studies show no difference in amount or kind of verbal interaction; patterns within subgroups, however, are possible.

3. *Parental warmth.* The nine available observational studies find no difference by sex. Girls, however, report receiving more parental warmth.

4. *Parental restrictiveness.* Most studies show no difference; those that do, find *boys* more restricted by parents.

5. *Reactions to dependency.* The results are inconsistent and show no overall trend.

6. *Reactions to aggression.* Interview reports are inconsistent. Observational studies of parents' responses to aggressive acts against them by their children are inconsistent; there is some tendency on parents' part, however, to respond more negatively to aggression shown by a son. No observational studies are available of parents' responses to aggression by their children against peers, which is probably more important. Maccoby and Jacklin make the commonsense observation that parents do not encourage aggression in children of either sex but favor, instead, teaching them other techniques.

7. *Encouragement of sex-typed activities.* There is little direct evidence, but what evidence exists (Lansky, 1967; Fling and Manosevitz, 1972) suggests that parents encourage sex-typed activities and discourage sex-inappropriate activities of boys more than girls.[3]

8. *Response to childrens' sexuality.* The three available interview studies indicate no difference in parental restrictiveness toward boys and girls.

9. *Physical punishment and other negative sanctions.* Boys clearly receive more punishment. Some evidence suggests a circular process: Boys get punished more because their initial responses to parental sanctions are weaker.

10. *Praise, reward, positive feedback.* Boys do receive more positive feedback, but also more negative feedback. Boys receive more evaluation and surveillance in general.

11. *Achievement pressure.* There is no differecce in the extent to which boys and girls are encouraged or expected to perform competently on tasks. But, boys are encouraged more to go to college and to pursue education generally.

Thus, Maccoby and Jacklin find consistent differential reinforcement in only three of these eleven areas. Several previous large-scale studies and reviews also conclude that the ways in which boys are treated differently from girls are relatively few. For example, Sears, Maccoby, and Levin's *Patterns of Child Rearing* (1957), perhaps the best-known study, in comparison between the self-reports of 202 mothers of boys and 177 mothers of girls concluded that "there were few dimensions on which the sexes were differently treated . . . and it may be that at least some of the differences here would not be found in a wider sample of mothers" (pp. 401–402). Mischel (1966) notes that "unfortunately, present evidence that the sexes are treated differently by their parents with respect to the above behaviors [aggression and dependency] is far from firm" (p. 75). Mussen's (1969) review of data concerning the differential socialization hypothesis also finds that "in fact there is very little evidence that infant boys and girls receive any significant differential treatment by either or both parents" (p. 713).

Block (1978), however, argues that parents' differential treatment of the sexes is substantial. In Block's study, 5 samples of mothers and 6 of fathers describe their behavior toward a particular child on a 91-item Child-Rearing Practices Report (CRPR).[4] Mothers of sons report significantly different behaviors than mothers of daughters on 26 of the 91 items (29%), and fathers report significantly different behaviors on 23 items (25%). Actually, the proportions of sex-differentiated behavior found by Block are comparable to Maccoby and Jacklin's conclusion that parents treat the sexes differently in only 3 of the 11 areas they review (3/11=27%). Ultimately, it is a question of judgment whether to regard these proportions—somewhat more than a quarter—as demonstrating a lot or only a little parental sex differentiation.

Block's data illustrate another issue of judgment. Block establishes differences in parental behavior according to children's sex by using a statistical procedure that combines the results across the samples in a special way. For example, Block concludes that mothers express significantly more physical affection to daughters than to sons. But this difference is not statistically significant within any of the samples of mothers: 4 show nonsignificant trends in this direction, while 1 shows the opposite trend. But the overall pattern of results—nonsignificant trends in the expected direction in 4 of the 5 samples—is statistically significant. Across all the items on which significant differences are found, the difference is significant within the individual samples examined less than a third of the time. Block's statistical procedure is legitimate, but most of the differences it yields are quite small; they are not sufficiently large to be evident to a statistically significant degree even a third of the time in individual samples of about 100 each (which, for studies of this type, are relatively large). To put it succinctly, differential socialization by sex must be a considerably weaker phenomenon than is generally thought if a pooled sample of over 500 has to be used in order to demonstrate it at statistically significant levels.

Does Differential Reinforcement Actually Lead to Sex Typing?

Even with strong and consistent differences in parents' behavior toward boys and girls, it still would remain to be shown that this differential treatment actually differentially affects child development. That is, in order to validate the theory, it is not enough to show that parents treat boys differently than girls; it must be shown that variations in the extent to which parents shape sex-typed behavior are actually related to variations in sex typing among children.

In fact, any such relationship has yet to be well established for global measures of sex typing. Mussen's (1969, p. 715) review of the evidence concludes that "there are no definitive studies relating reliable and objective observations of parental rewards and punishments to children's sex-typed behavior." Mussen and Rutherford (1963), for example, find no relationships between boys' sex typing and the extent to which parents report encouragement of their children to engage in sex-typed activities. Fling and Manosevitz (1972) find only one significant relationship between parents' reports of the degree to which they prefer only sex-typed activities in their children and their children's sex typing at the orientation, preference, and adoption levels distinguished by Biller and Lynn: Fathers who report that they prefer strong sex typing have daughters who are sex typed at the adoption level but not at the other two levels. Biller (1968) shows that a measure of the extent to which mothers report that they encourage (or at least do not discourage) assertive, aggressive, or independent behavior in their kindergarten sons (interpreted as their encouragement of masculinity) is positively correlated with sons' masculinity at the preference level (self-reported toy and game preferences) but not at the other two levels. Fagot and Patterson (1969) conclude that children's sex-typed behavior does not change in the direction of their teacher's reinforcement over the course of a year, and Sears, Rau, and Alpert (1965) find that the degree to which children engage in sex-typed activities does not relate to measures of the degree of parental encouragement of sex typing.[5] Thus there is actually quite little evidence that differential reinforcement by parents leads to sex typing in children, at least as assessed by global measures.

In summary, currently available evidence suggests that differential parental reinforcement of sex-typed traits may be considerably weaker than is generally thought; even when it does occur, its actual effect on global measures of children's sex typing has not been demonstrated. A more critical blow to the MSRI paradigm is that there is little evidence that reinforcement is a more important source of sex typing in males than in females.

Cognitive Learning

The third major approach to the development of sex typing is the *cognitive learning theory*, which holds that individuals acquire sex typing through cognitive internalization of the culture's sex role norms and stereotypes. In other words, individuals seek to develop characteristics consistent with cultural beliefs about their sex. This theory implies that the development of sex-typed traits depends on the maturation of cognitive capacities.

Cognitive learning theory has two different versions. In the MSRI paradigm, the cognitive learning of sex typing is considered complete when the individual successfully acquires traditional sex-typed traits. According to the paradigm, cognitive learning is more important as a source of sex typing among males than females. Other recent theorists, however, argue that cognitive development ideally proceeds beyond traditional sex typing to a later stage in which the individual no longer cognitively polarizes the roles of the sexes, and therefore becomes less sex typed (Block, 1973; Pleck, 1975a; Rebecca, Hefner, and Ole-shanksy, 1976). This latter view may be called the *cognitive transcendence theory.*

Mussen (1969) notes that the cognitive learning theory of sex typing usually is used to account for general trends in sex role development by age; relatively little research uses it to explain individual differences in sex typing within a given age group—a more definitive test. The most important of the latter kind of study is Kohlberg and Zigler (1967), who find that IQ is an important correlate of individual differences in sex typing. Specifically, among young children high IQ is associated with high sex typing, while among adolescents high IQ is associated with low sex typing. This result tends to discredit the MSRI paradigm by lending support to the cognitive transcendence theory. Also, the study concludes that these relationships between IQ and sex typing are no stronger for boys than for girls. Again, doubt is cast on the MSRI paradigm, according to which cognitive learning is a more important source of sex role identity for boys than for girls.

Cognitive learning theory also predicts that variations in sex typing are related to variations in the sex role norms and stereotypes that people perceive. Several studies examine sex role stereotyping in children's books and other media (Child, Potter, and Levine, 1946; Jacklin and Mischel, 1973). Two important studies by McArthur and Eisen (1976a, 1976b) go further and show that images of the sexes portrayed in such media affect children's actual behavior. McArthur and Eisen (1976a) read children ages 4–6 a stereotype story depicting achievement behavior by a male but not a female, a reversal story depicting achievement by a female, or a control story depicting no achievement for any character. Boys persist significantly longer on an achievement task after hearing the stereotype story, and girls show a nonsignificant trend in the opposite direction. In their second study, McArthur and Eisen (1976b) show children videotape stimuli including adult males and females acting in sex-stereotyped or reversed ways (determined by a separate study of activities representative of those played by each sex on television). Following this viewing, boys perform significantly more masculine than feminine activities if they watch the stereotyped program, but more feminine than masculine activities if they watch the reversed program. Opposite trends are evident in girls but not reaching statistical significance. These findings are consistent with predictions made by the MSRI paradigm.

Finally, Lynn (1969, pp. 28–30) reviews other sorts of data on the role of cognitive learning and concludes that "there is insufficient evidence to evaluate it with confidence." The studies reviewed by Lynn that provide the strongest support for the proposition involve comparing the degree of similarity between sons and their own fathers with the degree of similarity between sons and fathers (or other adult males) picked at random. The former is usually not significantly higher, and sometimes is even lower, than the latter, which may be interpreted as confirming the proposition by showing that a son models himself after a generalized male role image rather than after his father. The meaning of this comparison is inherently ambiguous, however, since it is impossible to tell whether the cognitive learning theory is being validated or the identification-modeling theory is being invalidated. Also, many of these studies make this comparison only among male subjects, so that systematic examination of the relative importance of cognitive learning of sex typing to males and to females is impossible.

Overall, evidence on the cognitive learning hypothesis is both insufficient and somewhat inconsistent. Kohlberg and Zigler (1967) and McArthur and Eisen (1976a, b) provide the strongest data in its support. Only the latter research, however, supports the identity paradigm's prediction that cognitive learning is more important for males than females.

Overview

No doubt, many readers will be surprised to learn that a critical review of the evidence for the three major theories of the development of sex typing yields such negative results (see also Constantinople, 1979). The second proposition of the MSRI paradigm, without whose support the paradigm is in very serious difficulty, receives only weak confirmation. Identification-modeling indeed does not appear to be a strong source of sex role development in boys, but it is not clear whether its effects are weaker on boys than on girls, as the paradigm requires. Nor are reinforcement and cognitive learning stronger. The evidence on the effects of reinforcement is generally negative for both sexes. While McArthur and Eisen's studies suggest that boys' sex typing responds more to cognitive input than does girls, other studies do not confirm this.

The research reviewed here has broader implications. In spite of several decades of research, the factors promoting or inhibiting the acquisition of sex typing within each sex are still not well understood. Better measures of sex typing, particularly androgyny-type measures, need to be used. Studies should compare the *relative* strengths of the three major casual factors rather than test them one at a time for the presence or absence of statistical significance. Also, the relative strengths of each factor need to be compared between the sexes.

5

Males tend to have greater difficulty than females in achieving same-sex identification. . . . More males than females fail more or less completely in achieving same-sex identification, making instead an opposite-sex identification. (Lynn, 1969, p. 103)

The passive male homosexual and the active female homosexual are individuals whose sexual behavior is to be understood as an outgrowth or expression of their overall inversion; the male invert psychologically perceives himself as a female, and accordingly looks to the "opposite" sex for sexual gratification. . . . Inversion has its roots in the earliest years of life when the child forms, at first involuntarily and later consciously, an identification-attachment to the parent of the opposite sex and thereby introjects the sex role of the opposite sex. The invert, then, is a psychosomatic misfit, having the body of one sex and the personality of the other sex. (D. Brown, 1957b, pp. 615, 618)

Proposition 3. *The development of appropriate sex role identity is a risky, failure-prone process, especially for males.*

The MSRI paradigm argues that, because it depends to a large degree on learning processes requiring favorable environmental conditions, the development of sex role identity is an inherently risky affair, especially for males, for whom same-sex parental identification is more difficult. The data most relevant to this proposition concern the prediction that more males than females fail to develop appropriate sex role identities and are of three basic sorts: transsexuality, sex typing in children, and sex typing in adults. (Data on the incidence of homosexuality are also often cited in support of this proposition; their discussion will be deferred until proposition 4.)

Transsexuality

The evidence cited most frequently in support of the notion that men more often than women fail to develop appropriate sex role identities is the higher incidence of transsexuality[1] among men than women (see, for example, Lynn, 1969, p. 59). *Transsexuality* is used here, and by most authorities, to refer to individuals of one biological sex who are convinced that they are, and psychologically experience themselves to be, members of the other sex. Transsexuality concerns individual sex self-classification (that is, the sex that individuals assign themselves), and must be distinguished from sex typing. A frequent image used by transsexuals to describe their experience is that they feel they have been trapped in a body of the wrong sex.

The ratio of biological males to biological females applying for transsexual surgery is usually estimated to be about 4 to 1 (see, for example, Money and Ehrhardt, 1972, p. 147). This skewed sex ratio seems a powerful piece of evidence, but two points make its implications ambiguous. First, the assumption that this sex ratio reflects the relative frequency of transsexuality itself is open to question. Lynn (1969, p. 70), for example, notes that the apparently greater feasibility of surgical procedures for removing compared to constructing male genitalia and the notoriety of certain male-to-female transsexuals (for example, Christine Jorgensen) may bias the application ratio. Second, the absolute rate of incidence of transsexuality among males is extremely low—certainly less than 1 in 1,000. Even if the rate of transsexuality is much higher among males than females, its rate among males is still minuscule, and can hardly be evidence that failure in sex role identity development is a major risk faced by males.

Sex Typing in Children

The It Scale

Past studies of sex typing in children have relied primarily on the It scale (D. Brown, 1956). Kohlberg's (1966) review of studies employing this measure suggests that boys develop sex typing both more strongly and earlier than girls. For example, in the sample on which the It scale was originally developed, girls' mean score averages 38 points from the extreme feminine end of the scale, while boys' mean score is only 18 points from the extreme masculine end.

It has been suggested that boys' stronger sex typing on this measure occurs because the figure depicting It actually looks more like a boy than a girl. Efforts to make the stimulus more sex neutral (by such techniques as concealing the figure in an envelope or using a blank card) have not produced consistent results, however. Fling and Manosevitz (1972) find that boys are not significantly more sex typed than girls when the concealed It is used, but Endsley (1967) still finds stronger sex typing in boys. It has also been argued that boys' greater problems in sex role identity are shown by their greater variance (that is, breadth of the distribution of their scores) on the It scale (Lansky and McKay, 1963), but other studies find boys' scores have lower variance (Endsley, 1967).

The Draw-a-Person (DAP) Test

Another measure of sex typing that presumably measures a deep level of sex role identity is the sex of the figure drawn first when subjects are asked simply to draw a person; drawing a figure of one's own sex that is thought to indicate appropriate sex role identity. Brown and Tolor (1957) review a group of studies using this technique and note that among younger children a higher proportion of girls than boys draw a same-sex figure first. Among older children, however, this trend is reversed, and by college age 91% of male subjects draw a male figure first and only 61% of the women draw a female first.

The age reversal poses certain problems to the theory. If these results show that boys have more difficulty acquiring appropriate sex role identity early in life, they also show that the difficulty is more than overcome later in life. It is possible to argue that the test does not assess the same thing at different stages in development, but this leads to logically arbitrary interpretations. For example, some might argue that young boys' cross-sex drawings indicate their deep-lying feminine identifications, while girls' cross-sex drawings in later childhood and adolescence reflect the fact that in our society persons (and other sex-neutral terms) are assumed to be male unless specified otherwise. But could not an alternative argument be made that young boys' drawings of women simply reflect the fact that females are the most salient figures in children's social worlds, while older girls' drawings of men indicate their deep-seated sex role identify confusion? There is no clear logical or empirical basis for interpreting what the test means or whether it means the same thing at different times.[2]

Behavioral Preferences

The problems in the DAP test perhaps can be avoided simply by asking children to describe their own actual preferences for sex-typed activities. The majority of such studies (Ross, 1971; Ward, 1968, 1973; Rabban, 1950; Pulaski, 1970; De Lucia, 1963; Hall and Keith, 1964; Ferguson and Maccoby, 1966; Wolf, 1975) find that boys are more sex typed, either in the sense of (1) having mean scores closer to the maximum masculine score than girls' mean score is to the maximum feminine score or (2) resisting playing with an opposite-sex toy.

There is a critical assumption that must be made for these results (as well as those with the It scale) to be meaningful, however. One must assume that the measures are constructed so that the maximum feminine score is as exactly as extremely feminine as the maximum masculine score is extremely masculine. This may be true, but there is no clear way to test such an assumption. The second kind of study illustrates this same problem even more clearly. Wolf (1975) compares the frequency of boys playing with dolls to the frequency of girls playing with a fire engine after the boys and girls have been exposed to a same-sex model playing with the sex-inappropriate toy and finds that girls play with the cross-sex toy more than boys. But is a fire engine as sex-inappropriate for a girl as a doll is for a boy? Using another sex-inappropriate toy for girls, such as a gun, might have produced quite different results. Such studies in the future will need to establish that the stimuli used are equivalently sex inappropriate. One study using stimuli that seem, on their face, equivalent (willingness to play the role of the other sex in a telephone game) does not find a sex difference (Sears, Rau, and Alpert, 1965).

There is still another interpretive ambiguity in these studies. In the Wolf (1975) study, during a free-play period following exposure to the model girls touch their sex-inappropriate toy (a fire engine) more than boys do theirs (a doll), but when the children are asked to play in unusual or novel ways this sex difference disappears: the boys' rate could easily be raised to the girls'. In another example, when Ross and Ross (1972) have teachers suggest to children that they play with sex-inappropriate toys, the boys argue with the teachers more about this than do girls but *actually choose* a sex-inappropriate toy at the same rate. The issue raised by these studies is that boys may be spontaneously or ordinarily more sex typed in their behavior than are girls but that this can be overcome rather easily.

Time in Other-Sex Activities

Several studies classify various nursery school activities as boys' or girls' simply according to the amount of time each sex spends in them. Fagot and Patterson (1969) find that 3-year-old boys spend 13.5% of their time in girl's activities, while girls spend 7.6% of their time in boys' activities.[3] Etaugh, Collins, and Gerson (1975) report similar results in a 2-year-old sample. This find of more frequent cross-sex activities in boys disagrees with the other behavioral studies. Two factors may account for it. First, the most frequent activities classified as girls' in the time use studies are art work and listening to stories. Whether boys who engage in these specific activities should be regarded as exhibiting cross-sex behavior is open to question. Second, nursery teachers probably encourage children to draw and listen to stories and, as shown by Wolf (1975) and Ross and Ross (1972), this encouragement may overcome boys' avoidance of cross-sex behavior.

Sex Typing in Adults

The relative degree of sex typing in adults can also be examined. Older studies, which use bipolar sex typing measures, cannot be easily used for this purpose since these scales provide no way of deciding whether men's or women's average scores show a higher degree of sex typing. Newer studies, employing androgyny measures, are more promising. The best available study for this purpose, Bem (1974), using presence or absence of a significant difference between masculinity and femininity scores (as determined by t-test) as the criterion for classifying individuals as sex typed, sex reversed, or androgynous, finds that 30% of the men are sex typed compared to 20% of the women. Although these date do not show that men are more sex typed than women by an absolute criterion, they do show that a higher proportion of men than women have relatively more sex-typed than sex-reversed traits.

Other androgyny studies using the median-split rather than the t-test method of classification yield different results. Bem (1977), reanalyzing her 1974 data with the median-split method (dividing both m and f scores at their respective combined-sex sample medians), finds almost equal proportions of exclusively sex-typed persons in both sexes (37% versus 34%). Spence, Helmreich, and Stapp (1974), however, conclude that the proportion of sex-typed males is less than the proportion of sex-typed females (27% versus 38%). One generally unrecognized problem with the median-split method in which sexes are combined is that the relative proportion of males and females in the sample will systematically affect the proportions of persons of each sex classified in the four sex typing groups.[4]

Overview

The MSRI paradigm holds that males have more difficulty attaining sex role identity than do females. Empirically testing this hypothesis requires comparing males and females on their relative degree of sex typing using the various measures available. But examining the evidence makes it clear that there is no simple answer to the apparently simple question, "Which sex is more sex typed?"

In studies of children, there is a slight preponderance of evidence that boys are more rigidly sex typed than girls. But the value of this evidence actually depends in large part on untested (and probably untestable) assumptions about the meaning of the It scale and the equivalence of the sex-inappropriate stimuli used in the behavioral-preference studies. Further, spontaneous behavioral differences appear to be easily overcome by social influence. A direct comparison of willingness to play the role of the other sex reveal no sex difference. Studies of time spent by very young children in other-sex activities in classrooms suggest boys show less sex typing than girls, but this finding may be due to the specific behaviors studied and also teacher influence. Studies in adults yield results that are inconsistent and appear highly dependent on the classification procedure used. The inconsistency of these data simply underlines the point that sex typing is more complicated and poorly understood than has been widely realized.

Such results can be reconciled with the MSRI paradigm only by selective emphasis on some data (for example, transsexuality and DAP performance in young children) and selective reinterpretation of other data (for example, greater sex typing in males reflects overcompensation for their true insecurity in their sex role identities). But doing so means emphasizing the data drawn from the more controversial and ambiguous measures at the expense of the more concrete and unambiguous ones. Overall the evidence that males are more vulnerable than females to failures of sex role identity development is weak.

Proposition 4. *Homosexuality reflects a disturbance of sex role identity.*

Male homosexuality has always been one of the central preoccupations of the MSRI paradigm. For example, comparisons between homosexuals and heterosexuals have often been employed in the development of simple m-f sex typing scales, and homosexuality has been one of the phenomena studied most frequently with them. Nearly a fifth of Terman and Miles's (1936) *Sex and Personality,* the first book-length analysis and empirical study of sex typing, is devoted to studies of homosexuals (almost all of which concern male homosexuals). It is common among identity theorists to treat homosexuality as a sex role identity defect (see, for example, D. Brown, 1957b, 1958b).

In most popular discussions about insecure or inadequate sex role identity, concern about homosexuality is not far below the surface. When traditionalists argue against various childrearing or school practices that, it is feared, cause boys to have sex role identity problems, increased likelihood of homosexuality is usually what is really meant. The various terms for difficulties in sex role identity (insecurities, conflicts and so forth) are often simply pseudoscientific euphemisms for homosexuality.[5]

Sex difference in rates of homosexuality are often interpreted to support the idea that the attainment of sex role identity is more problematic for males than females. It is difficult, though, to get reliable data on this since the social stigma against homosexuality makes it doubtful that people will truthfully report in general surveys past or present homosexual behavior. The well-known Kinsey studies (Kinsey, Pomeroy, and Martin, 1948; Kinsey et al., 1953), using an extremely intensive interview technique with large samples of men and women, do find homosexuality to be considerably more frequent in men than women according to all indices, but these samples are neither representative nor comparable to each other in educational level.

Moreover, it is a problem for the MSRI paradigm that men should show weak sex role identity more often than women when homosexuality is the criterion, but show stronger identity than women by other criteria of sex typing. Lynn's (1969, p. 60) attempt to resolve this problem is inconclusive; male identity is more difficult to establish, he holds, but it "typically progresses satisfactorily if it 'once gets off the ground,' that is, if the initial step is taken early in life." Homosexuality simply contributes more inconsistency to the data on sex differences in sex typing.

The data most relevant to the proposition that homosexuality is a manifestation of insecure sex role identity concern the relationship between homosexual behavior and measures of sex typing. Studies that bear directly on this question appear to be rare. Harrington (1970) assesses the frequency of sexual behaviors "inappropriate to the male role" (this includes exhibitionism and masturbation in addition to homosexuality) in a sample of 118 adolescent males seen in inpatient and outpatient mental health services. Males coded as showing this cluster of behaviors have markedly more feminine scores on the Gough Fe scale but do not show appreciably more feminine sex typing on the m-f scale of the SVIB, or the Franck test. Further, this cluster is only weakly related to eleven other behaviors interpreted as masculine or feminine (Harrington, 1970, pp. 65, 67–68).

Another kind of data concerns comparisons of the scores of homosexuals and heterosexuals on m-f tests. Many such studies find that male homosexuals have more feminine sex typing than heterosexuals. It is interesting to note, though, that a number of these studies do not. Indeed, the first study to examine this relationship, Terman and Miles (1936), finds that while so-called passive male homosexuals have more feminine scores, active male homosexuals actually have more masculine scores than do the control samples. Renaud (1950) cannot distinguish male homosexuals from heterosexuals on the basis of the MMPI m-f scale alone. Frass (1970) likewise does not find significant difference between small samples of male homosexuals and heterosexuals on the MMPI m-f scale. Manosevitz (1970) concludes that MMPI masculinity-femininity has a correlation with homosexuality of 0.72 in one sample but only 0.30 in another, Thompson et al. (1973) that male homosexuals have significantly more feminine scores on Heilbrun's Adjective Checklist m-f measure but do not have more feminine Franck scores. Freund et al. (1974) finds no significant difference between homosexual and heterosexual males on a sex typing measure.

There are several methodological problems in comparisons of homosexuals and heterosexuals on sex typing scales. The sex typing scale most often used in these studies, the MMPI m-f scale, is based on a particularly unrepresentative sample. Many of these studies are conducted in prison populations, resulting in atypical samples of homosexuals and heterosexuals. As an extreme example, Burton (1947) actually uses heterosexual rapists as the control group against whom homosexuals are compared! (He finds, incidentally, that homosexuals do not have significantly more feminine scores.) Because of these and other problems, even early reviews of the use of m-f tests for diagnosing homosexuality (for example, Grygier, 1957) note their considerable inadequacies. Manuals for most m-f tests now strongly caution against this use.

Three recent studies examining the relationship between homosexuality and androgyny sex typing scales, all using student samples, report inconsistent results. Bender, Davis, and Glover (1976), who compare sexual-preference groups of both sexes on the scales of both the Bem BSRI and the Spence and Helmreich PAQ, find no significant differences on the PAQ scales, but they do find homosexuals score higher on BSRI femininity. Their analysis does not specifically compare homosexuals and heterosexuals separately within each sex, but inspection of their data suggests that the difference on BSRI femininity is not significant for males alone. Ward (reported in Spence and Helmreich, 1978, pp. 65–67), however, concludes that college male homosexuals score significantly higher than heterosexuals in PAQ femininity and lower in masculinity.[6] Homosexual males appear more likely to be sex reversed and (to an even stronger degree) undifferentiated than heterosexual males, as well as less likely to be sex typed. Heilbrun and Thompson (1977), using Heilbrun's Adjective Checklist androgyny scale, find that homosexual males, compared to heterosexuals, are somewhat less likely to be sex typed (masculine) and more likely to be sex reversed (feminine). But these differences do not attain statistical significance, nor are there any differences in the frequency of androgynous and undifferentiated types in the two samples. (In the latter point they are at variance with Ward.)

These studies use more adequate measures of sex typing and better samples than studies based on older m-f scales. Their results are no more consistent, however—certainly not sufficiently consistent to suggest that sexual preference is directly related to other aspects of sex typing and therefore interpretable as a critical manifestation of sex role identity.

Interpreting Anomalous Data on Homosexuality and Sex Typing

Since the data on the relationship between homosexuality and sex typing are anomalous for the male MSRI paradigm, an interpretation had to be found that would reconcile the data with the theory. Thus, a distinction was made between inversion and homosexuality (D. Brown, 1957b): The male invert plays the passive or receptive role in homosexual relations; all inverts are homosexuals, but not all homosexuals are inverts. In effect, the idea is that the paradigm's theory about homosexuality holds true, but only for a subgroup, the inverted homosexuals. D. J. West, the foremost British authority on homosexuality, illustrates this qualified theory well. In his first book about homosexuality, West (1960) claims that

the notion that all male homosexuals have effeminate characteristics and all lesbians have masculine traits is not without a certain justification, for a minority among homosexuals do show a marked temperamental bias toward features more characteristic of the opposite sex. (P. 58)

In a more recent book, West (1977), asserts that

a minority of homosexuals do suffer to a certain degree from disturbance of gender identity. In some cases it amounts to no more than an inner feeling of dissatisfaction or incompetence when performing the social or occupational roles expected of a man or woman. Sometimes the disturbance is more overt. The effeminate male homosexual (queen) who advertises himself with a falsetto voice, make-up, and girlish mannerisms is only too well known. (P. 5)

This theoretical distinction is vulnerable to at least one criticism and has a surprising implication. It assumes that homosexuals can be readily and reliably classified as inverted or noninverted. Actually, research indicates that male homosexuals and lesbians do not have exclusively so-called active or passive roles in their sexual relationships (Bell and Weinberg, 1978), which casts doubt on the primary basis for differentiating the inverted from the noninverted. And even if these groups could be reliably discriminated, the resolution proposed requires giving up any psychodynamic interpretation of noninverted homosexuality. Among males, there would no longer be any theoretical basis for differentiating between males who play active sexual roles with women from males who play active sexual roles with men.

One of the central underlying themes in the MSRI paradigm is that sex role identity problems are often hidden or disguised due to individuals' unconscious defense mechanisms (and often their conscious dishonesty as well). Since identity disturbances are thought to be serious, it becomes permissible for psychologists to use diagnostic techniques designed to circumvent these defenses. Nowhere has this been more true than in the assessment of male homosexuality. An extreme example appears in a study by Greenstein (1966) concerning the relationship between paternal characteristics and sex typing in a sample of delinquent boys. The section of the published report describing the methodology of the study indicates that "part of the routine examination at the Diagnostic Center is a psychiatric interview conducted under sodium amytal medication [popularly known as truth serum]. During this interview, questions regarding the subjects' past behavior are asked which permit the measurement of frequency of overt homosexual experiences" (p. 273). Greenstein's passive language deadens the full impact of what he describes. A more active description is that a psychiatrist is drugging minors so as to better interrogate them about possible homosexual experiences.

Such practices are, of course, hardly the worst infringement of civil liberties that homosexuals have suffered. There is no way to know how widespread such procedures have been; most researchers' and clinicians' reports are less revealing than Greenstein's. His ethically questionable diagnostic method, nonetheless, both expresses in extreme form a fundamental theme in the MSRI paradigm and illustrates how the paradigm deals with disconfirming data. If homosexuality (and other sex role identity problems) is concealed, then psychologists develop m-f tests to reveal it; if these tests do not accomplish the task (as research indeed suggests), then psychologists turn to even more drastic procedures. That such a report could be published in an official journal of the American Psychological Association as late as 1966 indicates how deeply the MSRI paradigm has taken hold in American psychology.

6

Personal normality presupposes that an individual has assimilated not
only those values and ideals which are regarded as necessary and
proper for all persons, but also those which are uniquely appropriate
to one's sex role, as a man or as a woman. When identification has
occurred predominantly with the opposite-sexed parent rather than
the parent of the same sex, the individual is predisposed to homosexuality. Where there is a divided sexual identification, the resulting personality is likely to be neurotic. (Mowrer, 1950, p. 15)

Some children either resent or experience anxiety over the behaviors
that are assigned to their biological sex. This assumption is not inconsistent with the fact that some adolescents and adults strive to avoid
adoption of sex-typed responses because of anxiety over the behaviors
that are prescribed for their sex role. These individuals are typically in
conflict and are likely to manifest a variety of psychopathological symptoms. (Kagan, 1964a, pp. 145–146)

The father is an important model for his child. The father's positive
involvement facilitates the development of the boy's cognitive functioning, self-concept, his ability to control his impulses and to function
independently and responsibly, and his overall interpersonal competence. Much of the father's influence is related to his impact on the
boy's sex role development. (Biller, 1974, p. 84)

Proposition 5. *Appropriate sex role identity is necessary for good psychological adjustment because of an inner psychological need for it.*

The MSRI paradigm asserts that sex-appropriate sex typing is
correlated with measures of good psychological adjustment. Underlying this hypothesized relationship is the assumption that
individuals have an inner psychological need to validate or affirm
their biological sex by developing sex role identities, manifested

in their behavior by sex-appropriate sex typing. In doing so they become psychologically mature as members of their sex, and not doing so indicates a failure of normal development.

This proposition generates different predictions depending on which of the three conceptions of sex role identity is adopted. The simple conception leads to the *simple sex-appropriateness hypothesis*: Good adjustment requires exclusively sex-appropriate sex typing. The androgynous conception implies the *androgyny hypothesis*: Good adjustment requires both masculine and feminine sex typing. The multileveled conception produces a more complex set of predictions, considered separately in another proposition.

The Simple Sex-Appropriateness Hypothesis

The body of literature potentially relevant to this hypothesis is enormous; I consider here only the most frequently cited and most important studies.

Gray and Webb

In an examination of the relationship between sex-typed interests, anxiety, and social acceptance in 40 sixth- and seventh-grade boys and girls, Gray (1957) argues that women's sex role is changing in such a way that, to be well adjusted, girls need many traits traditionally considered sex inappropriate; but boys' adjustment, she argues, still necessitates exclusively sex-appropriate traits. For this study, sex typing is assessed by peer ratings; the measures of adjustment include social acceptance (assessed by classmates' ratings on leadership, friendship, practical intelligence, aggression, and withdrawal) and a questionnaire measure of anxiety. Gray predicts that masculinity is associated in both sexes with being rated as leader, friend, practical, aggressive, and not withdrawing and as scoring low on anxiety.

Gray's predictions are confirmed for girls on anxiety and withdrawal, but the relationships between sex typing and the other measures of social acceptance are not significant. For boys masculinity is related as predicted to three of the five social-acceptance measures (leadership, friendship, and withdrawal) but has no significant relationship to the other two. Contrary to prediction, however, masculinity is related to high rather than low anxiety. Gray suggested that it is possible that striving to maintain a masculine role is for the boy of this age group stressful enough to be associated with manifest anxiety. Or one could argue contrariwise that only the boy who is secure in his masculine role is willing to admit to such unmanly characteristics. (P. 212)

Thus Gray's study provides validation as well as invalidation of the proposition. Interestingly, however, the conclusion of Gray's report summarizes the study as "indicating a lack of clarity in the expectancies of the girl nearing adolescence as she is faced by the task of achieving an appropriate sex role" and makes no mention of the unexpected findings for boys. Later reviewers of this study usually report only that part of its findings that confirms the traditional proposition about sex typing and adjustment. Biller and Borstelman (1967, p. 256), for example, summarize this study by saying only that "Gray (1957) found leadership and social acceptance strongly related to masculinity in sixth and seventh grade boys."

Webb (1963) replicates Gray's study, making the same predictions, with a much larger sample of 317 seventh, eighth, and ninth graders and using the Gough Fe scale as the measure of sex typing, classmates' ratings on a five-item social-distance scale as the single index of social acceptance, and the same questionnaire anxiety measure used by Gray. Going beyond Gray's design, Webb employs the number of school absences as an additional behavioral measure of adjustment, and also tests for differences among grade levels in the relationship between sex typing and adjustment to determine whether the relationship changes during this period in development. Webb's predictions for girls are confirmed for anxiety and absences for all grades but not for social acceptance. For boys there is no relationship between m-f score and social acceptance in any grade, thus failing to replicate Gray. As predicted, anxiety is significantly associated with low masculinity in the eighth grade. But, contrary to prediction. anxiety is significantly related to high masculinity in the ninth grade, and seventh graders show a nonsignificant trend in the same direction. Also contrary to prediction is the finding that high masculinity is significantly associated with frequent rather than infrequent absences.

Webb's discussion of these discrepant results illustrates the lengths to which researchers have gone to maintain the identity paradigm in the face of contrary data. To start, Webb asserts that the reason that his predictions are not confirmed for boys is that changes in women's role are confusing them:

> The new freedom and new activities of women and girls may affect the boy's role and confuse his conception of his proper place in the culture. In short, the masculine role may be becoming more complicated by reason of the woman's assumption of roles which were previously masculine. (P. 615)

Webb shows considerable agility in redefining the meaning of his dependent measures in order to make the data fit his hypothesis. He accounts for the results on anxiety among seventh-grade boys by arguing that they are making "the adjustment to greater independence and the breaking of ties with a single teacher, usually a mother figure" (p. 616), while for ninth-grade boys his argument is that "the pressure to select a major and prospective vocation may be anxiety arousing to the boys, especially perhaps the extremely masculine one who begins to see his adult male responsibilities facing him more clearly" (p. 616). Thus Webb argues, in effect, that anxiety in these two grades actually reflects good, not poor, adjustment. But for the eighth-grade sample, in which anxiety is related to low masculinity (as originally predicted), Webb seems content to accept the initial assumption that anxiety is an indicator of poor adjustment.

Webb's explanation for the high absence rate among masculine boys is particularly ingenious.

> It may be that certain forms of absenteeism at this age represent the individual's attempts at becoming more independent of authority. It may also be that excessive absence represents an aggressive protest against other aspects of school attendance such as pressures from the home for outstanding achievement. . . . From a mental health point of view, the individuals who handle their emotional problems in this way may fare better than those who show a feminine role preference, who may be more readily intimidated, and who may attend school through passive compliance but react with other symptomatic behavior. . . . It may . . . be that boys and girls who have high femininity scores find their greatest satisfactions and security in good school attendance. Since the peer group does not appear to exert any special social stigma upon high femininity, the school may actually serve as a refuge for the boy and girl who are troubled by their femininity. Such children might be expected to throw all their psychic energies into being model students and fail to become well integrated personalities. (Pp. 616–617)

Thus frequent school absence is actually a measure of good, not poor, adjustment.

As with anxiety, Webb's reinterpretation of absenteeism is not necessarily wrong. The point, however, is that such interpretive ingenuity is applied only to contrary findings. Data showing that masculinity has either no relationship or a negative relationship to adjustment are discounted or used to criticize women (for confusing men) or nonmasculine males; data suggesting that masculinity has positive correlates are accepted at face value.

These studies also illustrate identity researchers' different attitudes toward sex-inappropriate behavior in males compared to females. Gray and Webb find it relatively easy to give up the idea that among girls positive adjustment requires only sex-appropriate traits but—in spite of data to the contrary—continue to hold this idea for males. This greater concern about traditional sex typing in males is evident throughout the MSRI paradigm.

Kagan and Moss

Kagan and Moss (1962) examine the relationship between sex typing and sexual adjustment. Their statistical analysis shows that weak sex typing in childhood is significantly related to males' "avoidance of premarital sexuality," defined as the individual's "reluctance to establish heterosexual relationships during late adolescence and early adulthood and the degree of inhibition placed on erotic behavior (necking, petting, coitus)" (p. 159). Kagan and Moss also illustrate this finding with case studies. The nonmasculine boy described earlier in chapter 3

reported much tension and anxiety with girls and a strong reluctance to initiate erotic activity with them. He was afraid that a girl would reject him if he were to become sexually aggressive, and he usually waited for her to initiate any romance. He had never petted with a girl or experienced sexual intercourse. (P. 165)

By contrast, the masculine male dated "frequently and consistently during his last two years of high school" with "episodes of erotic activity," followed by "frequent occurrences of coital activity" in college. What this "coital activity," supposedly a measure of good psychological adjustment, really means becomes apparent in the following excerpts from the interview with the masculine subject (Recall that E means experimenter, and S means subject.)

E: "What about dating during college?"

S: "In my sophomore year I went on a rampage, I guess—I mean, I went out every weekend."

E: "Any intercourse?"

S: "Some. Do you mean on dates, permeditated dates? There weren't many girls I took out on a premeditated date that I didn't know I couldn't lay before I took them out. Some girls I know go: some girls I'm not sure about. Some girls I know don't. Those I wasn't sure about, I didn't—very few of them I ever laid."

E: "This first group that you knew would lay, you took them out occasionally?"

S: "I would take them out to get laid."

E: "Only for that reason?"

S: "Yeh, but not very often, 'cause that's not my philosophy. I was, I can name about 60 girls that I have taken out on a premeditated basis."

E: "Have your intercourse experiences been with girls whom you always took out for this one purpose, or are there some girls whom you like and didn't take out specifically for sex?"

S: "Most of the girls that I have had intercourse with I have taken out purely for that purpose." (Pp. 162–163)

Kagan and Moss apparently believe that the more masculine male is the better sexually adjusted of the two but few today would view him as a model of good sexual adjustment. The less masculine male does not necessarily have better adjustment, though his is less damaging to women. Actually, in the changing culture of today it is not easy to say just what good sexual adjustment is for a male adolescent. Perhaps these two males simply reveal two alternative solutions to the same underlying problem. In any event, this case study should make two things clear: researching the relationship between sex typing and adjustment inevitably raises value questions; and the values of MSRI researchers have been traditional.

Mussen

Paul Mussen (1961, 1962) presents what is probably the single most important study of the relationship between sex typing and adjustment within the identity paradigm. It is so important because it is longitudinal, that is, it follows a group of subjects through the life cycle: Sixty-eight males in the University of California Adolescent Growth Study were observed during their senior year in high school (at ages 17 and 18, in 1940) and again in adulthood. Their sex role identities are assessed with the m-f scale of the SVIB, administered when they were high-school seniors, and the 20 most masculine boys in this sample are compared with the 19 least masculine on a variety of personality scales and staff ratings.

Mussen's 1961 report, in which the two groups are compared as adolescents, concludes that the highly masculine boys are better adjusted. The 1962 report, which examines the two groups as adults, finds the exact opposite: The males who had been highly masculine in adolescence are relatively lacking in the CPI traits called *dominance, capacity for status*, and *self-acceptance,* and are high in the Edwards Personal Preference Schedule (EPPS) trait called *need for abasement.* Personal interviews with a subsample of the subjects in the research confirm the impressions yielded by these personality questionnaire measures; the highly masculine males are rated as less sociable, showing less social leadership, and less introspective.

Mussen (1962, p. 439) speculates that the source of the highly masculine males' adjustment problems in adulthood is their lack of social-emotional skills. This deficiency, argues Mussen, does not hamper them in adolescence, for this is an age at which stereotyped masculine behavior is highly valued. As a result, however, these highly masculine males have little incentive to develop social skills; later in life this lack holds them back, causing personal, social, and vocational frustrations that weaken their self-confidence and sense of adequacy. Noting how inconsistent this result is with the traditional view that masculinity leads to good adjustment in males, Mussen (1962) cautiously concludes that

high masculine identification during adolescence, as measured in this study, is conducive to the development of feelings of adequacy and contentment at the time but is insufficient per se to ensure enduring favorable consequents. In fact, it appears that the development of strongly masculine interests, if unaccompanied by certain social characteristics, may have deleterious long range results. The extent to which this conclusion may be generalized is, of course, limited by the nature of the sample (only high and low extremes of the distribution of masculinity of interests) and by the criterion of adjustment employed. (P. 439)

Actually, certain aspects of these data suggest that masculinity has negative correlates even during adolescence. For example, as adolescents the highly masculine boys are rated lower than the other boys on most measures of social orientation, but are nonsignificantly higher on one called "smoothness in social functioning." This nonsignificant difference provides the basis for the following interpretation (Mussen, 1961):

In view of this result, it hardly seems likely that the relatively low level of social orientation among the highly masculine adolescent boys reflects ineptitude or awkwardness in social relationships. Instead, their low sociability ratings and gregariousness may represent . . . the extinction of responses generally considered to be aspects of female role behavior.

Furthermore, the relatively low standing of the boys low in masculinity of interests in "smoothness of social functioning," considered in light of their high levels of outgoingness and social initiative, may be interpreted to mean that their sociability is essentially of an immature sort, perhaps reflecting their attention-getting and dependency needs rather than skill in the establishment of mature relationships with others. (P. 19)

Mussen's argument, in effect, is that the measure of social orientation on which the strongly masculine boys excel is an indicator of good psychological adjustment, whereas the measures on which the weakly masculine boys excel reflect "female role behavior" and "immature relationships."

To take another example, the weakly masculine boys are rated higher than the strongly masculine boys in heterosexual orientation during adolescence, which would seem to contradict the generalization that the weakly masculine males are more poorly adjusted. This is Mussen's (1961) interpretation:

In view of their strong dependency and approval needs, however, it may be inferred that their high interest in girls probably reflected their general sociability and gregariousness rather than any marked ability to establish mature relationships with members of the opposite sex. It is also possible that the relatively high heterosexual interests of those low in masculinity of interests resulted from the fact that they were more likely to find social success and social gratifications in interactions with girls than in interpersonal relationships with boys. (Pp. 7–8)

Once again, if a measure ordinarily indicating good adjustment occurs in nonmasculine males, it is arbitrarily reinterpreted to indicate poor adjustment.

Bem (1974) and others have generally accepted Mussen's interpretation that it shows that masculine sex typing in males leads to good adjustment in adolescence but poor adjustment later in life, but Kuhn's analysis of paradigm shifts in scientific progress suggests a different interpretation. In the 1961 report, Mussen notes a number of serious anomalies in the data but is able to reconcile them with the MSRI paradigm. By the 1962 report, however, the anomalies are too far reaching and fundamental to explain away. Actually, Mussen's data show that the most masculine males are poorly adjusted in both adulthood *and* adolescence.

More Recent Studies

More recent studies also suggest that masculinity in males is associated with variables indicating poor adjustment.[1] Harford, Willis, and Deabler (1967) study the relationship between the m-f scale from the SVIB and various scales from the 16 Personality Factor (16PF) test in a sample of 213 adult males. These investigators find that masculinity is associated with being aloof, dull, emotionally dissatisfied, tough, suspecting, practical, unpretentious, guilt prone, anxious, unresponsive emotionally, and neurotic. Not all of these traits are clearly psychologically positive or negative, but of the ones that are, more are negative.

In another study, Vincent (1966) analyzes the relationship between Gough's Fe (m-f) scale and other CPI indices in a sample of 260 high-school senior males. The weakly masculine males have more favorable scores on two thirds of the CPI scales. Vincent (1966) concludes that

If today's male is to be "successful" in terms of current role expectations of the middle class male, he will tend to score high on *Fe* when items are included which formerly described the more dependent, intuitive, sensitive, "peace-making" role of the female in a tradition-oriented society, but which now tend to describe the "other-directed," "organization man" in-the-gray-flannel-suit whose success depends more on a psychological than a physical manipulation of environment and people. (P. 198)

Effects of Paternal Absence

Another body of literature frequently cited in support of the view that appropriate sex role identity among males leads to good adjustment is research on the effects of paternal absence on boys.

The premise is that paternal absence leads to an insecure male identity, which in turn leads to poor adjustment. Herzog and Sudia (1971) examine the effects of paternal absence on school performance, mental illness, and marital instability; they conclude that there is little support for the belief that, controlling for other factors, paternal absence is associated with these three indicators of maladjustment. They do find that boys without fathers are slightly overrepresented among delinquents but that this relationship is dwarfed by the impact of other factors such as socioeconomic status and home climate and has little practical significance.

Sex Typing and Social Class

One problem in studies relating sex typing to adjustment reveals that these studies generally fail to take into account how sex typing varies by social class. One of the most consistent findings of m-f research is that working-class individuals are more sex typed on the average than those from the middle class (Manosevitz, 1971). Thus, if males scoring masculine on the SVIB as adolescents show signs of poor adjustment in adulthood (as in the Mussen study), this may simply show that working-class males are more poorly adjusted in adulthood than middle-class males. The negative traits characterizing the strongly masculine males in Mussen's study—low dominance, low capacity for status, low self-acceptance, and need for abasement—read like a catalogue of the psychological costs of being working class in a middle-class society (see Sennett and Cobb, 1972).

Psychology has generally overlooked the obvious and potentially confounding effect of social class on sex typing. As one illustration, Mussen (1962) finds that the males assessed as most masculine during adolescence have more masculine adult occupations than do males assessed in adolescence as weakly masculine. Mussen asserts that this finding demonstrates the continuity of sex role identity over two decades of the life cycle. But a simpler interpretation is that, since sex-typed occupational aspirations are a major component of the m-f measure that Mussen uses (the SVIB), Mussen has found only that working-class adolescents attain working-class occupations as adults, while middle-class adolescents attain middle-class occupations. Rather than demonstrating the continuity of m-f assessments, Mussen's findings more likely demonstrate the continuity of social class.

Another illustration is Kagan and Moss's (1962, p. 169) analysis of the adult occupations of the ten boys rated most masculine and the seven boys rated least masculine at ages 3–6 in the study discussed earlier. The adult occupations of the highly masculine boys include three businessmen, two farmers, two athletic coaches, a carpenter, a machinist, and an engineer. The group rated least masculine produces three high-school teachers, a chemist, a biologist, a physicist, and a psychiatrist. Kagan and Moss conclude that the major difference between these two groups of occupations is that the first is more masculine than the second, thus demonstrating the importance of sex role identity in determining adult occupational choice. They fail to note that the first group of occupations have generally much lower social status than the second.

On reflection, the fact that one of the few truly consistent findings in m-f research is that males of lower socioeconomic status score higher in masculine sex typing should have led to more skepticism about the traditional view that masculinity leads to adjustment. Since middle-class values so dominate society, it would be quite remarkable if a trait more associated with working-class than middle-class males should lead to good adjustment. Similarly, findings that weak sex typing is associated with good adjustment simply may demonstrate that the middle class shows better adjustment than the working class.

The relationship between sex typing and social class is perhaps the single most profound fact about sex typing. The interpretations made of this fact are, in the broadest sense, political interpretations. Findings that black males have lower average masculinity scores than whites has often led to the conclusion that black males have sex role identity conflicts (proposition 9). The parallel observation that middle-class men have lower masculinity scores than working class-men has been interpreted as showing that working class males are overcompensating for insecure sex role identities (proposition 7). White, middle-class behavior is always the standard by which other groups are compared, whatever the direction of difference.

The Definition of Psychological Adjustment

A second methodological problem in these studies concerns the definition of adjustment. Scores on questionnaire tests of self-esteem, ego strength, neurosis, anxiety, and the like interpreted as indicating good adjustment may simply reflect unwillingness to admit problems (see Mischel, 1969, pp. 13–15). Men with differing masculinity ratings may differ not in psychopathology but only in *willingness to admit* psychopathology.

Mussen's (1962) study provides a good illustration. One of the few respects in which strongly masculine males in this study show apparently better adjustment in adulthood than weakly masculine males is in sexual adjustment. But Mussen notes that

the ratings in sexual adjustment are difficult to interpret because they were, of necessity, made entirely on the basis of subjects' self reports. Since these men tended to be nonintrospective, they probably did not analyze or examine the subtler aspects of their sexual relationships but simply accepted—and reported—the more superficial satisfactions and tension reduction of sexual activity. In addition, since they regarded themselves as highly masculine, they may have found it extremely threatening to admit or discuss any sexual problems or dissatisfactions. (P. 439)

A study by Holmes (1967) concerning the relationship between ego strength and sex typing in the MMPI points up a related problem; several of the items on the MMPI m-f scale are also on the ego-strength scale—for example, not liking to work and not wanting to paint flowers. Thus the two scales appear to be correlated because they include some of the same items!

The general point is that the relationship between adjustment and sex typing is a matter of definition and interpretation. One researcher's "ego strength" or "low anxiety" is another's "denial of problems"; one researcher's "low social skills' is another's "low dependency" or "low approval needs." The traditional approach in psychology has been, on the basis of rather slim evidence, to make the most favorable possible interpretation of masculine males and the least favorable interpretation of nonmasculine males. This bias must be exposed and corrected. But in doing so it is essential to avoid making the same error in the opposite direction.

The Androgyny Hypothesis

Research on psychological androgyny makes an important contribution to our understanding of the relationship between sex typing and psychological adjustment, but not in the way that many think.

Two Lines of Research

Early androgyny research took the position that for either sex good adjustment requires both masculine and feminine characteristics, so that the androgynous person will show better adjustment than the masculine, feminine, or undifferentiated. This prediction is tested in two quite different lines of research. In the first, Spence, Helmreich and Stapp (1974, 1975a) investigate the relationship between the PAQ and a measure of social self-esteem, the Texas Social Behavior Inventory (TSBI), and find that the androgynous group has higher self-esteem than the other three sex-typing groups.

In the second line of research, Bem (1975) and her colleagues (Bem, Martyna, and Watson, 1976) investigate the behavior of the various sex typing groups in experimental situations, testing the prediction that androgynous persons will perform equally well in situations requiring masculine or feminine skills while masculine and feminine individuals will be less flexible. For a situation requiring a masculine skill, subjects are placed in small groups and asked to rate the humor of a set of cartoons. Everyone in the group except the subject is a confederate of the experimenter, and it is arranged that the confederates rate certain cartoons as being much more funny or much less funny than they really are (as determined by prior ratings of independent judges). The ability to resist group pressure for conformity and not going along with these implausible group ratings is considered a masculine skill. Bem uses three different experimental situations calling on feminine nurturant and expressive skills: playing with a kitten, playing with a baby, and listening to another student (actually a confederate of the experimenter) talk about problems of adjusting to college. Subjects are observed in each situation and rated as to how confortable and helpful they are in each. Bem's prediction for males is clearly confirmed: Exclusively masculine men show marked deficits in the three kinds of situations requiring nurturant or expressive skills; they are inhibited and restricted in playing with the kitten or baby; and they are unresponsive to the student talking about problems in adjusting to college. Bem suggests that this inability of sex-typed men to be nurturant is a major limitation, with important social consequences.

Anomalous Results

These results are relatively well known, and many believe that they prove that androgynous persons are indeed the best psychologically adjusted. Actually, there are reasons to question this conclusion. In the self-esteem studies, while the androgynous group has higher self-esteem than the other groups, they do not have *significantly* higher self-esteem than the masculine (Wetter, 1975; Kelly and Worell, 1977). The real difference among the sex typing groups is that the two groups that score high on masculinity (androgynous and exclusively masculine) have higher self-esteem than the two groups that score low on masculinity (exclusively feminine and undifferentiated). Having feminine traits has an additional positive but nonsignificant effect on self-esteem, but considerably smaller than the effect of having masculine traits (see also Spence and Helmreich, 1979; Silvern and Ryan, 1979).[2]

Bem's behavioral studies (1975; Bem, Martyna, and Watson, 1976) also reveal an anomalous result: Among women, the feminine group performs less adaptively than the others in two of the three situations thought to require feminine skills. Lenny (1979a) notes that, just as research conducted within the identity paradigm overlooked anomalous and contrary results, so too has androgyny research, which prompts the suggestion that it is time to undertake a more fundamental reconsideration of the concept itself (see, for example, Lenney, 1979b; Kaplan, 1979).[3]

The Real Contribution of Androgyny Research

If this research simply showed that the androgynous are the best adjusted, it would represent only a new stage within the MSRI paradigm, differing from earlier ones only in the particular form of sex typing thought to be ideal. While the androgynous ideal has more positive implications for change in sex roles than does the traditional ideal, nonetheless it continues to impose a sex role standard that women and men should attain. The real contribution of androgyny to sex role research, I believe, lies elsewhere.

In essence, androgyny is a transitional concept; while rooted in the old paradigm, it points the way to the new. The self-esteem studies initiated by Spence, Helmreich, and Stapp are identical in their basic design to the adjustment studies conducted earlier within the identity paradigm. Bem's behavioral studies, however, suggest an entirely new way of understanding *why* sex typing is related to adjustment. While the identity paradigm derives this relationship from a hypothesized inner psychological need for identity, Bem's research implies that the mechanism underlying the relationship is situational adaptation: Patterns of sex-typed traits may help or hinder individuals in meeting the demands of their social roles. The functional adaptiveness (and possible maladaptiveness) of sex-typed traits is one of the central ideas of the strain paradigm, and Bem helps develop it.

The situational adaptation argument implies that particular personality characteristics, whether sex typed or androgynous, lead to good or bad psychological adjustment only in the context of particular situations; no intrinsic relationship exists between sex typing and global measures of adjustment (see also Lenney, 1979a). Bem and others are probably right in holding that individuals of both sexes increasingly are required to function in situations calling for both masculine and feminine skills. At the same time, many individuals still function primarily in environments requiring only traditional sex-typed skills. If consistent relationships are found between sex typing and adjustment, the situational adaptation argument implies that they result from similarities in the demands individuals face, not from an inherent theoretical relationship. Thus, androgyny research signals the end of the long search for an intrinsic relationship between sex typing and adjustment that has been at the core of the MSRI paradigm.

Hypermasculinity and Men's Attitudes toward Women

Structural features of contemporary societies create a problem of masculine identification. Boys initially identify and depend on their mothers, but they realize that they must, when they grow up, become men and not women. Much of the exaggerated roughness and toughness of preadolescent and adolescent boys should be understood . . . as the result of unconscious needs to repudiate a natural identification with their mothers. (Toby, 1966, p. 20)

One might expect high-scoring [that is, authoritarian] men to think of themselves as very masculine, and that this claim would be the more insistent the greater the underlying feelings of weakness. Low-scoring men, on the other hand, having actually more personal and masculine identity—perhaps by virtue of having had less threatening parental figures—can afford to admit failures and doubts along these lines. In fact, there seems to be, in the high-scoring men, more of what may be called *pseudo-masculinity*—as defined by boastfulness about such traits as determination, energy, industry, independence, decisiveness, and will power—and less admission of passivity. . . . The typical low-scoring man more readily accepts his own femininity than the high scorer. (Adorno et al., 1950, pp. 428, 405)

A boy, in his attempt to gain an elusive masculine identification, often comes to define his masculinity largely in negative terms, as that which is not feminine or involved with women. There is an internal and external aspect to this. Internally, the boy tries to reject his mother and deny his attachment to her and the strong dependence on her that he feels. He also tries to deny the deep personal identification with her that has developed during his early years. He does this by repressing whatever he takes to be feminine inside himself, and, importantly, by denigrating whatever he considers to be feminine in the outside world. (Chodorow, 1974, p. 50)

Since it is "girl-like" activities that provoked the punishment administered in an effort to induce sex-typical behavior in boys, then, in developing dislike for the activity which led to such punishment, boys should develop hostility toward "girl-like" activities. Also, boys should be expected to generalize and consequently develop hostility toward all females as representatives of this disliked role. (Lynn, 1966, p. 469)

Proposition 6. *Hypermasculinity in males (exaggerated masculinity, often with negative social consequences) indicates insecurity in their sex role identities.*

The *hypermasculinity hypothesis* holds that certain kinds of exaggerated masculine (or hypermasculine) behaviors are a manifestation of a male's insecurity in his sex role identity. A male with an insecure sex role identity at the deepest level of his personality may compensate for it by developing characteristics at a more superficial level that assure him and others of his masculinity. The hypermasculinity hypothesis has been applied to delinquency and violence, conservative social attitudes (for example, authoritarianism and homophobia), and bodybuilding.[1]

The hypermasculinity hypothesis extends proposition 5 concerning identity and adjustment to the multileveled conception of sex role identity: Males with masculine identities at both the unconscious and conscious levels (Miller and Swanson's MM) show good psychological adjustment; those with feminine identities at both levels (FF) show poor adjustment; and those with unconscious feminine identities but masculine conscious identities (FM) show a distinctive form of poor adjustment—hypermasculinity.

Delinquency and Violence

The idea that insecurity in sex role identity among males is a source of crime and violence is a venerable one in the social sciences. Talcott Parsons (1959), summarizing his original formulation of this hypothesis (1947), suggests that

the boy. . .has a tendency to form a direct feminine identification, since his mother is the model most readily available and significant to him. But he is not destined to become an adult woman. . . . Hence, when boys emerge into what the Freudians call the latency period, their behavior tends to be marked by a kind of compulsive masculinity. . . . This universal pattern bears all the earmarks of a reaction formation. It is the result not simply of masculine nature but largely of a defense against a feminine identification. . . [The mother] focuses in herself the symbols of what is "good" behavior, of conformity with the expectations of the respectable adult world. When he revolts against identification with his mother in the name of masculinity, it is not surprising that a boy unconsciously identifies goodness with femininity and that being a "bad boy" becomes a positive goal. . . . There is a strong tendency for boyish behavior, in striking contrast to that of pre-adolescent girls, to run in antisocial if not directly destructive directions (Pp. 186–187)

Walter Miller's (1958) well-known article, "Lower Class Culture as a Generating Milieu of Gang Delinquency," argues that the lower class concern with toughness

is probably related to the fact that a significant proportion of lower class males are reared in a predominantly female household and lack a consistently present male figure with whom to identify and from whom to learn essential components of a "male" role. Since women serve as a primary object of identification during pre-adolescent years, the almost obsessive lower class concern with "masculinity" probably resembles a type of compulsive reaction-formation. (P. 9)

Rohrer and Edmonson (1960) develop a similar analysis of the origins of adolescent male gangs among New Orleans blacks:

Thus an organizational form that springs from the little boy's search for masculinity he cannot find at home becomes at first a protest against femininity and then an assertion of hyper-virility. On the way it acquires a structuring in which the aspirations and goals of the matriarchy or the middle class are seen as soft, effeminate, and despicable. The gang ideology of masculine independence is formed from these perceptions and the gang then sees its common enemy not as a class, nor even as a sex, but as the "feminine principle" in society. (Pp. 162–163)

Whiting, Kluckhohn, and Anthony (1958) extend the hypothesis by arguing that "insofar as there has been an increase in juvenile delinquency in our society, it probably has been accompanied by an increase in the exclusiveness of mother-child relationships and/or a decrease in the authority of the father" (p.70). While this interpretation of delinquency as hypermasculinity has been widely popularized, the empirical research evaluating it is quite limited.

Silverman and Dinitz

Silverman and Dinitz (1974) study a group of 284 delinquent boys ages 14–19 in an Ohio training school, of whom about half are black and half white. The subjects fill out a "compulsive masculinity" scale, assessing their "self-identification with tough behavior (e.g., weapon-carrying, maintaining a reputation as a tough guy) and sexual athleticism" (p. 505). Subjects also rate themselves and the others in their residential group on manliness and toughness, as does the correctional staff. In addition, several personality tests are administered. (Actual past criminal behavior is not examined.) The compulsive masculinity index, the boys' self-rating, the other boys' and the staff's ratings, and the discrepancies among the latter are analyzed according to the boy's family type. Female-headed households contribute 35% of the sample; natural two-parent households, 24%; and households with a natural parent and stepparent, 29%.

Delinquents from female-headed households rate themselves as tougher than delinquents from the other household types, but there are no other differences among these three groups on any other variables or the various discrepancy scores.[2] This difference on only one of several self-rating measures, with no corroboration by other observers' ratings, can hardly be regarded as strong support for the hypermasculinity hypothesis.

This study provides a dramatic illustration of the misreporting of data to fit a hypothesis. In spite of the near absence of findings, Silverman and Dinitz assert that "data from this study clearly suggested that delinquent boys from female-based households were more hypermasculine than delinquents from other types of households" (p. 511). Their summary of the evidence supporting this generalization is directly contradicted by the results they actually report. In this summary (p. 511), they state that delinquents from female-headed households (a) had the highest self-perceptions on manliness and toughness (true for toughness, not true for manliness, on which delinquents from stepparent families score higher); (b) "emphasized" the two components of compulsive masculinity, toughness and sexual athleticism (actually, delinquents from stepparent families were nonsignificantly higher); (c) "were more impulsive" and "more hostile," as assessed by the Lykken Scale (but on the preceding page they state that "delinquents from mother-based homes did not have appreciably different mean Lykken scores as compared with delinquent boys from other types of households"). Silverman and Dinitz then conclude with the declaration that these specific findings "lend support to the Parsonian thesis that the mother-based home generates problems of compulsive masculinity which in turn promote antisocial conduct" (p. 512).

Harrington

Harrington's (1970) *Errors in Sex-Role Behavior in Teen-Age Boys* is perhaps the single best-designed study of hypermasculinity and delinquency. Harrington studies 118 adolescent males in inpatient or outpatient facilities in upper New York State. On the basis of case records and interviews with parents, he classifies these males as hypermasculine, feminine, or controls. (The presence or absence of each of 18 specific behaviors interpreted as reflecting these three patterns is also rated for separate analysis.) Harrington compares the three groups on measures of unconscious sex role identity (the Franck Drawing Completion Test) and conscious sex role identity (the Gough Fe scale, the SVIB m-f scale, and the ratio of the number of household tasks performed by the boy with his father to those performed with his mother). Information is collected also on the composition of the household during the boy's upbringing to test the hypotheses about the etiology of the hypermasculine and inverted patterns. Finally, social class and physical strength are rated as possible additional factors accounting for differences among the three groups on sex typing variables.

Regarding unconscious sex role identity, Harrington finds that both hypermasculine and feminine boys have significantly more feminine Franck scores than do the control boys. The three groups also differ significantly in social class and physical strength, but the differences among the three groups on Franck scores are still significant when these factors are controlled.

While this result appears to support the hypermasculinity hypothesis, Harrington observes several anomalies in the data. First, the variance in Franck score for the hypermasculine and feminine groups is four times as large as in the control group. Hypermasculine and feminine boys have both more feminine *and* more masculine scores on this test. In fact, several members of both the hypermasculine and feminine groups have more masculine Franck scores than anyone in the control group. Harrington notes that this surprising result may be due to inadequacies in the test or its scoring. But he also suggests that "the possibility remains, however, that excessively male *primary* [unconscious] sex identity may also predict errors in sex-role behavior [the hypermasculine and feminine patterns]" (p. 79).

Second, in an alternative mode of analysis examining the relationship of clusters of specific hypermasculine, feminine, and control behaviors to the Franck test, Harrington finds that the most feminine behaviors are associated with feminine scores; however, the average Franck scores associated with the most hypermasculine behaviors are only slightly more feminine than those associated with the control behaviors. Harrington observes that "the Franck scores seem to lose effectiveness on the negative (male) side of the continuum" (p. 70). In other words, this alternative procedure finds that the hypermasculine behavioral cluster (as opposed to the global classification of hypermasculinity) is *not* associated with the measure of unconscious feminine identity.

Finally, Harrington examines the individual behaviors in each cluster in relationship to the Franck test and concludes that elevated Franck scores are related to behavior classified as defiant but not to any of the other hypermasculine behaviors, including aggressive behavior, troublemaking, or sexual acting-out (pp. 64–65). Harrington summarizes that

this throws into some question the view of *aggression* as "protest masculinity." . . . It may be that, not aggression per se, but rather the attitude or mental set which accompanies it, is predicted by primary cross-sex identity . . . . what our data seem to suggest is that primary cross-sex identity accompanied by conflicting secondary male identity predicts a defiant and rebellious attitude as an error in sex-role behavior. Because such an attitude is often associated with over aggression, we have been [erroneously] led to believe that aggression per se is explainable in this way. (Pp. 80–81)

Regarding conscious sex role identity, Harrington finds, as expected, that feminine boys are less masculine than the other two groups on the conscious-level sex typing measures, even when social class and physical strength are controlled. But the relative position of the hypermasculine and control boys varies according to the specific measure and type of comparison used. The boys classified as hypermasculine are almost identical in masculinity to the control boys on the Gough scale, significantly more masculine on the SVIB, and significantly less masculine as assessed by the ratio of household tasks performed with the father to those performed with the mother. Specific hypermasculine behaviors are associated with more masculine scores on both tests. The discrepancies among the relationships between various measures of sex typing and hypermasculinity are considerable. The important point is that hypermasculinity is not consistently or strongly related to either conscious or unconscious sex typing.

Harrington hypothesizes that the feminine pattern is likely to occur when the father has been absent throughout childhood, while the hypermasculine pattern is likely to occur when there is paternal absence in early childhood followed by significant male influence in later childhood. But in his data the relationship between family composition during childhood and the three behavior patterns is essentially random, except that complete paternal absence is markedly *under*represented in the feminine group. (This is the study noted in chapter 4, in which invalidation of the expected relationship between paternal absence and a measure of sex role identity led the researcher to suggest that both the boys and their families are not accurately reporting whether the father had been present.) Thus the hypermasculinity hypothesis suffers yet another serious setback.

Rosenfeld

Rosenfeld (1969) compares 20 institutionalized male delinquents, 20 male delinquents on probation who had no more than two adjudications, and 20 male nondeliquent high-school students on the Franck and Gough tests. The two delinquent groups combined have more feminine Franck scores and more masculine Gough scores than the nondelinquents, providing support for the hypermasculinity hypothesis. But the delinquents have less education than the nondelinquents, which could account for the results on the Gough test. Rosenfeld then tests the prediction that the more serious delinquents (the institutionalized) will have more feminine Franck and more masculine Gough scores than the less serious delinquents (the probationers). The expected differences are not found in this equally important comparison.

Paternal Absence and Delinquency

Herzog and Sudia's (1971) comprehensive review concludes that paternal absence has a slight relationship to delinquency, but one that is too small to have any practical or social significance. Rosen (1970) reviews this literature as well and comes to the same conclusion. Rosen (1969) provides a good example of the findings typical of the best-designed research in this literature. This study concerns the relationship between paternal absence and delinquency specifically in black males, to whom the hypermasculinity

hypothesis has been applied particularly often (for example, Moynihan, 1977, pp. 38–40). Many studies of this relationship simply
compare the rates of paternal absence among a sample of delinquents and a more or less imperfectly matched sample of nondelinquents. Rosen employs a more rigorous procedure, drawing
a probability sample of 1,098 black male youths in a ten-square-
mile area of Philadelphia and then comparing the reported delinquency rates of those with and without a father (or stepfather)
in the household. Statistical analysis indicates that paternal presence or absence accounts for only 1.2% of the variance in delinquency.

Rosen also examines the effects of three other measures of the
presence of positive role models on delinquency and its two major
subcategories: acts against persons and acts not against persons.
He reasons that insecure male identity should be related more to
the former, which are more serious and violent than the latter.
Two of the alternative measures of male role modeling—sex of
the main wage earner in the family and sex of the main decision-
maker in the family—have about the same relationship to overall
delinquency as does paternal absence, while the third alternative
measure—sex of the most influential adult in the family—has no
relationship to overall delinquency. Moreover, these three measures have no relationship to the type of crime committed. The
only significant interaction between paternal absence and the
three other measures on delinquency is that in households without the father, male dominance in decisionmaking is associated
with a *higher* rate of personal crimes. In sum, Rosen's results do
not lend much support to the hypermasculinity hypothesis.

Cross-Cultural Studies

Another type of evidence cited in support of the hypermasculinity hypothesis is cross-cultural research on the correlates of crime
and violence. This line of research considers whole societies as
the units of analysis, analyzing differences between those with
high and low incidence of crime and violence.

In one widely cited study, B. Whiting (1965) analyzes the correlates of crime and violence in the Six Cultures Study. The two
societies with the highest rates of physical violence and murder
are the Nyansongo in Africa and the Rajput in Khalapur. These
two societies differ from the four others in that husbands and
wives in Nyansongo and Khalapur do not eat or sleep together

and rarely work or play together. Whiting argues that mother-father contact may be used as an index of father-infant contact on the grounds that infants spend most of their time with their mothers, and that low father-infant contact theoretically leads to a greater incidence of insecure sex role identities among males because sons will have more difficulty identifying with their fathers. Thus, Whiting argues, the association of physical violence with low husband-wife contact supports the hypothesis that violence in men reflects hypermasculine overcompensation for insecure sex role identity.

The chain of reasoning in this study is quite indirect. The most suspect link in this chain is the use of mother-father contact as an index of father-child contact. Also, Whiting's descriptions of the Nyansongo and Rajputs make clear that both sexes commit violence at high rates, which casts doubt on an explanation concerning the hypothetical dynamics of sex role identity in only one sex.

Bacon, Child, and Barry (1963) conduct another frequently cited study in which 48 cultures are rated for frequency of theft (defined as stealing the personal property of others) and personal crime (defined as intent to injure or kill a person, including assault, rape, suicide, sorcery intended to make another ill, murder, and false accusations). The boy's opportunity to form an identification with his father is assessed by a classification of the household structure typical in each society (ranging from monogamous nuclear to polygamous mother-child households) and by a rating of the presence or absence of exclusive mother-child sleeping arrangements (a residential pattern in which the child sleeps in the same room, and sometimes in the same bed, with its mother, while the father sleeps in a different room or even a different house). According to the theory, a polygamous mother-child household and mother-child sleeping arrangement increase a boy's identification with his mother and decreases his identification with his father. Bacon, Child, and Barry find that theft and personal crime occur more frequently in societies in which sons have less opportunity to identify with their fathers as assessed by both variables, in accord with the hypermasculinity hypothesis.

But both types of crime are related also to many other cultural characteristics investigated in the study. Frequency of theft is significantly associated with 11 other variables out of the 34 examined: absence of childhood indulgence; anxiety aroused in the child about failure to live up to cultural standards of responsibility, self-reliance, achievement, and obedience; and social stratification, political integration, elaboration of social control, concern about property, distrust about property, and lack of kindness expressed in folk tales. Frequency of personal crime is associated with 3 other variables: anxiety aroused in the child about failing to live up to cultural standards for dependency; distrust as a cultural trait; and hostility expressed in folk tales. Since crime is associated with so many other cultural variables, many of which may be associated with each other, it is difficult to assess the theoretical importance of any particular relationship. For example, the study may actually show that the arousal of anxiety during childhood is the source of adult crime, and polygamous household structure only appears to be correlated with crime because polygamy is associated with anxiety during child-rearing. Without more sophisticated statistical analysis, the meaning of Barry, Child, and Bacon's results is unclear.

Conservative Social Attitudes

Identity theorists assert that certain conservative social attitudes derive from insecurity in sex role identity. This is one of the central hypotheses in Adorno et al., *The Authoritarian Personality* (1950), one of the most important works in the history of American personality psychology. This study is a large-scale effort to understand the psychological dynamics of authoritarianism, a hypothetical personality disposition characterized by rigidity, belief in authority and power, contempt for weakness, and intolerance of deviance, especially sexual deviance. As Sanford (1966), one of the study's staff, later put it, "The authors of *The Authoritarian Personality* became convinced that one of the main sources of this personality syndrome was ego-alien femininity—that is to say, underlying femininity that had to be countered by whatever defenses the subject had at his disposal" (p. 196). The idea is that a male with insecure sex role identity defends against it by repressing it, and this repression generalizes to a more global intolerance of softness, weakness, and sexual deviance, an identification with power, and psychological rigidity.

In *The Authoritarian Personality,* this interpretation is a clinical inference. Strodtbeck and his students (Lipsitt and Strodtbeck, 1967; Strodtbeck and Creelan, 1968; Bezdek and Strodtbeck,

1970; Strodtbeck, Bezdek, and Goldhamer, 1970; Cottle, Edwards, and Pleck, 1970), however, quantitatively test this hypothesis using the Franck and Gough tests. This line of research does not generate strong support for the hypothesis. Bezdek and Strodtbeck (1970) conclude that the Franck test taps a fundamental value dimension of idealism versus pragmatism, not unconscious sex role identity. Two studies illustrate the ambiguous results of this line of research.

In Lipsitt and Strodtbeck (1967), a sample of 380 male naval enlisted personnel listen to a one-hour tape recording of what is described as a military trial and are asked to render a verdict. The case at issue, which concerns a sailor who has killed an officer, is modeled loosely after Herman Melville's story *Billy Budd*. Four different versions of the trial are used, systematically varying (1) the presence or absence of testimony suggesting that the defendant is a homosexual, and (2) the presence or absence of instructions from the military judge that the jury should consider testimony bearing on the defendant's character in rendering a verdict; each subject hears only one version. The percentages of each of the four sex role identity groups (derived from the Franck and Gough tests[3]) that give a guilty verdict for each of the four versions of the trial are compared. The hypothesis is that FM subjects are most sensitive to the suggestion that the defendant is homosexual, feel most threatened by it, and are therefore most likely to submit a verdict of guilty.

In the experimental condition in which it is implied that the defendant is a homosexual but the judge does not instruct the jury to consider the defendant's character, a significantly higher proportion of FMs render guilty verdicts (86% versus 51%, 55% and 59% in the other groups). This finding at first appears to support the hypermasculinity hypothesis, and is often cited as such. Yet other data make Lipsitt and Strodtbeck reject this conclusion. In the condition in which it is implied that the defendant is homosexual *and* the judge instructs the jury to take evidence of moral character into account, there is no significant difference among the groups. In other words, the tendency among FMs to react more punitively to the allegation of homosexuality is not a powerful effect, in the sense that a simple instruction from the judge suffices to wipe it out. Lipsitt and Strodtbeck conclude that

if males who earn feminine scores on the Franck test are "unconsciously feminine" in the psychoanalytic sense . . . and if unconsciously feminine males invoked defense mechanisms to manage the threat of the homosexual suggestion, then the strength of these defense mechanisms should not be as strongly influenced by other variations in the trial stimulus as it in fact is. While this study may not be a crucial test of the Miller and Swanson theory, it does cast doubt on the defensive formulation. (P. 15)

Cottle, Edwards, and Pleck (1970) administer the Franck and Gough tests and a 35-item inventory assessing attitudes on current social and political issues to a sample of 85 men and 80 women in Boston-area communities. The hypothesis is that unconscious femininity, and especially the FM pattern, is associated with conservative political and social attitudes. The social-political attitude inventory is factory analyzed, revealing five clusters labeled political liberal (or dove), pro birth control, sex role morality, pro discrimination, and puritan achievement (or intolerance of expressivity). FM males score significantly higher in the political liberalism (dove) factor, contrary to prediction. The birth control factor is unrelated to either conscious or unconscious sex role identity. Traditional sex role morality is significantly associated with unconscious masculinity (not femininity, as predicted), but this relationship becomes nonsignificant when education is controlled. FM males score significantly higher in support of racial discrimination, inconsistent with their general political liberalism and dovishness. There is no relationship between sex role identity and the puritan-achievement factor. Thus this study yields a finding confirming the hypermasculinity theory of the origin of repressive social attitudes for one factor (racial discrimination), significant findings contrary to the theory for two factors (political liberalism and sex role morality), and no findings in either direction for the remaining two factors (birth control and puritan achievement). In sum, there is little support for the hypermasculinity hypothesis.

Bodybuilding

The third and final line of research on hypermasculinity examined here concerns bodybuilding. If bodybuilding is a manifestation of hypermasculinity deriving from insecure male sex role identity, it is certainly not as socially significant as crime and violence or repressive social attitudes. Nonetheless, it is perhaps the archetypal expression of male identity insecurity.

Research in this area is extremely limited; only two quantitative studies appear in the literature, and neither is very elaborate. Thune (1949) compares 100 weightlifters active in a California YMCA to 100 YMCA members who are not weightlifters on a heterogeneous 108-item personality questionnaire. Thune concludes that "basically the YMCA weight lifter would appear more shy, lacking in self-confidence, and more concerned with body build. On the other hand the lifting group wants to be strong, healthy, and dominant, to be more like other men" (p. 306). R. Harlow (1951) compares 20 weightlifters with 20 nonweight-lifter athletes. The responses of the two groups to a 6-card TAT and a 23-item sentence completion test are scored for feelings of masculine inadequacy, exposure early in life to a depriving and frustrating environment, failure to identify with an adequate male figure, narcissism, and dependency. Harlow's report claims that the results show that the weightlifting group had more feelings of masculine inadequacy, is more narcissistic, has more homosexual and fewer heterosexual impulses, has more maternal hostility, has strong dependency needs, and so on. Unfortunately, details or examples of the scoring of the projective test data for these variables are not given. The significance of these data depends entirely on the extent to which one accepts the validity of projective data in general, and more specifically on the extent to which one can accept Harlow's interpretations (with no details given) of what kinds of responses reflect characteristics like masculine inadequacy and homosexual impulses.

Overview

The hypermasculinity hypothesis has been applied most exclusively to delinquency and violence. When the studies believed to confirm this hypothesis are examined closely, they reveal little definitive support. The hypermasculinity hypothesis has been used also to explain conservative social attitudes and bodybuilding behavior. Here, too, the studies often believed to confirm the hypothesis actually do not do so. Thus, one of the fundamental propositions of the MSRI paradigm has little empirical support.

Proposition 7. *Problems of sex role identity account for men's negative attitudes and behaviors toward women.*

Identity theorists have developed three different arguments to explain men's negative attitudes toward women. These can be termed the *maternal domination, maternal identification,* and *maternal socialization hypotheses.*

The Maternal Domination and Identification Hypotheses

Horney (1932), the first exponent of the maternal domination hypothesis, holds that in the early mother-child relationship the child inevitably experiences the mother as powerful and over-whelming. To Horney, mythology about powerful, evil female forces such as witches and sirens are symbolic expressions of this early experience. The mother's power is particularly threatening to the male child and his sex role identity development because he cannot potentially identify or ally himself with her. In later life a man carries with him the psychological residue of the fear of his mother he had as a child. As summarized by Chodorow (1971):

One consequence of the fact that women are primary socializers for boys (who later become men) is what Horney calls the "dread of women." This has both psychological and cultural aspects. Psychologically, Horney believes that fears of the mother (women) in men is even greater and more repressed than fear of the father (men). The mother initially has complete power over the child's satisfaction of needs and first forbids instinctual activities and therefore encourages the child's first sadistic impulses to be directed against her and her body. This creates enormous anxiety in the child. (P. 274)

Consequently, men seek to control and restrict the fantasied power of women and avoid or eliminate situations in which they are potentially subordinate to women. These psychological needs are reflected in negative attitudes toward women.

In the maternal identification hypothesis, of which Chodorow (1974) is a leading proponent, the key issue is the male's psychological identification with his mother, not his perception of her power. As discussed in proposition 3, the MSRI paradigm postulates that one of the major reasons why the development of sex role identity is so problematical for males is that the boy's early psychological identification with his mother predisposes him toward a feminine sex role identity, which must later be overcome. One way for men to cope with this unconscious feminine identity, this feared part of themselves, is by restricting and controlling those who actually are feminine—women. Adorno et al. (1950) use this hypothesis to explain the authoritarian's negative attitudes toward women:

Since the typical low-scoring [that is, nonauthoritarian] man more readily accepts his own femininity than the high scorer . . . one important source of hidden aggression toward the opposite sex—and toward other people generally, as it seems—is reduced. (P. 405)

As Chodorow (1974) later put it,

A boy, in his attempt to gain an elusive masculine identification, often comes to define his masculinity largely in negative terms, as that which is not feminine or involved with women. There is an internal and external aspect to this. Internally, the boy tries to reject his mother and deny his attachment to her and the strong dependence on her that he still feels. He also tries to deny the deep personal identification with her that has developed during his early years. He does this by repressing whatever he takes to be feminine inside himself, and, importantly, by denigrating whatever he considers to be feminine in the outside world. (P. 50)

In short, males externalize their intrapsychic conflict about unconscious feminine sex role identity by transforming it into an intergroup conflict.

Though these first two psychodynamic hypotheses have widespread currency, there has been little empirical investigation of their validity. Testing the domination and identification hypotheses requires measuring the extent to which males in early childhood are dominated by, or closely attached to, their mothers and correlating such measures with later adult attitudes toward women. Such research has not been conducted. There are several studies, however, using men's *retrospective* perceptions of their mothers that can be examined in light of these hypotheses. Two of these find that a man's negative attitudes toward women are associated with reporting a distant rather than close relationship with his mother (Meier, 1972; Rapoport and Rapoport, 1971). Worell and Worell (1971) find that a man's attitudes toward women are correlated with characteristics of his reported relationship with his father (specifically, traditional attitudes are associated with a high degree of paternal control) but not his mother.

At first glance these findings appear to invalidate the hypotheses that traditional attitudes among males derive from either dominating or close relationships with their mothers. Concerning the maternal identification hypothesis in particular, it certainly seems more plausible that negative attitudes toward women are associated with distant rather than close maternal relationships. But the protean nature of the MSRI paradigm makes it possible to explain these apparently contradictory data by arguing that retrospective ratings are distorted by the very process being studied. That is, if a close or dominating maternal relationship in early life can lead to negative attitudes toward women, it may lead also to reporting the early relationship as distant. One could also argue that if the relationship with the mother is extremely dominating or close, the male will have pro-female attitudes as a product of that domination or that identification.

The theory, however, does not specify the circumstances under which a close mother-child relationship will need to be defended against (leading to anti-female attitudes) or accepted (leading to pro-female attitudes). Further, Worell and Worell's finding that anti-feminist attitudes are related to qualities of the paternal relationship is hard to reconcile with the psychoanalytic hypotheses under consideration, although other psychodynamic hypotheses probably can be devised to account for it. Because of these interpretive ambiguities, these studies neither clearly validate nor invalidate these hypotheses about traditional male attitudes toward women.

Bowman, Worthy, and Greyser (1965) provide less direct evidence used to support the domination hypothesis. In a study of male managers' attitudes toward women managers, younger men have significantly more negative attitudes. Bowman, Worthy, and Greyser suggest this occurs because younger men have stronger unresolved fears of domination by women. There are two difficulties with this interpretation, however. First, the negative association between age and traditional attitudes toward women appears to be unique to this sample. For example, two recent large studies with representative national samples find, more predictably, that younger men have more favorable attitudes toward women (Roper Organization, 1974, p. 3; Pleck, 1978a). Second, in this study negative attitudes are also related to low rank in the firm. Since age and rank are highly correlated, the apparent relationship between attitudes and the former may simply be a consequence of the relationship between attitudes and the latter. The relationship between negative attitudes and low rank can be interpreted with a social-psychological rather than psychodynamic hypothesis: men lower in rank have more negative attitudes toward women because they are more likely to be in actual competition with women for promotion and other rewards. Since the relationship between age and attitudes toward women is opposite to that found in other studies, this alternative explanation is all the more plausible.

Overall, available data do not provide much support for the maternal domination and maternal identification hypotheses. Definitive research directly assessing the qualities of the mother-child relationship in early life in relation to later male attitudes toward women, however, has not been conducted.[4]

The Maternal Socialization Hypothesis

Lynn (1966, 1969) develops another argument about the sources of men's negative attitudes toward women that derives from the second proposition of the MSRI paradigm, which holds that the differential reinforcement of sex-typed behavior is a more significant source of sex typing in boys than in girls. Lynn (1966, p. 469) argues that socialization among boys is reinforced more by punishment of feminine behavior than by reward for masculine behavior; further, punishment is exercised by mothers more than fathers simply because of the greater time mothers spend with their children. As a result, suggests Lynn, boys develop hostility to their mothers, which they generalize to all women as representatives of this disliked role. Matteson (1975) puts it this way:

As males become more firmly identified with the masculine role, they also become more rejecting of the feminine one. Masculinity appears to be bought at the cost of a hostility toward females which continues into adulthood. . . . Boys learn masculine behavior in part by being punished for any display of feminine behavior. Playing with girls' toys or doing things considered "sissy" result in ridicule. . . . Much of the punishment is inflicted on the boy by women. Since the learning is a negative experience, he rejects the teachers who provided him with that experience. The boy is led to reject not only the behavior that is punished but the punishers—and in both cases this is a rejection of the feminine. . . . The rejection of femininity is largely a consequence of the negative methods women use in teaching masculinity in the absence of male models. (Pp. 76–77, 82)

Adequately testing the maternal socialization hypothesis requires assessing the extent to which men were punished by their mothers (or other females) during childhood for feminine behaviors and the relationship between such punishment and their attitudes toward women. Unfortunately, no such evidence is available, so the hypothesis cannot be evaluated. There is also a latent contradiction between the maternal identification and maternal socialization hypotheses: the former holds that men hate women because women make men feminine, while the latter attributes this hatred to women making men masculine. Identity theorists agree that women are responsible for men's negative attitudes toward them, but contradict each other about exactly what it is that women do to earn this resentment.[5]

Are Psychodynamic Theories to Account for Men's Attitudes toward Women Necessary?

Since women have been subjected to a large volume of devaluating psychodynamic analyses, there is a temptation to turn the tables and subject men, and especially men's behavior and attitudes toward women, to the same kind of psychodynamic scrutiny. Some contemporary feminists have availed themselves of this opportunity by adopting one or another of the arguments discussed here (see, for example, Chodorow, 1971, 1974).

But tempting as these arguments are, we ought to ask whether such complex psychological explanations for men's traditional negative attitudes toward women are necessary. There are, no doubt, some men who hate women because of complex psychological dynamics rooted in their maternal relationships. But this does not mean that these dynamics should provide the basis for a general theory of men's traditional attitudes toward women, which can be explained in intellectually simpler, more parsimonious ways. The simplest explanation is that men hold these attitudes because to do so is in their self-interest; such attitudes justify men's relative privilege. Another explanation is that men (and women) hold these attitudes simply because they are widespread in the culture; given that the culture holds these attitudes, one does not need complex psychological theories to explain why individuals adopt them (see Pleck, 1978a).

Data about similarities between the sexes' attitudes toward women provide evidence against the psychodynamic hypothesis. On questionnaire scales of attitudes toward women used frequently in college samples, men show slightly more traditional overall scores. Analyses of items in national surveys, however, reveal mixed results: Men hold more traditional attitudes on some but similar or less traditional attitudes on others. Further, the correlations between attitudes toward women and such other personality variables as sex typing, self-esteem, and authoritarianism do not differ by sex. It is difficult to reconcile these similarities between the sexes with theories postulating unique psychological dynamics underlying men's traditional attitudes (Pleck, 1978b).

Male Sexual Violence against Women

One final feature of the MSRI paradigm's view of men's attitudes toward women is its interpretation of male sexual violence as deriving from men's insecurities in their sex role identities, particularly latent homosexuality. For example, Blanchard (1959) offers this interpretation in a study of two gangs of male adolescents who had committed gang rape. He introduces his report with the observation that "the idea of 'sharing the girl among us fellows', congregating around a common sexual object, and being sexually stimulated together as a group certainly have their homosexual implications" (p. 259). The strongest clinical evidence Blanchard cites to support this interpretation concerns the two groups' responses (as groups) to the Rorschach inkblot test. One of the adolescents, Pete, reports seeing in one blot a person with both a penis and a breast, a response classically interpretable as severe sex role identity confusion. But the others in Pete's group disagree. Further, Blanchard's transcription of the group discussion indicates that Blanchard was actively prompting and encouraging Pete in this perception.

In describing the police investigation of the Boston Strangler case, Brownmiller (1975) provides another clinical illustration of the hypermasculinity theory of male sexual violence:

A Medical-Psychiatric Committee, upon invitation of the stymied police, had put together an imaginative, detailed profile of the phantom Strangler. Or, to be more precise, they put together an imaginative profile of the Strangler's mother. Struck by the advanced age of the victims, one of whom was 75, the committee postulated with the kind of certainty that seems endemic to their profession that the elusive killer was a neat, punctual, conservatively dressed, possibly middle-aged, probably impotent, probably homosexual fellow who was consumed by raging hatred for his "sweet, orderly, neat, compulsive, seductive, punitive, overwhelming" mother. The Strangler's mother was probably dead, they agreed, but during his childhood she had walked about "half-exposed in their apartment, but punished him severely for any sexual curiosity." Consumed by mother hatred, the psychiatrists divined, the Strangler had chosen to murder and mutilate old women in a manner "both sadistic and loving." (P. 203)

Albert DeSalvo, the actual Boston Strangler, had a mother who was not particularly neat, sweet, or overwhelming. DeSalvo's rage was not toward his mother but his brutal alcoholic father, who had regularly beaten him, his siblings, and his mother (in fact breaking all her fingers and knocking out her teeth) and had smashed all the furniture in the house during periodic rampages (Brownmiller, 1975).

As a final illustration of the hypermasculinity hypothesis, consider the following summary of a study of rapists' wives by Abrahamsen (1960):

The conclusions reached were that the wives of the sex offenders on the surface behaved toward men in a submissive and masochistic way but latently denied their femininity and showed an aggressive masculine orientation; they unconsciously invited sexual aggression, only to respond to it with coolness and rejection. They stimulated their husbands into attempts to prove themselves, attempts which necessarily ended in frustration and increased their husbands' own doubts about their masculinity. In doing so, the wives unknowingly continued the type of relationship the offender had had with his mother. There can be no doubt that the sexual frustration which the wives caused is one of the factors motivating rape, which might be tentatively described as a displaced attempt to force a seductive but rejecting mother into submission. (P. 165)

In actuality, clinical studies do not agree about the characteristics of rapists' wives. In a recent study, for example, West, Roy, and Nichols (1978) conclude that

with one isolated exception, the histories of the members of the treatment group did not suggest that suffering at the hands of domineering or covertly hostile wives was an important contributory factor. Most of the group were or had been living as married men before coming to prison. Judging from their own accounts, and from talking to wives who still visited, there was no instance of an offender being driven to crime by his wife's behaviour. Marital tension, and failure of communication between husband and wife, certainly prevailed, but, contrary to what might have been expected, the wives seemed to play a relatively small part in producing these problems. There were men who would have found difficulty in sustaining an intimate heterosexual partnership with anyone. In fact, some of them had failed several times in attempts at a marital relationship with different women. (P. 128)

Abrahamsen develops the theory of hypermasculinity a step further: The husbands' insecurities about their masculinity are exacerbated by the sex role identity problems of their wives, who allegedly "latently denied their femininity and showed an aggressive masculine orientation." This example makes particularly explicit an underlying theme in the hypermasculinity hypothesis: While it acknowledges that certain male behaviors are undesirable, it places the responsibility for them not on men but women. According to the hypermasculinity hypothesis, women are the source of all undesirable male behaviors—either directly, as in the Boston Strangler and Abrahamsen examples, or indirectly, because these behaviors reflect insecurity in male sex role identity ultimately caused by women, particularly mothers.

Proposition 8. *Problems of sex role identity account for boys' difficulties
in school performance and adjustment.*

In light of contemporary concern that the educational system
discourages women from developing their full potential (see, for
example, Stacey, Bereaud, and Daniels, 1974), it is surprising to
see that recent studies of education express grave worries about
discrimination against *men.* A well-known book by Patricia Sexton,
*The Feminized Male: Classrooms, White Collars, and the Decline of
Manliness* (1973), develops this view:

Though run at the top by men, schools are essentially feminine
institutions, from nursery school through graduate school. In
the school, women set the standards for adult behavior, and
many favor students, males and female, who most conform to
their own behavior norms—polite, clean, obedient, neat and
nice ones. . . .

The feminized school simply bores many boys but it pulls
some in one of two opposite directions. If the boy absorbs
school values, he may bacome feminized himself. If he resists,
he is pushed toward school failure and rebellion. (Pp. 25, 33)

This view can be formally stated as the *school feminization hypothesis:*
Boys experience academic and psychological difficulties at school
because it exacerbates their sex role identity problems, due to the
predominance of female teachers, teachers' encouragement of
femininity, and the image of school as feminine (see also Biller,
1973, pp. 103–116; 1974, pp. 143–152).

Effects of Female Teachers

There is no dispute that most elementary teachers are women; Lee (1973) estimates that proportion to be about 85%. The more controversial question is whether the predominance of female teachers has negative effects on boys. At first glance, the most direct way to test this aspect of the school feminization hypothesis is to compare the school performance and adjustment of boys whose teachers are males with those whose teachers are females. Sexton, however, implies that this simple comparison may not be meaningful:

Putting a man, any man, in place of women in the school will not do. A man who is less than a man can be more damaging to boys than a domineering mother. The chances of getting feminized men in the school are fairly good because those eligible and willing, given present hiring codes and salaries, are usually those who made it through a feminine school system without conflict or failure. (Pp. 29–30)

Sexton develops here analysis of male teachers further in the following passage:

Still I must honestly report the striking neutral-to-feline nature of many males who function in educational institutions and related spheres. Some seem almost neuter in gender. Many others have a rather feline quality, a personality trait commonly ascribed to women. Many others are "nice boys" and "mama's boys" gone bad. It is as if they had always submitted, done what they were told, kept nice and clean, and loved mother—then suddenly they come into positions of great authority in the classroom. Now they can release all their contained rebellion, arrogance, and urge to be undisputed authorities. They act up, like spoiled children. They say whatever comes into their heads, no matter how malicious. They become the little Caesars mama wanted them to be. They do not have to be "nice" ever again. Some of them (especially in the field of literature) will bite and scratch their rivals—verbally, of course—and otherwise conduct their disputes in a way commonly ascribed to women. They are narcissistic, egoncentric, spoiled, the screamers and scratchers, the bad boys among feminized males. (Pp. 37–38)

If male teachers are "feminized," "neuter in gender," and "less than men," it is questionable whether they will have a positive effect on boys' sex role identities. Therefore, before turning directly to studies comparing the effects of male and female teachers, it is necessary to examine the available data about the characteristics of male teachers.

Are Male Teachers Masculine?

Three studies find only weak and inconsistent differences between male teachers and other males on m-f tests (Nance, 1949; Biedenkamp and Goering, 1971; Robinson and Canady, 1978). And, as I have argued earlier, even if a difference in scores on m-f scales is found in such comparisons, its meaning is highly questionable.

The actual classroom behavior of male and female teachers may also be compared. Lee and Wolinsky (1973), in a particularly thorough study, find that the major respect in which male teachers differ from female teachers is that the former initiate and involve themselves in male-typed activities and the latter in sex-neutral activities. Milgram and Sciarra (1974) provide further evidence that male teachers reinforce the traditional male role:

Many of the male teachers we spoke to felt that their female counterparts kept accusing them of being too tolerant of certain classroom behaviors. Perhaps the difference is in perspective. "Toilet talk" and painting pictures of a penis at the easel didn't seem to bother the men we spoke to, though several indicated that they would be bothered by seeing two four-year-old boys embracing and kissing each other. Some of them said they would step in immediately in order to stop this behavior. One young man stated that such a sight would bother him but, based on his knowledge of growth and development, he would check his urge to intervene. On the other hand, most of the women teachers we spoke to did not feel any need to place any significance on the act of boys kissing and embracing. (P. 246)

Since male teachers do act in masculine ways, comparison of male and female teachers' effects on children is a fair test of the feminization hypothesis.

Effects of Teachers' Sex on Boys

Six studies compare the academic achievement of boys having a male or female teacher. Four of these find no differences (Triplett, 1968; Cascario, 1971; Forslund and Hull, 1972; Asher and Gottman, 1973). McFarland (1969) concludes that boys in a class with a regular male volunteer assistant teacher do worse in mathematics than boys in a control class but perform no differently in other subjects. In the one study finding a positive difference, Brophy and Laosa (1971) determine that, in one of two samples, boys in kindergarten whose teachers are males do better on tasks involving spatial skills (though not in other areas); the second sample does not show this effect at a statistically significant level, however. Lee's (1973) review of these studies reaches the conclusion that they "have not generally found significant differences" (p. 87).

Kagan (1964a) and Biller (1974) assert that Preston's (1962) finding that boys' reading scores are lower than girls' in the United States, but higher than girls' in Germany, is the result of the higher proportion of male elementary teachers in Germany. Kagan and Biller fail to note, however, that Preston interprets this pattern as due to differences in the languages and methods of teaching reading that interact with subtle cognitive differences between the sexes. Also, Preston finds that in most comparisons American boys score higher than German boys—a fact hard to square with the hypothesis that female teachers cause boys to have reading problems.

Triplett (1968) and Forslund and Hull (1972) conclude that boys whose teachers are males like school more. Sciarra (1970) finds no such effect, however. Lee and Wolinsky (1973) observe that boys whose teachers are males are no more likely than boys whose teachers are females to think their teachers favor or prefer boys; boys with male teachers, however, are more likely to list a boy as the child most liked by the teacher. (There are no data from the teachers to check this perception.)

Tripplett (1968) finds also that boys whose teachers are males have higher self-esteem than other boys. McFarland (1969), however, concludes that male classroom volunteers have no effect on boys' self-perceptions. Both McFarland (1969) and Brophy and Laosa (1971) find that the presence of male teachers has no apparent relationship to the extent to which boys have masculine sex-typed traits.

Sciarra (1970) hypothesizes that the absence of male models in early education decreases boys' self-esteem, thereby increasing their aggression and susceptibility to peer-group influence, so that introducing male models should reduce both these effects. Sciarra introduces volunteers for eight weeks in three classrooms in an inner-city daycare center serving primarily black children ages 3–5. One class has a male volunteer every day, another a male volunteer intermittently, and the third a female volunteer. Boys in the three classes show no significant differences in aggression and susceptibility to peer-group influence. There is a nonsignificant trend, however, for boys exposed to the male model every day to become more susceptible to peer-group influence. Using a mode of reasoning common in MSRI research, Sciarra argues that this result shows that exposure to the daily male model increases boys' peer-group *cooperation* and therefore demonstrates that male models do indeed have positive effects.

Several of these studies suffer from the drawback that the male teacher or volunteer is inexperienced or spends little time in the classroom. For example, in Sciarra (1970) a male is present for only eight weeks, and in McFarland (1969) many different males rotate through the same class. Thus these studies cannot be regarded as definitive tests of the possible effects of full-time, experienced male teachers. It is interesting to note, however, that many school administrators so strongly believe in the need for male models that they make the most of even a limited male presence. Woodbridge (1973), for example, describes a Masculine Teacher Program in one Indiana school district, in which "the lone 'man teacher' in a school spends half his time 'on call' for 'masculine activities'" (p. 44).

Teachers' Reinforcement of Sex-Typed Behavior in Boys

The school feminization hypothesis asserts that teachers negatively reinforce masculine behaviors and positively reinforce feminine behaviors in boys.

Classroom Reinforcement

Lee and Wolinsky (1973) find that of the children's activities that female teachers positively reinforce, 17% are male typed, 14% are female typed, and 69% are neutral. These results do not support the notion that female teachers feminize boys.

A widely cited study by Fagot and Patterson (1969) finds, however, that female teachers reinforce feminine activities in boys six times as often as masculine activities. The study includes only four teachers (two in each of two nursery school classes), and detailed examination of the results reveals that what they really mean is a matter of definition. Behaviors are classified as sex typed if they are performed significantly more often by one sex in at least one of the two time periods studied.[1] In one class in the first observation period the feminine behaviors are art work, painting, and listening to stories; in the second observation period the only feminine behavior is art work. Thus, for half of the already small sample it is being asserted that teachers are feminizing boys because they are reinforcing boys for art work and listening to stories.

In the other class the behaviors do include sex-typed activities conventionally viewed as more feminine: doll play, dollhouse play, and kitchen play. But they also include painting, art work, and playing with clay. To a large extent, then, teachers' reinforcement of feminine behaviors in this study is only reinforcement of art activities. It stretches language beyond a reasonable limit to say that a teacher who tells a boy that he drew a nice picture is feminizing him.

Two other studies of this sort have similarly questionable definitions of masculinity and femininity. Etaugh, Collins, and Gerson (1975) replicate the Fagot and Patterson study in a sample of 2-year-olds and find that the feminine behaviors that five teachers reinforced are painting, helping the teacher, reading books, and listening to stories. Robinson and Canady's (1978) list includes these behaviors along with sitting and doing nothing. The evidence is consistent and incontrovertible: Teachers encourage these activities in children of both sexes. But it is certainly arguable that painting, helping teachers, and verbal activities are devastating to boys' sex role identities.

Evaluative Rating Studies

Levitin and Chananie (1972) provide a more indirect kind of evidence. Elementary teachers are given descriptions of three different kinds of male and female students—achieving, aggressive-disobedient, and obedient-dependent—and rate how much they like each student and approve of the student's behavior. Levitan and Chananie conceptualize aggression-disobedience as masculine, obedience-dependency as feminine, and achievement as neutral. Teachers react more negatively to disobedience-aggression than obedience-dependency in boys in terms of approval, but not liking. Whether to regard disapproval of disobedience and aggression as feminizing to boys is a matter of judgment. Etaugh and Hughes's (1975) replication of this study likewise yields mixed results.

Overall, then, there is little conclusive evidence that teachers favor feminine behaviors in boys.

Perception of the Schools as Feminine

The third argument in the feminization hypothesis is that boys see school itself as feminizing, so that simply being in school can give them academic and adjustment problems.

In a study by Kagan (1964b), second- and third-grade children are taught to associate one nonsense syllable with masculine objects and another nonsense syllable with feminine objects. To do this, the experimenter engages the child in a guessing game in which the child is first shown pictures of a man and of a woman and told that they are, respectively, DEP and ROV. The child is then shown other pictures, such as a man's trousers, a baseball bat, a woman's shoe, or a lipstick, and asked to guess whether these are DEP or ROV. (A third syllable, FAS, is used for objects related to farms.) Finally, after learning the correct associations, the child is shown a series of nineteen new pictures, including eight school-related objects, and asked to guess their categories.

Although Kagan concludes that boys perceive the schools as feminine, this is by no means clear from the data. First, of the eight objects designated in advance by the researcher as school related, only four—blackboard, book, page of arithmetic, and school desk—are labeled feminine significantly more often than masculine by all second graders (boys and girls combined). Of the other four items, two (school building, library) are classified as masculine or feminine about equally and two (pencil, map) are classified as masculine significantly more often. Second, of the four objects rated feminine by second graders, among the second-grade *boys* the differences are significant for only two (blackboard, page of arithmetic). Nor are these differences overwhelming; blackboards are rated feminine by 69% of the boys and a page of arithmetic by 60%, with substantial minorities (29% and 40%, respectively) perceiving them as masculine. In contrast, the masculine objects are more strongly masculine; pencils are rated masculine by 79% of the boys and feminine by only 15%; maps are rated masculine by 68% of the boys and feminine by only 16%. Thus boys' *average* rating of the sex-typed school objects is actually more masculine than feminine. Third, of the two items significantly more often rated feminine than masculine by second-grade boys, among third-grade boys one of them (a page of arithmetic) is more often rated masculine and one (blackboard) receives almost equal masculine and feminine ratings. Thus, far from showing that boys experience school objects as feminine, Kagan's study actually indicates that second-grade boys perceive a minority of school objects as feminine, but perceive an equal minority of school objects as even more strongly masculine and discard or even reverse their perceptions of the feminine objects only one grade later.

Another study often cited as demonstrating that boys view school as feminine, Kellogg (1969), yields similarly equivocal results. Lee and Wolinsky's finding, noted earlier, that teachers initiate and respond primarily to neutral and masculine activities provides further evidence contradicting this notion, as do studies of the overrepresentation of males and male activities in the educational curriculum (Jacklin and Mischel, 1973). Kagan (1964a) and Biller (1974) suggest that boys' deficit in school performance relative to girls becomes smaller at higher grade levels because boys begin to perceive school as more masculine. There is, however, a simpler explanation: boys, who mature somewhat more slowly than girls, catch up in the higher grades.

Sexton's Data

The Feminized Male: Classrooms, White Collars, and the Decline of Manliness (1970) is an extremely complicated and diverse book, presenting a wide variety of evidence and arguments about many different subjects. If one body of data in the book is more central than others, however, it is that drawn from her own study of ninth graders in an urban school system (presented at the end of her sixth chapter), which indicates that masculinity is negatively associated with school achievement: The boys who do best in school have undesirable feminized characteristics, while those who do worst have desirable masculine characteristics. The conclusion she draws is that school values are antithetical to true masculinity.

Once again sex typing and socioeconomic status are confounded. The masculine boys who do poorly in school come predominantly from lower socioeconomic backgrounds, so that the conflict reported by Sexton need not be between males and feminine values but between working-class youth and middle-class values. (Biller, 1974, pp. 147–148, makes a similar criticism, observing that Sexton's analysis does not take into account how definitions of masculinity vary by social class.) Even if these data do show an incompatibility between traditionally masculine working-class males and the schools, it remains an open question how this incompatibility should be resolved. While Sexton argues that it is the schools that need to change, one could equally well argue for change in the traditional masculine working-class values that lead to educational problems.

Sexton's argument also illustrates how research in the MSRI paradigm redefines outcomes as good or bad depending on their relationship to sex typing. Good academic performance is, of course, usually regarded as desirable. But since good performance in school is correlated with femininity, Sexton instead interprets it as revealing conformity to feminized values.

Even without these considerations, there is a more fundamental reason to doubt Sexton's argument that the schools are driving truly masculine males out and psychologically crippling those who remain. If true, the proportion of males should decrease at each successive level of education, men should be underrepresented in jobs requiring advanced education and, the men with the most education should be the most psychologically crippled, so that even those few men with advanced education should be less successful than similar women. It is obvious, however, that this is not the way things are.

Overview

The school feminization hypothesis asserts that boys do worse academically when their teachers are women, teachers encourage femininity, and boys perceive school as feminine. A review of the relevant data, however, indicates that these assertions are closer to stereotypes than factual descriptions.

It is true that in the early grades boys do not do as well academically as girls and have more adjustment problems. The femininization hypothesis assumes that school itself is the source of boys' difficulties. But until recently no such assumption was made about girls' school problems. For example, that girls perform less well than boys in mathematics and science traditionally has been interpreted as due to lack of aptitude or interest. Similarly, girls' lower rates of entry into, and completion of, higher education are explained as resulting from lack of motivation or greater desire for homemaking and motherhood. Few regarded the schools as having a responsibility to counter these characteristics.

But poor school performance among boys is something else. Biological factors, to be sure, are sometimes suggested as a source, as is a socialized lack of interest in school. But most often these problems are traced to the schools themselves. Some go so far as to argue that the schools should change their curriculum to give greater emphasis to things in which boys will be interested and do well, such as sports. It is simply taken for granted that the schools have a responsibility to counteract any factors impairing boys' performance. And, as a point of fact, schools have done more to deal with boys' educational problems than girls'. There are more remedial reading programs than remedial mathematics programs, and more programs to keep boys from dropping out of high school than to get girls into college. Further, it is often assumed that the changes in the schools now being proposed to help girls will hurt boys, but the question whether changes proposed to help boys may hurt girls is not even considered. Most of the studies of the effect of the sex of the teacher on student performance examine only *boys'* performance, as if this were the only grounds on which to decide whether to increase the proportion of male teachers.

Some educators are at last beginning to think about male role issues in education in new ways. Woodbridge (1973), for example, compares the role of male teachers as "super stereotypes" who reinforce traditional male roles with their role as "image breakers" who help both boys and girls toward a view of masculinity in which caring and warmth are no longer excluded. Kobliska (1974) presents a fascinating account of his experiences in an elementary school as leader of a "boys' group" set up to discuss the male stereotype. Boressoff (1977) and Sadker (1977) describe many useful strategies for working on male role issues in classrooms. It is clear that such new ways of thinking about men's issues in education are needed.

Proposition 9. *Black males are particularly vulnerable to sex role identity problems.*

According to the MSRI paradigm (for representative statements, see Woronoff, 1962; Pettigrew, 1964, pp. 17–24; Abrahams, 1965, pp. 31–39; Moynihan, 1967; Clark, 1965, pp. 67–74; Hare, 1971; Vontress, 1971; Wilkinson and Taylor, 1977), the black male has already been "emasculated" by the experience of slavery. Moreover, the acquisition of appropriate male identity is difficult for blacks because black fathers fail as role models since they are so often absent, and often are inadequate models even when present. And then black males' sex role identity problems are reinforced in adulthood by high rates of unemployment as well as their overrepresentation in low-paying, low-prestige jobs, expecially ones that carry the connotation of servility or women's work. Thus, as Pettigrew (1964, p. 21) puts it, "The sex-identity problems created by the fatherless home are perpetuated in adulthood." The most widely read expression of this *black emasculation hypothesis* is probably Grier and Cobbs's best-selling *Black Rage* (1968):

For the black man in this country, it is not so much a matter of acquiring manhood as it is a struggle to feel it his own. Whereas the white man regards his manhood as an ordained right, the black man is engaged in a never-ending battle for its possession. For the black man, attaining any portion of manhood is an active process. He must penetrate barriers and overcome opposition in order to assume a masculine posture. For the inner psychological obstacles to manhood are never so formidable as the impediments woven into American society. (P. 59)

MSRI researchers have argued that two kinds of data reveal sex role identity problems among black males: first, black males score more feminine than white males on m-f scales (Pettigrew, 1964, pp. 17–24); second, black males show high rates of delinquency and adult crime. Erikson (1968) and Staples (1971) note that many of the items in m-f scales interpreted as showing that black males are more feminine that whites may have different meaning in black culture. Black males may endorse the item "I would like to be a singer" (specifically cited by Pettigrew as an item indicating black males' femininity) because many black singers are cultural heroes among blacks. Of the two studies on which Pettigrew bases his interpretation of black males' sex role identity problems, one involves a sample of Alabama convicts and the other working-class veterans with tuberculosis in Wisconsin—certainly not the most representative of samples. A more recent study, using a better measure (the BSRI) in a less skewed sample (midwestern college students), finds that black males score significantly higher than whites on masculinity and do not differ on femininity (Hershey, 1978).

Ryan (1966), as part of a general critique of the so-called Moynihan report (Moynihan, 1967), notes that the data showing higher crime and delinquency rates among black males concern only reported or adjudicated crime and that many factors may cause blacks to be overrepresented in these rates. Also, as discussed earlier, paternal absence appears to have only a weak effect on rates of delinquency, and the only study attempting to relate paternal absence among black delinquents to hypermasculinity (Silverman and Dinitz, 1974) is inconclusive.

Part of the appeal of the black emasculation hypothesis is its implication that racism not only keeps blacks poor and in ghettoes but, even worse, damages black men's very manhood. This hypothesis was in vogue in the 1960s and became the official view of the federal government through the Moynihan report. Nonetheless, the hypothesis fails on empirical grounds and derives from a deeply conservative perspective on sex roles and a patronizing view of blacks. Moynihan (1967), for example, argues that the humiliations suffered by blacks during Reconstruction had a particularly devastating effect on black males because "the very essence of the male animal, from the bantam rooster to the four-star general, is to strut" (p. 62). Moynihan also argues that military service is an ideal solution to black men's frustrated masculinity: "Given the strains of the disorganized and matrifocal family life in which so many Negro youth come of age, the Armed Forces are a dramatic and desperately needed change: a world away from women, a world run by strong men of unquestioned authority" (p. 42). In a book on fatherhood, Biller and Meredith (1975) include material on black fathers in a chapter titled "Fathers with Special Problems," of which the only other example is fathers with physical handicaps.

Up to the present, the debate on black masculinity has been polarized between proponents of the black emasculation hypothesis, who ascribe sex role identity problems among blacks to racism, and critics of the hypothesis, who not only deny such problems but even argue that black males have a more masculine identity than whites (see examples in Wilkinson and Taylor, 1977). But both sides fail to question the assumptions of their debate. Neither side questions the construct of sex role identity itself. No one asks how the concept of sex role identity *really* adds to our understanding of the negative consequences to black (or, for that matter, any other) males of paternal absence, unemployment, or poorly paid jobs.

Proposition 10. *Male adolescent initiation rites are a response to problems of sex role identity.*

Burton and Whiting (1961) argue that the greatest sex role identity conflict in a male occurs when he is extremely close to, and dependent on, his mother early in life, leading to a feminine sex role identity, but then is exposed to a society in which men have control over resources, leading him to seek a masculine sex role identity. They argue further that one way in which cultures deal with this conflict is the adolescent inititation rite, which formally gives the boy social status as a man. They summarize as follows:

In societies with maximum conflict in sex identity, e.g., where a boy initially sleeps exclusively with his mother and where the domestic unit is partrilocal and hence controlled by men, there will be initiation rites at puberty which function to resolve this conflict in identity. This hypothesis suggests that initiation rites serve psychologically to brainwash the primary feminine identity and to establish firmly the secondary male identity. (P. 90)[2]

Of the 13 societies that Burton and Whiting coded as having "elaborate initiation ceremonies with genital operations" out of a sample of 64 studied, all had exclusive mother-child sleeping arrangements, and 12 of these also had patrilocal residence. This result is quite dramatic, and the study is widely cited and reprinted. There are, nonetheless, two major issues in research of this nature that considerably undermine the conclusions of the study.

The first problem is that the methodology of this kind of cross-cultural research is more subjective than it first appears. Norbeck, Walker, and Cohen (1962) discover many coding ambiguities in the Burton and Whiting study, both regarding the definition of initiation rites and the definition of a society. Indeed, it is their feeling that the ambiguities suffice to case doubt on the empirical relationships that Burton and Whiting find. (Most scholars citing the Burton and Whiting study, unfortunately, are unaware of this critique.)

A more substantive problem in the Burton and Whiting study is that initiation rites are strongly related to *other* variables, which in turn are related to sleeping arrangements and residence patterns, thus permitting other interpretations. Two examples of such alternative interpretations will illustrate the point. The first is expecially striking since it is from an earlier study involving

Whiting himself. Whiting, Kluckhohn, and Anthony (1958) show in a sample of 56 cultures that male initiation rites are associated with the simultaneous occurrence of exclusive mother-child sleeping arrangements and a postpartum sex taboo (prohibition of sexual intercourse after childbirth for a period of time) of a least a year's duration. This is interpreted not in terms of sex role identity conflicts, however, but rather in terms of the psychoanalytic theory of the Oedipal conflict. Burton and Whiting (1961) later assert that the interpretation in terms of sex role identity conflict is "more valid and fruitful," but do not indicate how this judgment is made.

Young (1962, 1965) provides a second alternative interpretation: Adolescent male initiation rites are needed when the problem of fulfilling the standards of the adult male role is intensified by the cultural pattern of "male solidarity," which Young (1962) defines as

cooperation of the men in maintaining a definition of their situation as one which is not only different from that of women, but which involves organized activities requiring the loyalty of all males. . . . A crucial threshhold [in male solidarity] develops when the men of a village come to see themselves as a consciously organized group with the power to exclude or discipline its members. (Pp. 381–382)

In societies characterized by this male solidarity, there are special standards that men must live up to in order to belong to the male group; since the discontinuity between preadult and adult male status is especially great, males need a special social institution to prepare them for, dramatize, and mark their transition to the adult male status, and this need is met by the initiation rite. Using Whiting, Kluckhohn, and Anthony's (1958) sample, Young finds somewhat stronger empirical support for this interpretation than for Burton and Whiting's.

Much as I prefer Young's interpretation to both of Whiting's, the data fail to support any of them definitively. Young's analysis makes clear that male solidarity is associated not only with initiation rites but with mother-child sleeping arrangements, and there is no basis for considering the relationship between initiation rites and male solidarity any more fundamental than that between initiation rites and sleeping arrangements. Whiting and Young each argue that his relationship is the primary one on logical or theoretical grounds, but there does not seem to be any way to resolve the issue on these grounds alone. To sum up the situation, given the strong interrelationships among the many cultural variables that predict initiation rites, at present no theoretical explanation is compelling.

Proposition 11. *Historical changes in the character of work and the organization of the family have made it more difficult for men to develop and maintain their sex role identities.*

The MSRI paradigm includes an interpretation of the history of the male role. Ruitenbeck (1967) provides the following representative statement:

The average man may not yet be aware that he is in crisis. He believes that as a male his position—social, economic, and sexual—makes him superior to the female. Nevertheless, all through American society, the male's behavior shows that he actually is experiencing a change which affects his traditional roles as father, lover, and provider. This change may be summed up in a single word: emasculation. The American male is being operated on by a force other than the castrating female, however; he is being shaped by a technologically oriented culture. (P. 17)[3]

This thesis leads to a corollary: Certain political and social phenomena are responses to, or defenses against, the insecure male identities caused by this historical process of feminization.

This *historical feminization hypothesis* has been applied to the foreign policy of the Progressives, and especially of Theodore Roosevelt. McGovern (1966), for example, interprets the aggressively masculine foreign policy statements of David Graham Phillips, an important Progressive, as a result of the sex role identity conflicts caused by his early relationship with his mother. Dubbert (1974) argues that various Progressive figures, especially William Allen White, admired what they perceived as Roosevelt's quintessential manliness because of their own sex role identity conflicts. The hypothesis can also be applied to the emergence of the Boy Scouts in the early twentieth century. Greven (1977) applies the hypothesis to an earlier period by analyzing the Great Awakening in the mid-eighteenth century in terms of evangelical ministers' sex role identity problems caused by their close relationships with their mothers, sisters, and aunts. He also interprets the colonists' concern about British trickery and exploitation as "political paranoia" deriving from their insecure sex role identities.

Such arguments cannot, of course, be proved or disproved. In the SRS paradigm, however, I develop an alternative interpretation of the impact of recent historical change on male roles. The historical feminization hypothesis has strongly taken hold in psychohistory, currently in considerable vogue. Unfortunately, the concepts psychohistorians have borrowed from the social sciences have often been its most traditional ones, such as sex role identity.

Sex-Role Strain (SRS): An Alternative Paradigm

In an important sense there is only one complete unblushing male in America: a young, married, white, urban, northern, heterosexual Protestant father of college education, fully employed, of good complexion, weight, and height, and a recent record in sports. Every American male tends to look out upon the world from this perspective, this constituting one sense in which one can speak of a common value system in America. Any male who fails to qualify in any one of these ways is likely to view himself—during moments at least—as unworthy, incomplete, and inferior. (Goffman, 1963, p. 128)

The birthright of every American male is a chronic sense of personal inadequacy. (Woolfolk and Richardson, 1978, p. 57)

Social scientists influenced by the feminist analysis of women's and men's roles are developing an alternative to the male sex role identity paradigm: the sex role strain (SRS) paradigm.[1] This paradigm is the general theory that implicitly underlies the new research on sex roles. Presenting the paradigm systematically and explicitly makes each of its individual lines of research more meaningful. The following quiz tests the degree to which your interpretation of sex roles is in agreement with the SRS paradigm (the more questions checked as true, the greater the agreement).

A Second Quiz on Sex Roles

	True	False
1. Society has very definite ideas about what men and women should be like.	——	——
2. There is no way that people can do all the things expected of them as men and women.	——	——

3. People who flaunt society's expectations about
how men and women should act are usually
ostracized.   ____ ____

4. There is greater tolerance of tomboys than
sissies.   ____ ____

5. Many masculine and feminine traits are
undesirable.   ____ ____

6. Many people have ideas about masculinity or
femininity that they cannot live up to.   ____ ____

7. Many men who seem too masculine are
concerned about not living up to society's
expectations.   ____ ____

8. Probably most people fail to live up to society's
expectations for men and women.   ____ ____

9. Masculinity does not have to exclude
emotionality.   ____ ____

10. Masculinity and femininity would be less
stressful if less stereotyped.   ____ ____

11. Masculinity should not require
aggressiveness.   ____ ____

As noted in chapter 2, a relationship between sex-typed traits
and psychological adjustment can be explained by three different
hypotheses. While an *innate psychological need* for sex-typed traits
is the underlying assumption of the MSRI paradigm, the implications of sex-typed traits for *social approval* and *situational adaptation* are the central arguments of the SRS paradigm.

Like the MSRI paradigm, the SRS paradigm consists of a series
of propositions (see listing in chapter 1). Proposition 1* is a
fundamental definition. Propositions 2*–7* develop what can be
called the *self-role discrepancy theory* of sex role strain, based on the
social approval hypothesis: Individuals suffer negative consequences when they fail to live up to sex roles. Proposition 8*
presents what can be called the *socialized dysfunctional characteristics
theory* of sex role strain: Because of sex roles, individuals are
socialized to have personality characteristics that are dysfunctional. For women, these are dependency and achievement in-

hibitions; for men, aggression and emotional constriction. Proposition 9* applies these sex role strain theories to men's and women's roles in employment and the family. Proposition 10* considers the historical aspect of sex role strain. While these propositions apply to both sexes, they are discussed here primarily in relation to men.

Proposition I.* *Sex roles are operationally defined by sex role stereotypes and norms.*

In the United States a *real* boy climbs trees, disdains girls, dirties his knees, plays with soldiers, and takes blue for his favorite color. When they go to school, real boys prefer manual training, gym, and arithmetic. In college the boys smoke pipes, drink beer, and major in engineering or physics. The real boy matures into a "man's man" who plays poker, goes hunting, drinks brandy, and dies in the war. (Brown, 1965, p. 161)

As discussed in chapter 1, sex role *stereotypes* are widely shared beliefs about what the sexes actually are like, that is, descriptive beliefs about the sexes. Sex role *norms* are widely shared beliefs about what the sexes should be like, that is, prescriptive beliefs about the sexes.

The concept of stereotype is borrowed from studies of prejudice against racial and ethnic groups that argue that prejudice results in part from negative and presumably inaccurate beliefs about a group's actual characteristics (Brigham, 1971). The concept of norm has a long history in sociology and social psychology but derives most immediately from research on occupational and family roles (for example, Gross, Mason, and McEachern, 1958). Researchers postulate that widely shared beliefs exist prescribing how individuals holding particular roles should act, and that individuals compare themselves and are compared by others to these beliefs. Both stereotypes and norms are essential to the definition of sex roles. A sex role is similar in some ways to an ethnic identity, but similar in other ways to an occupational or family role.

Stereotypes

While the results of recent research on sex role stereotypes are widely known (see Broverman et al., 1972; Cicone and Ruble, 1978; Brannon, 1978), several conceptual issues have not heretofore received adequate attention.

Ambiguous Meaning

In popular usage, the term sex role stereotype usually means inaccurate perceptions of the sexes rooted in traditional sex role ideology. As assessed in research studies, however, stereotypes are simply perceptions of the way each sex actually is; their accuracy and sources cannot be determined. For example, suppose that on a 7-point scale ranging from aggressive (=7) to unaggressive (=1), a particular individual rates the typical man as 6 and the typical woman as 4. There is no way to decide whether this individual perceives each sex by itself, or the difference between the two, accurately or not.

Even if these scores' accuracy could be determined, their implications would be ambiguous in another respect. One individual making these ratings may believe that a difference between men and women is biologically based, inevitable, and socially desirable. Another, however, may view this difference as an undesirable but fortunately changeable outcome of traditional sex role socialization. It is often erroneously assumed that perceiving the sexes to be different is inherently conservative; actually, it becomes so only when combined with a particular view of the sources and desirability of the difference.

Relative versus Absolute Stereotypes

The relative stereotype of a sex includes the traits that most *differentiate* that sex from the other; the absolute stereotype includes the traits that most *characterize* that sex, whether sex differentiating or not. While almost all analyses of sex role stereotypes conceptualize them in relative terms, several researchers note that this can be quite misleading. Sherriffs and McKee (1957, p. 455) note that the relative stereotype excludes many items seen as highly characteristic of each sex because they do not discriminate, but includes many uncharacteristic attributes that do. In their data, for example, a majority of respondents describe both men and women as clever, but not to different degrees. On the other hand, only a tiny fraction rate men as witty, but none rate women this way; the difference is statistically significant. As a result, the relative male stereotype includes wit (even though few think it characteristic of men) but not cleverness (even though most do rate it a male characteristic).

Spence, Helmreich, and Stapp (1974) note in another study that for all but a tiny minority of traits, the average ratings assigned to males and females are on the same side of the mid-point of the scale. For example, while men are rated as stronger than women, women are still rated on the strong side of the strong-weak dimension. Thus, suggest these investigators, it is misleading to say that women are perceived as weak.[2] Nonetheless, such conclusions are extremely common in discussions of such research, as in the oft-repeated claim that Broverman et al. (1972) show that women are perceived as weak, passive, and illogical. As stated, such generalizations are simply false.

While both kinds of stereotypes are meaningful, absolute stereotypes are the more important to the SRS paradigm. The stereotypes that members of a sex are compared to, and compare themselves to, are absolute, not relative. A man worries "Am I as aggressive as most other men are?", not "Am I more aggressive than women, the way other men are?"

Absolute stereotypes lead to different conclusions about sex roles than do relative stereotypes. Spence, Helmreich, and Stapp's observation that men and women are rated on the same side of the midpoint on most traits implies that, in absolute terms, the sexes are perceived to be comparatively similar. These researchers further note that the traits on which each sex is rated high include both masculine and feminine ones.

While these statements may seem startling, they are consistent with two other ideas now widely accepted in sex role research: the replacement of the bipolar (masculinity-femininity) conception of the structure of sex typing with the androgynous (that is, dual-unipolar) conception, and the realization that the traditional focus on sex differences obscures the fact that women and men are more alike than different. As evidence accumulates that women and men have both masculine and feminine traits and are more similar than different, it is not surprising that a reconsideration of data on sex role stereotypes suggests precisely the same result about how the sexes are perceived.

Is the Male Stereotype More Favorable?

Research on relative stereotypes is invariably interpreted as demonstrating that the male stereotype is more favorable than the female. In the study most often cited in this regard, Rosenkrantz et al. (1968) find that their procedure for investigating relative sex role stereotypes yields 29 socially desirable male-valued and 12 socially desirable female-valued traits. Since this study also determines that, on the average, male and female traits have equal social desirability, the conclusion that the male stereotype is more favorable than the female depends entirely on the relatively greater number of positively valued items in the male stereotype. But it is clear that the number of adjectives deduced for each sex's stereotype depends entirely on the initial pool of adjectives. Newer studies (for example, Silvern, 1977) using broader item pools that include more socially undesirable masculine traits find that in many respects the male role is perceived as less desirable than the female role (see also Best, Williams, and Briggs, 1980).

Norms

One of the most surprising facts about contemporary sex role research is that, although it has devoted considerable effort to investigating stereotyping, it has hardly given any attention to sex role norms. Some studies provide limited information (see Jenkin and Vroegh, 1969; Spence, Helmreich, and Stapp, 1974; Roper Organization, 1974; Tavris, 1979; Yankelovich, 1974; Allen, 1954; Steinmann and Fox, 1966), but they are inadequate as an empirical base for a description of male sex role norms.

The most popular methodology for investigating norms collects ratings of the "ideal man" (or "ideal woman") or qualities most admired in a man (or a woman). There is clearly something normative about these ratings; but it is not clear that such ratings represent the standards against which average persons are compared or compare themselves. Individuals more likely compare themselves to some standard of minimum acceptable fulfillment, not maximum ideal performance. In effect, available research assesses only the extreme upper end of what is clearly a continuum of norms. But this continuum is important because there is an inverse relationship between the level of idealization in the norm and the degree to which the norm is actually applied to the self in self-evaluation. The more idealized the norm, the less most people actually compare themselves to it.

Different levels of norms vary in another respect as well. Available research using the ideal man or qualities most admired methods (for example, Roper Organization, 1974; Tavris, 1977) finds that the male norm at this level includes many sex-neutral and feminine characteristics, for example, intelligence, sensitivity to the needs of others, warmth, and romanticism. Reece (1964) and Jenkin and Vroegh (1969) likewise find that the ideal male and female share many traits. But these studies show that the male sex role norm is androgynous only at the most highly idealized extreme of the continuum. At the more realistic (minimum acceptable standard) end of the continuum, male norms are probably considerably more sex typed. In fact, most people probably focus on sex differentiating characteristics precisely because they are more realistically attainable then the androgynous characteristics required at a higher level of sex role idealization. For example, it demands less of a man to be competitive or interested in male sports than it does to be intelligent or sensitive. Many men, therefore, spend their time competing with each other or watching sports rather than trying to be intelligent or sensitive.

Factors and Types
Future research in sex role norms (and stereotypes) will also have to concern itself with factors (or types). According to Broverman et al. (1972), the adjectives differentiating the sexes fall into distinct instrumental and expressive factors. Cicone and Ruble (1978) propose an interpretation of the male role in terms of four factors. But the most sophisticated factorial conception of the male role is Brannon and David's (1976). Their four factors are

1. No Sissy Stuff: the stigma of anything even vaguely feminine;
2. The Big Wheel: success, status, and the need to be looked up to;
3. The Sturdy Oak: a manly air of toughness, confidence, and self-reliance;
4. Give 'Em Hell: the aura of aggression, violence, and daring.

Brannon and David note that there is no reason to assume that these factors are orthogonal, that is, empirically independent and mutually uncorrelated. (In fact, the assumption of orthogonality has highly restrictive consequences; Brannon, 1978). They further argue that fulfilling the demands of the male role requires that a man score high on some but not necessarily all factors (see also Brannon, Juni, and Grady, 1981).

Traditional versus Modern
There have been a number of persistent inconsistencies in images of manliness. For example, physical strength is a dominant stan-

dard of masculine worth, but intellectual and interpersonal competence are necessary for the kinds of achievement that society most rewards in men. Men are expected to show greater emotional control and are often described as being more alienated from their feelings than women. But men appear to become angry or violent more easily—and are often rewarded for doing so. Men appear to have stronger social bonds with others of the same sex than do women (a thesis popularized by Tiger, 1969) but men are also reputed to avoid emotional intimacy with others of the same sex and have greater fears of homosexuality.

One way to resolve these inconsistencies is by distinguishing between traditional and modern versions of male role norms (Pleck, 1976a). The traditional male role is depicted in the ethnographies of many primitive societies, such as those cited in Tiger's *Men in Groups* (1969), and such working-class and ethnic community studies as W. F. Whyte's *Street Corner Society* (1943), Komarovsky's *Blue Collar Marriage* (1964), and LeMasters's *Blue Collar Aristocrats* (1975). The modern male role, by contrast, is depicted in such studies of middle-class communities and groups as W. H. Whyte's *The Organization Man* (1956), Seeley, Sim, and Loosey's *Crestwood Heights* (1956), Mills's *White Collar: The American Middle Classes* (1956), and most explicitly in Komarovsky's *Dilemmas of Masculinity: A Study of College Youth* (1976).

In the traditional male role, masculinity is validated ultimately by individual physical strength and aggression. Men are generally expected not to be emotionally sensitive to others or emotionally expressive or self-revealing, particularly of feelings of vulnerability or weakness. Paradoxically, anger and certain other impulsive emotional expressions, particularly toward other males, are expected or tolerated.

In the modern male role, by contrast, masculinity is validated by economic achievement and organizational or bureaucratic power. Interpersonal skills and intelligence are esteemed insofar as they lead to these goals. Emotionally, the modern male role strongly values the capacity for emotional sensitivity and self-expression in romantic relationships with women. It holds, however, that these emotional behaviors should occur only with women. Overall, maintenance of emotional control is a crucial role requirement. Anger and other traditional male impulsive emotional behavior are thus discouraged.

The traditional male prefers the company of men to the company of women and experiences other men as the primary validators of his masculinity. Though bonds of friendship among men are not necessarily emotionally intimate, they are often strong. In the traditional male role in marital and other relationships, women are seen as necessary for sex and for bearing children, but these relationships are not expected to be emotionally intimate or romantic, and often seem only pragmatic arrangements of convenience. The traditional male expects women to acknowledge and defer to his authority. There is also strong adherence to a sexual double standard that views sexual freedom as appropriate for men but not women. Further, men often view women in terms of the madonna-whore complex, in which some women are categorized as morally superior, and other women morally inferior to men.

The modern male prefers the company of women. Women, rather than other men, are experienced as the primary validators of masculinity. Men's relationships with women are now expected to be intimate and romantic. As Burgess and Locke (1945) argue, the marital relationship has evolved from "institution" to "companionship." Men now see heterosexual relationships as the only legitimate source of the emotional support they need. Women now soothe men's wounds and replenish their emotional reserves rather than defer to their authority in the family. Though it still persists, the sexual double standard is less marked. Masculinity is now proved less by many sexual conquests than by truly satisfying one woman's sexual needs. Men's emotional relationships with other men have become weaker and less emotionally important though a high level of competence in conducting work relationships is expected. Komarovsky (1977), for example, reports in an elite college sample that men now disclose more to female than male friends. It is now men's relationships with other men—rather than with women—that seem to be only arrangements of convenience. Male-male relationships often appear now to derive primarily from workplace contacts and to be expressed primarily through drinking and watching sports on television.

This distinction parallels a more general shift in the national character; see, in particular, Reich's (1970) analysis of the transition from "Consciousness I" to "Consciousness II" character types. It also parallels a distinction between working-class and middle-class culture. My argument is not that all males once had traditional roles and now have modern ones. Rather, as contemporary culture has evolved, the modern male role has emerged and increasingly represents the expectations against which males evaluate themselves. Elements of the traditional male role clearly persist, both in culturally conservative groups and in the personalities of many males, but these elements are becoming less dominant.

Future Research

Future research should first give more attention to sex role norms. McKee and Sherriffs, who initiated the first contemporary line of research on beliefs about sex roles, first studied stereotypes (McKee and Sherriffs, 1957; Sherriffs and McKee, 1957), but later shifted their focus to norms (McKee and Sherriffs, 1959). When Rosenkrantz et al. (1968) reinitiated the investigation of sex role beliefs a decade later, unfortunately they turned the attention of the field back to stereotypes (with one exception—Elman, Press, and Rosenkrantz, 1970).

Second, scales measuring absolute rather than relative stereotypes and norms about each sex are needed (for example, Brannon, Juni, and Grady, 1982). Many currently available scales claim to assess attitudes toward women (Spence and Helmreich, 1972a) or attitudes toward men (Doyle and Moore, 1978; Moreland and Van Tuinen, 1978), but since they contain large proportions of items on relative differences and male-female relations, these scales do not really focus on either sex by itself. The relationship between attitudes toward women and men needs to be analyzed. Do these attitudes overlap or are they independent? Perhaps many individuals who hold modern attitudes toward women nonetheless cling to traditional attitudes toward men.

Proposition 2.*   *Sex roles are contradictory and inconsistent.*

Several kinds of contradictions and inconsistencies make it difficult, if not impossible, to conform to sex roles: life-cycle inconsistencies; historical change; and inconsistencies between men's and women's expectations.

Komarovsky (1946, 1953) first proposed that sex roles are internally contradictory in a study finding that girls are expected to do well in elementary and secondary school, but need to downplay their intellectual abilities in college so as not to threaten men. Hacker (1957), Hartley (1970), and Knox and Kupferer (1971) observe that boys' socialization emphasizes physical strength and skill and the avoidance of anything feminine, including girls, but that men are rewarded primarily for intellectual and social skills and are expected to be capable of intimate relationships with women. Mussen's (1961, 1962) research (see chapter 6) provides evidence that masculine characteristics facilitating psychological adjustment in adolescent males do not do so in adults.

New male norms have emerged, but traditional role expectations still persist (Hacker, 1957). As an example, Komarovsky (1973, 1976) suggests that the contemporary norm that men should have intellectual companionship with their dating partners leads them to select women who are their equals, but the persistence of the traditional expectation of male intellectual superiority then causes them to feel intellectual rivalry. Komarovsky finds that this intellectual rivalry is a problem for one third of the Ivy League college sample she studied.

McKee and Sherriffs (1959) and Steinmann and Fox (1974) observe that women have (or are perceived by men to have) different expectations for the male role than do men themselves. Women want men to be more expressive and emotional than men themselves feel is appropriate.

Proposition 3.* *The proportion of individuals who violate sex roles is high.*

Sex roles generate strain because it is difficult for individuals to develop and maintain the characteristics that their sex roles prescribe for them. This can happen for several reasons.

Individuals vary in their personality characteristics. Therefore, no matter what the normative sex role patterns are, inevitably some will not fit them. In *Sex and Temperament in Three Primitive Societies*, Mead (1935) shows how a person perfectly adapted to the norms in one society may be a complete misfit in another. Komarovsky (1976) labels role strain of this sort "idiosyncratic malfit" between the personality and the sex role.

Living up to male sex role norms often depends upon the availability of socially determined external resources. For example, a man's ability to be a good economic provider for his family, a cardinal component of the male role, depends on the state of the economy, his race, education, age, and so on. Komarovsky

calls role strain of this sort "socially structured scarcity of resources."

The norms for each sex role may be so idealized that only the
tiniest minority, no matter what personal characteristics or resources they have, can fulfill them. In this sense, everyone feels
they fail to live up to their sex role.

Several studies provide data on men's perception of discrepancies between themselves and the ideal male (McKee and Sherriffs, 1959; Ehrenberg, 1960; Rosenkrantz et al., 1968; Elman,
Press, and Rosenkrantz, 1970; Steinmann and Fox, 1974; Komarovsky, 1976; Tavris, 1977; Gilbert, Deutsch, and Strahan,
1978; Moore and Nutall, 1980). Tavris (1977) shows particularly
clearly that large proportions of men believe they lack certain
desirable masculine traits (self-confidence, independence, competitiveness)—as well as feminine traits (ability to love, warmth,
gentleness).

Proposition 4.* *Violating sex roles leads to social condemnation.*

This proposition describes one way in which self-norm discrepancies generate the negative consequences experienced as sex
role strain. Sociological literature refers to the social disapproval
resulting from the violation of social norms as *negative sanctions*
(or sometimes simply *sanctions*). Such negative sanctions help produce conformity to social norms.

Social psychologists have studied the consequences of sex role
violations in occupational or activity interests and personality
characteristics (O'Leary and Donoghue, 1978; Spence, Helmreich, and Stapp, 1975b; Kristal et al., 1975; Levitin and Chananie, 1972; Feinman, 1974; Costrich et al., 1975, Derlega and
Chaikin, 1976; Seyfried and Hendrick, 1973). Males with extremely feminine occupational activity interests or personality
characteristics are less well liked than other males and are more
often rated as psychologically maladjusted and in need of psy-
chotherapy. But mild sex role violation does not have these negative consequences, especially when it involves extreme
competence or a socially desirable activity. For example, Levitin
and Chananie (1972) find that sex role violation in boys is not
devalued by elementary teachers when it makes life easier for the
teacher. O'Leary and Donoghue (1978) show that a male pursu-
ing studies in special education on scholarship at Harvard is not

ostracized; in contrast, a male majoring in interior decoration or in home economics is (Spence, Helmreich, and Stapp, 1975b).[3]

Proposition 5.* *Violating sex roles leads to negative psychological consequences.*

Deutsch and Gilbert (1976) observe that "if sex role stereotypes do not correspond with what people think of themselves, with what they think others want them to be, or with what they ideally would like to be, then . . . psychological conflict results" (p. 373). The negative psychological consequences of violating sex roles result not only from social disapproval but also from self-devaluation.

Komarovsky (1973) reports that 45% of a sample of elite male undergraduates exhibit "mild to acute anxiety over their failure in relationships with women, to live up to the traditional ideal of superior masculine assertiveness, determination, decisiveness, courage, independence, aggressiveness, and stability in the face of stress" (p. 655). Ehrenberg (1960) and Deutsch and Gilbert (1976) confirm that a man having characteristics different from his perception of the male role tends to have poor psychological adjustment. Sex role violation should have the greatest negative consequences among those who believe that conformity to sex roles is important and desirable (Garnets and Pleck, 1979; Garnets, 1978).

Proposition 6.* *Actual or imagined violation of sex roles leads individuals to overconform to them.*

By this process, a man who fails to live up to a significant aspect of the male role, or imagines so, will compensate by conforming to other aspects of the role in an exaggerated way. This *role overconformity hypothesis,* while seemingly identical to the MSRI paradigm's hypermasculinity hypothesis, has quite different implications. According to the hypermasculinity hypothesis, the problem causing exaggerated masculine behavior lies in the man; in the overconformity hypothesis, the role itself causes the problem.

Turner (1970, p. 294) discusses the results of a masculinity-femininity study by Nichols (1962) in terms of this hypothesis. Nichols develops "obvious" and "subtle" m-f scales and finds that males who rated themselves as having the fewest "subtle" male characteristics (traits actually characteristic of males, but not often thought to be) rate themselves as having the most "obvious" male characteristics. Turner (1970) suggests that "one plausible judgment would be that those who fit less well into their ascribed sex roles, as indicated by their scores for the subtle scale, suffer role stress to which they react by adhering more narrowly to the stereotypic features of the role" (p. 294).

The most powerful data supporting the overconformity hypothesis concern male sexual aggression. Rape and other forms of male sex aggression are often interpreted as reflecting sex role identity problems and disturbed maternal relationships. Diana Russell (1973) argues, to the contrary, that rape is an instance of overconformity to male role norms about sexuality:

Rape is not so much a deviant act as an over-conforming act. Rape may be understood as an extreme acting-out of qualities that are regarded as super masculine in this and many other societies: aggression, force, power, strength, toughness, dominance, competitiveness. To win, to be superior, to be successful, to conquer—all demonstrate masculinity to those who subscribe to common cultural notions of masculinity, i.e., the *masculine mystique.* And it would be surprising if these notions of masculinity did not find expression in men's sexual behavior. Indeed, sex may be the arena where these notions of masculinity are most intensely played out, particularly by men who feel powerless in the rest of their lives, and hence, whose masculinity is threatened by this sense of powerlessness. (P. 1)

An important study by Kanin (1967) provides data relevant to this argument. In an interview of a random sample of males at a large, coeducational midwestern university, Kanin classifies 26% of the sample as sexually aggressive. Male sexual aggression is defined in a later summary of this study (Kanin, 1970) as

those male-female encounters where, although some erotic intimacy has taken place by mutual consent, the male reacts to the female's negative reponse to further erotic concessions and utilizes force in an effort to render his companion sexually accessible. . . . For the most part, these aggressions involve forceful efforts at removing the female clothing and forceful efforts to maneuver the female into a physically advantageous position for coital access. (P. 29)

In two thirds of these cases, the females scream, fight, cry, or plead for the male to stop.

Kanin rules out the notion that these males are sexually aggressive because they were sexually "frustrated"; the aggressive males had more sexual experience, and more recent sexual experience, than the nonaggressives. Kanin shows that the aggressive group has several characteristics that fit the overconformity hypothesis. In particular, despite greater sexual experience, they report themselves less satisfied with their level of sexual experience because they have higher expectations for the number of orgasms per week necessary for sexual satisfaction. Kanin finds that these high expectations result from having friends who exert social pressure for sexual activity. He concludes that "a high level of erotic aspiration is internalized from erotic-oriented significant others and for the average unmarried college male, this level is almost impossible to achieve" (p. 432).

Proposition 7.*   *Violating sex roles has more severe consequences for males than females.*

According to Goodenough (1957), Lansky (1967), and Fling and Manosevitz (1972), parents disapprove of sex-inappropriate behavior more in boys than in girls. Most studies (Seyfried and Hendrick, 1973; Feinman, 1974; Spence, Helmreich, and Stapp, 1975b; Derlega and Chaikin, 1976) show that males having characteristics deviating from traditional sex roles are perceived more negatively than females. (Levitin and Chananie, 1972, and Costrich et al., 1975, do not, however.)

Negative sanctions for violating sex roles are only one way individuals are restricted by their roles. While men appear to be more restricted than women in this sense, sex roles may also be restrictive by virtue of the social power associated with the role. In this other sense, women's role is clearly more restrictive.

Proposition 8.*   *Certain characteristics prescribed by sex roles are psychologically dysfunctional.*

This proposition expresses the *socialized dysfunctional characteristics theory* of sex role strain. As applied to men, it holds that even if they successfully live up to the male role, they suffer adverse consequences.

Male Aggression

All authorities agree that males are, on the average, more aggressive than females. Aggression is a primitive way of resolving disputes, with undesirable consequences for both its victims and perpetrators.

Future research needs to investigate further the extent to which males' greater aggression generalizes to other areas of their behavior and is affected by social factors. Maccoby and Jacklin (1974), for example, argue that there do not appear to be clear sex differences in behaviors seemingly closely related to aggression such as competition and dominance. Frodi, Macaulay, and Thome (1977) note circumstances under which the usual sex difference in aggression does not appear, such as conditions making aggression appear justified. Halverson and Waldrop (1973) observe that boys' aggressions seem to be heightened by being in a group of other boys.

Many note the obvious connection between male aggressiveness and war (Stone, 1974; Steinem, 1974; Komisar, 1976). Fasteau's (1974) detailed analysis of the Pentagon Papers demonstrates that governmental justifications for the expansion of the Vietnam war during the 1970s are filled with masculine imagery concerning the need for strength, power, and dominance. Etheredge's (1978) studies of current State Department staff and policy disagreements between US Presidents and Secretaries of State since 1898 reveals a connection between aggressive masculine traits and hard-line foreign policy.

Interpreting males' greater aggression as a consequence of the male role requires ruling out the possibility that it results from biological factors. Appendix A reviews evidence relevant to the biological hypothesis and concludes that it is unsupported (see also Brannon, 1981).

Male Emotional and Interpersonal Orientation

Compared to women, men show deficits in many (though not all) aspects of emotional and interpersonal behavior. Males are not necessarily less oriented or responsive to social stimuli (Maccoby and Jacklin, 1974) or less adept at assessing others' emotions or cognitive perspective, but they are less empathic, that is, their feelings are less affected by the feelings of others (Hoffman, 1977). Men are also less emotionally expressive (Allen and Hamsher, 1974; Allen and Haccoun, 1976; Bem, Martyna, and Watson, 1976; Balswick and Avertt, 1977).

Jourard (1964a) labels men's low self-disclosure a "lethal aspect of the male role." Men's problems with self-disclosure, however, appear to be more subtle than this. Many studies actually find no sex difference in this behavior (Jourard, 1964b; Plog, 1965; Cozby, 1973; Bender, Davis, and Glover, 1976). But men do disclose less about highly intimate topics (Morgan, 1976). Further, men tend to restrict their most intimate self-disclosures to a single relationship, while women typically have several relationships with a high level of disclosure (Komarovsky, 1976).

Men's friendships differ from women's (Pleck, 1975b; Lewis, 1978). Douvan and Adelson (1966), for example, observe that adolescent males tend to participate in male groups, while females are more likely to have dyadic friendships (that is, friendships in pairs). Boys are less articulate about the nature and meaning of friendship and do not think it is as important as girls do. Boys' criteria in picking friends are more concrete than girls'; they look for specific qualities or shared interests rather than the generalized warmth, understanding, and emotional rapport rated important by girls. Boys report reacting less strongly than girls to the loss of a friendship. Douvan and Adelson conclude that while males measure no lower than females in sociability, they do measure lower in intimacy.

In an excellent experimental study, Caldwell and Peplau (1981) confirm that men's friendships are less intimate. Booth (1972) finds that while men report a slightly greater number of friendships than women do, men's friendships are described as less close and spontaneous. A study of individuals' relationships with kin members by Adams (1968) observes that men report less closeness and contact with their brothers than women do with their sisters, even when differences in geographical proximity are taken into account.

Any discussion of men's social relationships must necessarily address Lionel Tiger's *Men in Groups* (1969). Tiger coined the term *male bonding* to describe what he argues is a culturally universal, biologically based male propensity to establish strong social ties and institutions with other men. This male-male camaradie, Tiger speculates, forms the backbone of social organization in all societies. In actuality, one part of Tiger's thesis can be substantiated, but interpreted in a different way. While men have more same-sex group involvements than do women, this does not mean men have closer relationships with each other. To the contrary, the evidence is relatively consistent that men have less intimacy than women in these same-sex relationships. As an example of this low intimacy, Margaret Mead (1949) makes the following observation about men's "buddy relationships":

> During the last war English observers were confused by the apparent contradiction in American soldiers' emphasis on the buddy, so grievously exemplified in the break-downs that followed a buddy's death, and the results of detailed inquiry that showed how transitory these buddy relationships were. It was found that men actually accepted their buddies as derivative from their outfit, and from accidents of association, rather than because of any special personality characteristics capable of ripening into friendship. (P. 114)

Male bonding is not a vehicle for male-male emotional relationships, but rather is a substitute for them. Komarovsky suggests, as does Pleck (1975b), that in recent history, men's intimacy has become increasingly directed toward women and away from other men.

Men's Lower Life Expectancy

Men die younger than women on the average. The life expectancy of men born in the United States in 1975 is 68.7 years, compared to 76.5 years for women—a difference of 7.8 years. The difference between men's and women's life expectancies has increased over this century. In 1900, they were 46.3 and 48.3 years, respectively, and differed by only 2 years (Harrison, 1978).

Purely biological factors account for some of this sex difference. For example, males have high rates of mortality even in the prenatal period, and sex hormones are a factor in heart disease (Harrison, 1978; Waldron, 1976). Further, Madigan (1957) and Madigan and Vance (1957) find that the sex difference in mortality persists even when males and females live in similar low-stress environments (cloistered religious communities). Nonetheless, the male role is hazardous to men's health in a variety of specific ways (Harrison, 1978; Waldron, 1976) such as

1. Aggressiveness and competitiveness cause men to put themselves in dangerous situations.
2. Emotional inexpressiveness causes psychosomatic and other health problems.
3. Men take greater risks.
4. Men's jobs expose them to physical danger.
5. Men's jobs expose them to psychological stress.

6. The male role socializes men to have personality characteristics associated with high mortality (for example, "type A" behavior; Friedman and Rosenman, 1974).

7. Responsibilities as family breadwinners expose men to psychological stress.

8. The male role encourages certain specific behaviors that endanger health, specifically tobacco smoking and alcohol consumption.

9. The male role psychologically discourages men from taking adequate medical care of themselves.

The psychological stresses of men's jobs may receive too much emphasis as source of men's shorter life expectancy. A large-scale study by Lee and Schneider (1958) compares men in the position usually regarded as a model for stress—corporate executive—with male nonexecutives of the same age in the same organization. The male executives actually have somewhat lower rates of the diseases perhaps most often thought to be produced by stress: hypertension and arteriosclerosis. In this study, all subjects participate in the same health plan, so that differences in the availability of medical care cannot account for the results. Other studies (for example, Kitagawa and Hauser, 1973; Metropolitan Life Insurance Company, 1974) confirm that males in higher-status jobs have lower mortality than do other males. But the possibilities cannot be ruled out that good health is a cause rather than a consequence of executive office or that executives' higher level of education leads them to seek more health care.

Current research suggests that drinking and smoking may be particularly important factors in men's lower life expectancy (Harrison, 1978). Retherford (1975) estimates that half of the current sex differential results from tobacco smoking alone.

Proposition 9.[*] *Each sex experiences sex role strain in its paid work and family roles.*

A substantial proportion of husbands feel inadequate as family breadwinners (Quinn and Staines, 1978), and many men feel thay are not doing a good job as husbands and fathers. Men experience these shortcomings because more is expected of them than they can realistically provide. These roles are also difficult to fulfill satisfactorily because they make conflicting demands on men. Husbands report considerable conflict between their work and family roles—as much, in fact, as do employed wives (Herman and Gyllstrom, 1977; Kelly, 1979; Pleck, Staines, and Lang, 1980).

Men may also be socialized to have traits that are dysfunctional in relation to their work and family roles. Some men are excessively oriented to achievement in a way that limits their family participation (Masih, 1967), although other evidence suggests that the average man may not necessarily be more achievement-oriented than the average woman (Stein and Bailey, 1970; Maccoby and Jacklin, 1974). Men show more psychological involvement in their jobs and less in their families than do women, although men nonetheless show much greater family than job involvement (Pleck and Lang, 1978; Pleck, 1981).

Fathers obviously spend less time with their children than do mothers (Robinson, 1977; Pleck and Lang, 1978; Pleck and Rustad, 1980), but this does not necessarily result from a socialized psychological unresponsiveness to, or lack of interest in, children. A variety of studies reveal a high degree of similarity between men's and women's responses to newborns (Greenberg and Morris, 1974; Cronenwett and Newmark, 1975; Parke and O'Leary, 1975; Parke and Sawin, 1976; Berman, 1980) and with older children (Mackey and Day, 1979). Men's greater investment of time in their jobs than their families is probably caused more by socialization to view economic support as their primary family function than by the socialization of more general personality traits predisposing men toward employment and away from childcare. (Trivers, 1972, Rypma, 1976, and Rossi, 1977, argue that biological factors help account for men's low participation in childcare; Appendix B provides a critical review.)

Proposition 10.* *Historical change causes sex role strain.*

Changes over time in sex role expectations cause strain, as already noted in proposition 2*. Historical change in the availability of the resources needed to fulfill sex roles also generates strain. Hantover (1978) applies the *historical strain hypothesis,* the alternative to the MSRI paradigm's historical feminization hypothesis, to the emergence of the Boy Scout movement in the United States. He finds that men's applications to become scoutmasters in the early twentieth century express strong desires to participate in the outdoor life and to build character in boys and help them become men, which he interprets as a response to the discrepancy between the rise of white-collar, middle-class occupations as an ideal for males and women's increasing participation in these occupations, making them more difficult for men to attain.[4]

Who in the world would dare to write a book about man—simply as a representative of the male sex? The question would at once be asked: "What man? One from an industrialized country, or from a backward part of the world? A young man, a grown-up, or an elderly person? Intellectual or farmer? And above all, how and on what assumption would the material be handled? Why, indeed, make such an assessment? Modern man in relation to what norms?" (Sullerot, 1971, p. 7)

The field of sex roles, like other disciplines, is more than the sum of many individual studies. Its lines of research inevitably are logically and philosophically related; the validity of any one such line can be understood only by putting it in a larger theoretical context. The issues fundamental to the study of sex roles can be addressed only by identifying its underlying paradigms.

Within the limits of available research methodologies, specific arguments in a paradigm can be validated or invalidated, but a paradigm as a whole cannot. Rather, it can be evaluated only as more or less intellectually useful in structuring the research questions in a field. The more the lines of research in a paradigm fail empirically or conceptually, the less theoretically useful is the paradigm.

The central argument of this book is that past and current research on sex roles can be organized into either of two comprehensive, yet radically different paradigms, MSRI and SRS; that on both philosophical and empirical grounds the MSRI paradigm is not a useful way of understanding sex roles; and that the SRS paradigm is.

The Persistence and Sources of the MSRI Paradigm

Several factors contribute to the contemporary persistence of the MSRI paradigm. First, one of its principal social implications—that fathers should be more involved with their children—is a desirable and widely supported social goal. Many support it, of course, because they believe it will help change traditional roles rather than because they believe (as does the identity paradigm) it will reinforce them (Seifert, 1973). But due to the strong historical association between calls for a greater paternal role and the MSRI paradigm, the broad social consensus favoring the former (though deriving from diverse sources) lends legitimacy to the latter. A clear example is Farrell's (1974) recommendation for greater paternal participation in one of the major early books of the men's liberation movement; he asserts it will help break down traditional sex roles but also claims it will reduce male homosexuality (p. 116). Farrell's inclusion of the latter argument—actu ally at variance with the broader inplications of his book—illustrates how powerful a link the MSRI paradigm has created in the public consciousness between fathering and male sex role identity, and how this link leads many to take positions unwittingly supporting the paradigm.

Second, the phenomenon of transsexuality (individuals psychologically experiencing themselves to be of the other gender) became widely known in the 1960s and 1970s (Stoller, 1968; Money and Ehrhardt, 1972; Green, 1974). To Money and Ehrhardt and other authorities, the study of transsexuality reveals that once a child learns to label its gender accurately, as all but the tiniest minority effortlessly do, behaviors violating traditional roles do not threaten this self-identification; through discovering transsexuality, researchers came to view mere nontraditional role behavior with equanimity. But to the public, transsexuality became instead a specter revealing the potential danger of nontraditional roles. Because of the notoriety of Christine Jorgensen, Jan Morris, Renee Richard, and other male-to-female transsexuals, parents came to worry that nontraditional roles might cause the same fate to befall their children. Contrary to its true implications, transsexuality appeared to confirm the MSRI paradigm and thus set back the acceptance of nontraditional roles.

Third, a new psychoanalytic critique of traditional sex roles by Dinnerstein (1976) and Chodorow (1978) bearing an apparent similarity to the traditional paradigm has aroused great interest. Like the identity paradigm, Dinnerstein and Chodorow take fathers' low participation in child care as their starting point. They use different theoretical arguments, however, to derive from it radically different consequences for sex roles: Weak paternal participation distorts the ego boundaries of both sexes, and fathers should have an equal role so that men and women can become more fully human. While this analysis actually falls within the SRS paradigm (proposition 8*), its popularity and superficial resemblance to the MSRI paradigm have helped delay more widespread recognition of the latter's deficiencies.[1]

These factors help account for the persistence of the MSRI paradigm, but the reasons for its emergence lie in more general trends in American intellectual and social history.

Psychoanalysis

Psychoanalysis, though not the underlying source of the MSRI paradigm, played an important part in its development. Social concerns about masculinity, manliness, and emasculation actually emerged in advance of Freudian psychology and its introduction to the United States in 1908 (Freud's visit to America). Articles with titles such as "The Effeminization of Men" appeared in popular magazines as early as 1893 (Dubbert, 1974). In the writings of Freud and his immediate followers, the concept of sex role identity is not explicitly developed. Freud did, it is true, give some attention to sex typing (he describes it as the "character traits" of masculinity and femininity); but he does this primarily in his early writings (notably in *Three Contributions to the Theory of Sex*) and only to observe that most individuals have both masculine and feminine psychological characteristics, not to prescribe only those appropriate to one's sex. The first explicit formulations of sex role identity in the psychoanalytic tradition appear to be Adler's (1936) concept of masculine protest and Boehm's (1932) and Horney's (1932) concept of the femininity complex in men. But these ideas were never fully integrated in the psychoanalytic literature. For example, Fenichel's (1945) encyclopedic *The Psychoanalytic Theory of Neurosis* contains only two brief references to sex typing and sex role identity (pp. 337, 506).

Freudian psychology did provide, however, a conceptual framework within which US academic psychologists could intellectualize their culture's preexisting concerns about masculinity. What Freud had left out, they filled in, and with a vengeance. Indeed, they made their preoccupation with the maintenance of masculinity the dominant feature of Freudian thought as it came to be understood and popularized in American culture. There is no question that the "psychoanalytic" idea that has been the most widely disseminated and deeply accepted in American culture is the concept of sex role identity.

The academic psychologists who founded the MSRI paradigm did all their work primarily with just three Freudian ideas, all of which are found in his earliest work: identification, psychosexual development, and homosexuality as a fixation in psychosexual development. After this initial borrowing, MSRI theorists developed their paradigm with little further exchange with psychoanalysis. Psychoanalysis has since gone through several intellectual paradigm shifts of its own, and there is now hardly anything intellectually in common between the MSRI paradigm and psychoanalytic theory. In brief, the MSRI paradigm can be interpreted as the product of the interaction between late nineteenth- and twentieth-century social concerns about masculinity in the United States and an early, immature stage of psychoanalytic thought.

From External to Internal Social Control

These concerns derive, I believe, from a breakdown of the institutions traditionally organizing and regulating women's and men's behavior beginning in the late nineteenth century. Traditional sex roles historically have been supported—indeed defined—by a rigid segregation of the social spheres of women and men, particularly in employment and the family.This segregation provided a social-institutional basis, external to the individual, for customary roles.

Between the late nineteenth century and the present, however, many all-male colleges and fraternities have become coeducational; the all-male saloon has given way to the singles bar; the military increasingly integrates women; corporations are beginning to bring women into management as well as traditional male blue-collar jobs (Pleck, 1975b). The fundamental axis around which social relations are organized is shifting, in Gagnon and Simon's (1975) terms, from homosociality to heterosociality. Simultaneously, women's participation in the work force has risen slowly but nonetheless dramatically, altering both women's traditional role as homemaker and men's as family breadwinner.

As Rieff (1966) argues, when a culture weakens one mode of regulating basic human activities and needs, it must strengthen others. The decline of the social institutions formerly externally controlling men's and women's behavior generated great social concern and stimulated the emergence of more internalized, psychologically based mechanisms. Foremost among these is the theory of male sex role identity. While in an earlier age males became men by participating in all-male social life and holding a job, they now came to do so by learning from psychologists that they must act in certain ways if they are to have male sex role identities.

The shift from external to internal control of sex roles and the concomitant rise of the MSRI paradigm are particularly evident in two periods: the 1930s and the 1950s. It is not a historical coincidence, I believe, that Terman and Miles published the paradigm's founding work, *Sex and Personality* (1936), in the midst of the Great Depression—the historical event causing perhaps the single greatest crisis in the traditional institutional basis of the male role, that of family economic provider. If holding a job to support a family could no longer be counted on to define manhood, a masculinity-femininity test could.

The MSRI paradigm clearly held greatest sway in American culture during the 1950s, another period of crisis in the male role. World War II provided institutional validation of the traditional male role as powerful as the Depression's invalidation: American men lived and worked together, away from women, in a popular war against clearly immoral enemies, and emerged victorious. How great, then, was their shock when, on returning home, they encountered wives and girlfriends who had acquired traditionally male jobs in war industries and new-found psychological independence from having to live without men; a job market transformed by wartime technological advances, requiring they obtain levels of training and education previously unprecedented; and postwar inflation making them less adequate as family providers. In response to these challenges to the traditional foundations of the male role, the MSRI paradigm rose to the zenith of its influence. Together with the "feminine mystique" (Friedan, 1963)—its counterpart for women—the theory of male sex role identity replaced the former institutional foundation of the male role with an internal psychological one; traditional roles, even if no longer required by social convention or law, came to be widely perceived as necessary for normal psychological development.

Beyond Male Sex Role Identity

The MSRI paradigm has helped generate sex role strain. The concept of sex role identity prevents individuals who violate the traditional role for their sex from challenging it; instead, they feel personally inadequate and insecure—the subjective experience of sex role strain. The deeper the acceptance of the MSRI paradigm in the culture, the more widespread the experience of strain. Through this process the MSRI paradigm paradoxically sowed the seeds of its own demise. As sex role strain continued to build, the women's and men's liberation movements arose in response, providing individuals a way of understanding the strain they experience, analyzing its sources, and reducing it. These movements also stimulated an intellectual critique of the old paradigm and the emergence of the new. In essence, the theory of male sex role identity dialectically created sex role strain as its social and ultimately intellectual antithesis.

Social scientific research and ideas often play a conservative role in society, holding back rather than facilitating change. The need for change in sex roles continues to be evident, if only because we can no longer return to a disappearing way of life. I can assign to the social sciences only a modest part in furthering the liberation of the sexes, but the part they can play for men is clear: understanding the roots of the strains men experience, analyzing men's aggression and their inability to find and express intimacy, and examining the burdens and conflicts arising from assigning men the role of family provider. This is the research agenda for the future, and it carries the promise of a more humane and egalitarian scientific study of the sexes.

Appendix A
The Biological Basis of Male
Aggression: A Critique

It is generally accepted that aggression and sex differences in
aggression are biologically based. Even Maccoby and Jacklin
(1974), while rejecting the notion of biological causes for average
sex differences in most areas of social behavior, make aggression
a clear exception.

Male Sex Hormones

Methodological Issues
It is essential to differentiate the effects of *prenatal* androgen
levels on aggression from the effects of *current* androgen levels.
Money and Ehrhardt (1972) suggest that prenatal hormone levels, by shaping brain development, have by far the more important effects of the two. (There is some evidence that levels of
prenatal hormones affect individual sensitivity to variations in
current hormone levels, thus further complicating attempts to
correlate current hormones and current behavior.)

Unfortunately, the effects of prenatal hormones in humans are
not easy to study. One method is to find individuals who, through
some abnormality or medical procedure, were exposed to excess
androgens prenatally but not postnatally. Such research necessarily uses small samples whose special medical problems may
make them unrepresentative. Another method is to assess infant
hormone levels prenatally, or as soon as possible after birth, and
examine the correlates in later life of naturally occurring variation in these prenatal hormone levels. Such long-term longitu-

dinal research is expensive to conduct and does not yield results for many years.

Current hormone levels are not much easier to study. Techniques for assessing androgens have changed dramatically in recent years and are continuing to be refined. Most older studies use the proportion of various metabolic breakdown products of sex hormones appearing in the urine to estimate the level of sex hormones in the blood. But, as Money and Ehrhardt (1972, p. 230) note, this assay procedure probably tells more about the functional efficiency of the liver than the amount of sex hormones circulating in the blood. There are now more sophisticated techniques for assessing testosterone levels in the blood, particularly radio-immunoassay (RIA). These techniques have been used in many of the more recent studies.

Moreover, current androgen levels can fluctuate. There is growing evidence of cyclical variations in male hormones (Doehring et al., 1974a). Noncyclical factors operate as well, as shown by a number of studies reviewed by Meyer-Bahlburg (1974) indicating that emotional stress and stress induced by surgery reduce androgen levels, while exercise increases them. Kolodny and Masters (1974), as another example, find that marijuana reduces androgen levels.

Because of these variations in androgen levels within the individual male, there are two possible forms of analysis. One, which correlates behavior and hormone levels *across* a group of subjects (that is, *inter*subject correlations), uses a single (or average) measurement of the behavior and androgen level for each subject. Another, which correlates the behavior and androgen level *within* each subject (that is, *intra*subject correlations), measures the behavior and androgen levels at many different points in time for each subject. Unfortunately, these two analyses do not always give the same results.

There is also evidence that androgen levels can be the effect, rather than the cause, of behavior; the evidence is particularly strong for aggression. A related problem is that there is little consensus about which of the many androgenic and estrogenic compounds are related to behavior. Many studies assay every conceivable hormone derivative and then include all these scores, their ratios, and often other arithmetic manipulations as well in the analysis so as to increase the chance of deriving a statistically significant finding. Nor are the basic mechanisms by which hormones affect behavior well understood.

Animal Hormones

The relevance of animal studies to human behavior has been a never ending source of debate in psychology. Still, there appears to be a wide variety of evidence in animal research, primarily with rodents, that male hormones are related to aggression (see reviews by Moyer, 1974; Conner, 1972; Maccoby and Jacklin, 1974, pp. 243–247). Such research demonstrates the independent as well as interactive effects of experimental manipulations of prenatal and postnatal androgens, both chemically and through castration, and also shows the effects of estrogens on behavior. There are, however, a number of exceptions. For example, Maccoby and Jacklin note that the female hamster is the more aggressive and that aggression is related to the level of progesterone, a female sex hormone. Maccoby and Jacklin also note that one study finds that administering testosterone to adult female chickens stimulates comb growth but not fighting. Another study finds that giving female hormones to newborn rats decreases aggressiveness later in life in male rats but increases it in females. In my view, given the small number of species studied, their great evolutionary distance from homo sapiens, and the reversals of effects in at least some species, there is little justification for extrapolating these findings to human beings.

Perhaps the most dramatic animal studies are those by Rose, Holaday, and Bernstein (1971) and Rose, Gordon, and Bernstein (1971, 1972) with rhesus monkeys, which find that the male's position in the dominance order is related to its testosterone level, with males in the highest quartile showing significantly higher levels than males in the lowest quartile. Further, manipulating testosterone levels leads to changes in dominance rank.

Even in a dramatic demonstration like this, there are several complicating factors. First, hormones appear to be both a cause and effect of rank in the dominance order. New males to the troop who settle low in the hierarchy show a marked drop in their testosterone levels, while low-ranking males placed in a position of dominance show a testosterone increase. There is also some evidence suggesting that the effect in animals of testosterone on dominance rank and aggression may be even more than a matter of androgens, Mugford and Nowell (cited by Moyer, 1974) suspect that sex hormone-dependent substances excreted by an animal in the urine helps touch off agression in other animals upon being smelled. For example, coating castrated male rats with the urine of aggressive, dominant males elicits aggression from other males toward them, while rats coated with the urine of nondominant males, or females, elicit much less attack. That is, testosterone may be related to aggression in an individual male monkey because it stimulates *other* monkeys to fight with him, whom he then fights back. Overall, while the relationship between testosterone and aggression in animal studies is fairly well established, it appears to work in both directions, and we are only beginning to understand its mechanisms.

Prenatal Hormone Levels in Humans

One kind of evidence relevant to the relationship in humans between sex hormones and aggression concerns the effects of *prenatal* hormone levels. Several studies examine small samples of females or males who were exposed to high levels of androgens or estrogens before birth (but not after birth). Money and Ehrhardt (1972, pp. 98–108) report on a sample of 10 females whose mothers were given progestin (an androgen-like drug once used to prevent miscarriage) during their pregnancies and 15 females with andrenogenital syndrome. (In andrenogenital syndrome, the andrenals produce excess androgens during prenatal fetal development. If the condition is recognized after birth, the production of excess androgens after birth can be corrected by regular administration of cortisone, as was the case in Money and Ehrhardt's sample.) Thus both samples provide an opportunity to examine the effects of high androgen levels before, but not after, birth. In comparison with matched controls, both samples are rated as tomboyish and as being more athletic. But they are *not* rated more aggressive or likely to pick fights. Ehrhardt and Baker (1974) study another sample of 17 females with the adrenogenital syndrome, ranging in age from 4 to 19 years. These subjects are compared with their unaffected female siblings and with their mothers' retrospective ratings of themselves as children. Consistent with the earlier Money and Ehrhardt study, the androgenized females are significantly more often rated higher in intense energy expenditure but not in aggressiveness.

Ehrhardt and Baker (1974) also study a sample of 10 males with the androgenital syndrome who also had been exposed to excessively high levels of prenatal androgens. When compared with their unaffected male siblings, the androgenized males are also rated significantly higher in intense energy expenditure but not significantly higher in aggressiveness. Finally, Yalom, Green, and Fisk (1973) study 20 6-year-old boys and 10 16-year-old boys whose mothers had been taking estrogenic drugs during their pregnancies as treatment for serious chronic diabetes. These boys are reported as less aggressive and assertive than matched controls. But it is noted that their mothers' serious illness complicates the interpretation. Thus research does not clearly indicate that prenatal male sex hormones are a factor in human male aggression.

Current Hormone Levels in Humans

A second kind of evidence bearing on the relationship in humans between sex hormones and aggression concerns the effects of *current* hormone levels. The studies most cited are by Kreuz and Rose (1972) and Persky, Smith, and Basu (1971). Kreuz and Rose select 10 "fighter" and 11 "nonfighter" young males from a prison population according to the number of times that a prisoner had been placed in solitary confinement per year; fighters had been in two or more fights during prison while nonfighters had been in none or one. All subjects' plasma testosterone is assessed from 6 blood samples over a 2-week period and was reported as stable for each individual. The fighting and nonfighting groups do not differ in testosterone level, contrary to expectation. Nor does testosterone level correlate with the number of physical or verbal fights or scores on the Buss-Durkee Hostility Inventory. Kreuz and Rose assert that testosterone level is significantly related to previous record of "violent and aggressive criminal behavior," but this appears to result largely from including in this category attempts at prison escape; this category is unrelated to prison fighting or the questionnaire aggression measure.

Persky, Smith, and Basu collect measures of testosterone level and production rate and several paper-and-pencil measures of aggression, depression, and hostility in 18 young men (ages 17–18), 15 older men (ages 31–66), and 6 male psychiatric patients. There are no significant relationships between testosterone level and production rate in the older group. In the younger group only, testosterone *level* is positively related to the total hostility score from the Buss-Durkee Hostility Inventory and to its aggressive feelings subscale. It is not related, however, to hostility on the Multiple Affect Adjective Checklist (MAACL). Testosterone *production rate* is significantly correlated with the Buss-Durkee Total Hostility score and its Negative Feelings and Aggressive Feelings subscales but again not to the Hostility scale of the MAACL. (Incidentally, Persky, Smith, and Basu regard aggressive feelings as leading to—not resulting from—testosterone production, a point omitted in nearly all reports of this study.) Thus two frequently cited studies find only limited, and not entirely consistent, relationships between testosterone and aggression. In particular, they obtain different results on the only measure used in both, the Buss-Durkee Hostility Inventory.

More recent research has not confirmed even the highly limited results of these two studies. Meyer-Bahlburg et al. (1974) replicate the Persky study using a sample comparable in age and educational level. On the basis of the aggressive feelings subscale of the Buss-Durkee Hostility Inventory, Meyer-Bahlburg selects 6 low-aggression subjects (score range 10–15) and 5 high-aggression subjects (score range 31–39). He finds no difference in blood testosterone level or production rate or in urinary androgen levels. Doehring et al. (1974a) follow 20 males ages 20–28 over a 2-month period, collecting blood samples for the assessment of testosterone levels and administering the MAACL every second day. Subjects kept diaries that were scored for the occurrence of stress and anger, among other variables. Subjects also took the Buss-Durkee Hostility Inventory once during the study. The correlation between average testosterone level and the average MAACL hostility level across the 20 subjects is found to be about 0.35. This is about the same level as in Persky's study, and just missing significance at the 0.05 level. Testosterone is not significantly related to the Buss-Durkee Total Hostility, Negative Feelings, or Aggressive Feelings scales, but is significantly related to another subscale for Indirect Aggression. Testosterone is not related to ratings of anger or stress made from the diaries. Doehring et al. also examine correlations between testosterone and aggression measures *within* each subject, using the MAACL and diary, and find no consistency in the relationship between the testosterone and aggression measures; for some subjects, the relationship is positive; but for others, negative. Once again, the biological hypothesis is not supported.

Physical and Hormonal Castration

Some limited data are available concerning the effects on human aggression of castration and the admininstration of estrogenic or antiandrogenic hormones (sometimes referred to as hormonal castration). Brief reviews appear in Moyer (1974, pp. 363–366) and Meyer-Bahlburg (1974, pp. 443–444). Castration is still practiced in several countries, particularly in Scandinavia, as a treatment for sexual offenders. Bremer's (1959) follow-up of 224 Norwegian cases (many of whom, incidentally, were castrated during the Nazi occupation) finds that castration reduces sex drive but does not reduce aggression (unless the aggression is sexually motivated) and does not have a pacifying effect. But Hawkes' (1950) study of 330 men castrated for sexual aggression in Kansas during 1920–1950 asserts that castration did reduce nonsexual hostility. Hawke also reports a program in which testosterone was administered to these castrates over a period of several weeks; in some cases the castrates became extremely aggressive, but their aggressive behavior stopped when the testosterone was no longer admininstered. (It is not well known how widely castration and hormonal manipulations have been practiced in the United States; see Katz, 1976, for more examples.)

Moyer (1974, pp. 364–365) reviews several clinical studies, each with far smaller numbers of cases, in which estrogenic drugs were used to suppress aggressive and sexual behavior in adolescents and young adults. While these studies are not well controlled, they indicate that estrogens do eliminate or reduce male aggression. There are several biochemical substances that are antiandrogenic, that is, act as androgen antagonists, and in small clinical studies there appears to be variation in the effects of these different drugs; some reduce only sexual libido and sex-related aggression, while other appear to reduce aggression more generally (Moyer, 1974, pp. 365–366). Meyer–Bahlburg (1974, p. 443) reviews studies that seem to show that antiandrogenic drugs reduce male aggression and that testosterone administration increases it, but notes a number of methodological problems with such studies. Thus this area yields only weak support for the biological hypothesis.

Male Chromosomes: The 47,XYY Syndrome

Jacobs et al. (1965) report finding an unusually high rate (9 out of 315, or 3%) of the 47,XYY chromosomal pattern among the male inmates of a maximum security state mental hospital. Since then, there has been a great deal of speculation about the possible chromosomal determinants of criminality and aggression in males. Since it is the presence of the Y chromosome that initiates the chain of events leading an organism to develop as a male, it is easy to understand how the double Y would be popularly interpreted as a "supermale" pattern.

There is actually considerable disagreement in the literature about the degree of overrepresentation of XYY males in mental and penal populations. The first report on the Carstairs Hospital in Scotland (Jacobs et al., 1965) suggests a rate of 30 per 1,000 (3%) in the institutional population compared to a presumed rate of 1 per 1,000 in the general population, a disproportion of 30 to 1. A review by the National Institute of Mental Health's (NIMH) Center for Studies of Crime and Delinquency (1970) suggests a prevalence rate of 7.1 per 1,000 in 8 studies of mental and penal institutions, compared to 1.8 per 1,000 in unselected newborns, or a ratio of about 3.5 to 1. Owen's (1972) review suggests a prevalence rate of only 4 or 5 times the theoretically presumed population rate of 0.5 per 1,000.

One of the problems in determining the XYY prevalence rate in mental and penal populations is that because of the expense of karotyping (the procedure for examining chromosomes), many studies karotype only a sample of the institutional population. This sample is invariably preselected on some criterion designed to maximize the probability of locating XYYs (most often height). Then researchers usually report the prevalence rate of XYYs in the preselected group without indicating the size of the *total* institutional population from which they are drawn, the appropriate denominator for calculating the prevalence rate.

XYY inmates do not actually differ from other inmates in aggression. Owen (1972) reviews a number of studies using psychological tests and concludes that "the extreme abendance of clinical impressionistic data coupled with the remarkable paucity of psychometric data—and the lack of any definitive findings with what psychometric data have been collected—should seem to call into question the validty of the "aggressive XYY" stereotype" (p. 244). Kessler and Moos (1970) concur in this conclusion. In the original Carstairs population, the XYY males had *fewer* crimes of violence than a control group: 8.7% in the XYY group and 21.9% in the control (Price and Whatmore, 1967b). In another analysis by Price and Whatmore, there is little difference between XYYs and controls in the rate of property crimes. The comparisons of crimes against persons show the XYYs to be *less* aggressive. The murder rates are approximately equal, but the rate of assault is 6 times lower and the rate of sexual assault 2.5 times lower in the XYY than the control males (Price and Whatmore, 1967a). Griffiths et al. (1970) find that XYY prisoners have more theft and breaking-and-entering offenses but not more violent crimes. Casey et al. (1973) find that XYY males have more sex and property offenses but fewer crimes against persons. Thus the evidence does not support the hypothesis that XYY males are more aggressive than other male prisoners.

Price and Whatmore (1967b) find that XYYs have earlier first convictions than controls (13.1 years versus 8 years); other studies reviewed by Owen (1972), however, do not generally support this finding. Griffiths et al. (1970) do not find a difference in mean number of offenses or mean length of total sentences; XYY males do have a higher average number of convictions, however (13 versus 9.2).

Another way to evaluate the hypothesis that something about the XYY chromosome pattern leads to aggressive criminality is to compare XYY males to males with other chromosomal abnormalities. Several studies have compared XYY males with males with Klinefelter's syndrome (47,XXY), characterized by small gonads, infertility, often with breast development at puberty, and with mental retardation. There is also an overrepresentation of Klinefelter males in mental and penal institutions, though, as for XYY males, exact estimates vary. In the most comprehensive study, Casey et al. (1973) compare XYY, XXY, and controls from the same institution. It was noted above that XYYs show more sex and property offenses but fewer personal offenses than do controls. XXYs show the same pattern compared to controls; XXYs and XYYs do not differ in sex or personal offenses, but XYYs show fewer property offenses. Of four other less comprehensive studies reviewed by Meyer-Bahlburg (1974, p. 441), only one shows XYY inmates to be higher in violent crime than Klinefelter males. Thus this evidence suggests that (1) chromosomal abnormality in general, rather than the XYY syndrome per se, is associated with mental or penal incarceration and (2) chromosomal abnormality, whether XYY or some other, is not associated with crimes of violence or crimes against persons.

Finally, there is no relationship between the XYY syndrome and testosterone levels. Both Owen (1972, pp. 219–220) and Meyer-Bahlburg (1974, pp. 444–446) review studies using a variety of assay techniques on this question. Blood testosterone is in the normal range, or comparable to controls, for almost all measures studied. One study indicates that testosterone by-products in the urine appear to be lower for a substantial minority of XYY males. A minority of subjects in several other studies have urinary excretion of testosterone products higher than occurs in noninstitutional controls, but not higher than in controls from the same institution. The elevations of urinary testosterone by-products in non-XYY prisoners parallel to those in XYYs may simply indicate that both groups are exposed to similar behavioral or environmental factors affecting testosterone production.

Summary

Given the social importance of aggressive behavior, it is clear that research on its possible biological sources will continue to receive serious attention. At the present time, the evidence in animals for hormonal factors in male aggression is strong (albeit complex). But comparable evidence for human male aggression is much weaker and less consistent.

Appendix B
The Biological Basis of Weak
Paternal Involvement: A Critique

It is actually not a biological universal that males have little to do with the nurturance of the young. Howells (1971; see also Rypma, 1976) cites a number of species in which males in fact have a primary childrearing role, for example, the stickleback fish studied extensively by the ethologist Tinbergen. After selecting a territory in which to build a nest, the male stickleback attracts females to lay eggs in his nest. The female leaves after laying the eggs, and the male then guards and cares for the eggs, fanning a flow of current over them. After the eggs hatch, the stickleback father keeps the young together in a swarm, chasing after any errant young and retrieving them in his mouth. Other examples are emperor penguins, whose young live in the father's pouch while the mother searches for food, and the male phalarope bird, which builds the nest and has the entire responsibility for incubating the eggs.

According to a review by Mitchell (1969), there is also wide diversity among primates in the behavior of adult males toward the young, ranging from extreme hostility to extreme nurturance. In one New World monkey with monogamous mating patterns, the titi monkey, the male holds and carries the infant at virtually all times, except when the infant nurses. In the marmoset, the male likewise has the primary nurturing role. In hamadryas baboons, young adult males show considerable nurturance toward the young. In most species of anthropoid apes, males show some protectiveness toward the young. Further, recent studies (Redican and Mitchell, 1973; Mitchell, Redican, and Gomber, 1974) indicate that even in primate species in which adult males are typically hostile to the young, such as the rhesus monkey, males will develop "maternal" behavior if they are exposed to the young for a sufficiently long time.

Some argue that males' hormonal patterns make them less responsive to children. It is certainly the case that males do not experience the hormonal changes associated with pregnancy, birth, and nursing. May this not limit their nurturant responses? The relationship between sex hormones and parental behavior has been studied most systematically in rodents. In Maccoby and Jacklin's (1974, pp. 215–218) review of several such studies, it appears that the hormones associated with pregnancy and parturition facilitate "maternal" behaviors such as retrieving, nest building, and licking the pups. But male rats as well as virgin female rats—neither of which have these hormones—will show such parental behaviors after several days of exposure to newborns. As Quadagno, Briscoe, and Quadagno (1977) note, "The effect of perinatal androgen on maternal behavior in rodents is (unclear) because both male and female rodents will show all aspects of maternal behavior when presented with newborn animals" (p. 62).

As noted in appendix A, Money and Ehrhardt (1972) suggest that prenatal sex hormones have a more important influence on behavior than sex hormones. As one demonstration of this effect, Ehrhardt and Baker (1974) report in a study of a small sample of females accidentally exposed to high levels of androgens (male sex hormones) before birth that these females are significantly less interested in caring for young children (for example, are less willing to babysit) and engage in fewer fantasies or role plays of motherhood than their normal female siblings. One might reason from this evidence that males are less interested in caring for children because, at least in part, of the androgens they normally produce. It is not as widely known, however, that in the same study the parallel analysis of *males* exposed to unusually high androgen levels finds that these excessively androgenized males are markedly (though not significantly) *higher* in fantasies and role plays of fatherhood and more interested in infant care than their normal male siblings.

In sum, there is actually considerable diversity across animal species, and specifically within the primates, in the role of males in childrearing. Also, while in nonhuman species paternal involvement is facilitated by sex hormones, this pattern develops anyway upon exposure to newborns. In humans, the presence of male sex hormones during prenatal development appears to suppress nurturant interest in females but not in males.

This is a checklist of printed works and media, ordered chrono-
logically and alphabetically by subject, recommended especially
for bookstores and libraries.

General

Myron Brenton, *The American Male,* Fawcett, 1966

Lionel Tiger, *Men in Groups,* Random House, 1969

Warren Farrell, *The Liberated Man,* Random House, 1974; Bantam, 1975

Marc Feigen Fasteau, *The Male Machine,* McGraw-Hill, 1974

Harvey E. Kaye, *Male Survival,* Grossett and Dunlap, 1974

Michael Korda, *Male Chauvinism!,* Random House, 1974

Gene Marine, *A Male Guide to Women's Liberation,* Avon, 1974

Jack Nichols, *Men's Liberation: A New Definition of Masculinity,* Penguin,
1974

Anne Steinmann and David J. Fox, *The Male Dilemma,* Jason Aronson,
1974

Thorkill Vangaard, *Phallos: A Symbol and Its History in the Male World,*
International Universities Press, 1974

Glenn R. Bucher, *Straight/White/Male,* Fortress Press, 1975

Herb Goldberg, *The Hazards of Being Male,* Nash, 1975

Andrew Goodman and Patricia Walby, *A Book About Men,* Quartet, 1975

Mirra Komarovsky, *Dilemmas of Masculinity: A Study of College Youth,*
Norton, 1975

William L. Malcolmson, *Success is a Failure Experience: Male Liberation and
the American Myth of Success,* Abingdon, 1976

Joyce Mitchell, *Free to Choose: Decision-Making for Young Men,* Delacorte, 1976

Phyllis Chesler, *About Men,* Simon and Schuster, 1978

Lloyd Etheredge, *A World of Men: Masculinity in U.S. Foreign Policy,* MIT Press, 1978

Natalie Gittelson, *Dominus: A Woman Looks at Men's Lives,* Farrar Strauss Giroux, 1978

Laurel Halliday, *The Violent Sex: Male Biology and the Evolution of Consciousness,* Bluestocking Books, 1978

Robert A. Johnson, *He: Understanding Male Psychology,* Harper and Row, 1978

Hal Lyon, *Tenderness Is Strength: From Machismo to Manhood,* Harper and Row, 1978

Hershel Thornburg, *Punt, Pop (A Male Sex Role Manual),* Help Books, 1201 E. Calle Elena, Tucson, AZ 85718, 1978

Herb Goldberg, *The New Male: From Self-Destruction to Self-Care,* Morrow, 1979

Fred Hapgood, *Why Males Exist: An Inquiry into the Evolution of Sex,* Morrow, 1979

Leonard Kriegel, *On Men and Manhood,* Hawthorn Books, 1979

The Playboy Report on American Men, available free from Director, Corporate Communications, Playboy, 919 N. Michigan Ave., Chicago, IL 60611, 1979

Andrew Tolson, *The Limits of Masculinity,* Tavistock, 1978; Harper and Row, 1979

Frank Rose and George Bennett, *Real Men: Sex and Style in an Uncertain Age,* Doubleday, 1980

Joseph H. Pleck, *The Myth of Masculinity,* MIT Press, 1981

Wayne Ewing, *Changing Men: Mission Impossible,* Research Center on Women, Loretto Heights College, 3001 S. Federal Blvd., Denver, CO 80236, n.d.

General Readers and Collections

Joseph H. Pleck and Jack Sawyer, *Men and Masculinity,* Prentice-Hall, 1974

John W. Petras, *Sex: Male/Gender: Masculine,* Alfred, 1975

Deborah David and Robert Brannon, *The Forty-Nine Percent Majority: The Male Sex Role,* Addison-Wesley, 1976; 2nd ed. 1982

Jon Snodgrass, *For Men Against Sexism,* Times Change Press, 1977

The Men's Survival Resource Book: On Being A Man in Today's World, Minneapolis: MSRB Press, 1800 W. 76th St., Minneapolis 55423, 1978

Joseph H. Pleck and Robert Brannon, "Male Roles and the Male Experience," special issue of *Journal of Social Issues 34* (1): 1978

Doris Wilkenson and Ronald Taylor, *The Black Male,* Nelson-Hall, 1978

Evelyn Shapiro and Barry Shapiro, *The Women Say/ The Men Say: The Women's Liberation Movement and Men's Consciousness,* Delta, 1979

Robert A. Lewis, *Men in Difficult Times,* Prentice-Hall, 1981

Family and Fatherhood

Leonard Benson, *Fatherhood: A Sociological Perspective,* Random House, 1968

Henry Biller, *Paternal Deprivation: Schools, Sexuality, and Society,* Heath, 1974

Henry Biller and Dennis Meredith, *Father Power,* McKay, 1974

David B. Lynn, *The Father: His Role in Child Development,* Brooks/Cole, 1974

Michael McFadden, *Bachelor Fatherhood,* McKay, 1974

James Levine, *Who Will Care for the Children? New Options for Fathers (and Mothers),* Lippincott, 1975

Michael E. Lamb (ed.), *The Role of the Father in Child Development,* Wiley, 1976

James Walters (ed.), "Fatherhood," special issue of *The Fmily Coordinator* 25(4): 1976, National Council on Family Relations, 1219 University Ave., S.E., Minneapolis, Minn. 55414, single copy $6.50

Alexander Humez and Keith Fitzgerald Stavely, *Family Man: What Men Feel About Their Wives, Their Children, Their Parents, and Themselves,* Contemporary Books, 1978

Celeste Phillips and Joseph Anzalone, *Fathering: Participation in Labor and Birth,* Mosby, 1978

Robert A. Lewis and Joseph H. Pleck, "Men's Roles in the Family," special issue of *The Family Coordinator, 28*(4): 1979, National Council on Family Relations, 1219 University Ave., S.E., Minneapolis, Minn. 55414, single copy $6.50

The Nurturant Male, quarterly journal of the National Men's Childcare Caucus, c/o Lakeview Child Care Center, 900 W. Oakdale, Chicago, IL 60657, $8.00/year

Nurturing News: A Forum for Men in the Lives of Children, c/o David L. Giveans, 187 Caselli Ave., San Francisco, CA 94114

Health and Sexuality*

Thaddeus Mann, *The Biochemistry of Semen and of the Male Reproductive Tract,* Wiley, 1964

Hendrik M. Ruitenbeek (ed.), *Psychoanalysis and Male Sexuality,* College and University Press, 1966

Paul J. Gillette, *Vasectomy: The Male Sterilization Operation,* Paperback Library, 1972

Michael Greenfield and William M. Burrus, *The Complete Reference Book on Vasectomy,* Avon, 1973

Gerhard Raspé (ed.), *Schering Workshop on Contraception: The Masculine Gender,* Pergamon, 1973

Philip R. Roen, *Male Sexual Health,* Morrow, 1974

Helmut J. Ruebsaat and Raymond Hull, *The Male Climacteric,* Hawthorn, 1974

Sam Julty, *Male Sexual Performance,* Grossett and Dunlap, 1975

Robert Bahr, *The Virility Factor: Masculinity through Testosterone, The Male Sex Hormone,* Putnam, 1976

E. S. E. Hafez (ed.), *Andrology and the Human Semen,* Mosby, 1976

G. L. Simmons, *The Phallic Mystique,* Pinnacle Books, 1976

William H. Spillane and Paul E. Roger, *Male Fertility Survey: Fertility Knowledge, Attitudes, and Practices of Married Men,* Ballinger, 1976

Diagram Group, *Man's Body: An Owner's Manual,* Bantam, 1977

Anthony Pietropinto and Jacqueline Simenauer, *Beyond the Male Myth,* New York Times, 1977

John Chesterman and Michael Marten, *Man to Man: Straight Answers to Every Man's Questions about Sexuality, Fitness, and Health,* Berkley, 1978

Barry McCarthy, *What You (Still) Don't Know about Male Sexuality,* Crowell, 1978

National Clearinghouse for Family Planning Information, *Information Services Bulletin,* "Men and Family Planning," Aug. 1978, P.O. Box 2225, Rockville, MD 20825

Karen Shanor, *The Shanor Study: The Sexual Sensitivity of the American Male,* Ballantine, 1978

Bernie Zilbergeld, *Male Sexuality,* Little Brown, 1978

Richard Milsten, *Male Sexual Function: Myth, Fantasy, and Reality,* Avon, 1979

* These references deal primarily with heterosexuality. For a bibliography on homosexuality and gay liberation, send a stamped, self-addressed long envelope to Task Force on Gay Liberation, P.O. Box 2383, Philadelphia, PA 19103.

Nancy Friday, *Men in Love: Men's Sexual Fantasies—The Triumph of Love over Rage,* Delacorte, 1980

Sam Julty, *Men's Bodies, Men's Selves,* Delta, 1980

Mark Strage, *The Durable Fig Leaf: A Historical, Cultural, Medical, Social, Literary, and Inconographic Account of Man's Relations with His Penis,* Morrow, 1980

Michael Castleman, *Sexual Solutions: An Informative Guide,* Simon and Schuster, 1981

Male Involvement Newsletter (male sexuality and family planning), Human Services and Studies, 215 Stone Building, Florida State University, Tallahassee, FL 32306

Men and Family Planning (annotated bibliography), Douglas Beckstein, Center for Population Options, 2031 Florida Ave., NM, Washington, DC 20009

The Men's Letter: Family Planning Services for Men, National Institute for Community Development, 1815 N. Lynn St., Suite Arlington, VA 22209

Mental Health

Thomas Skovholt, "Counseling Men," special issue of *The Counseling Psychologist,* 7(4): 1978, Washington University, Box 1180, St. Louis, MO 63130, single copy $5

Thomas Skovholt, Paul Schauble, and Richard Davis (eds.), *Counseling Men,* Brooks/Cole, 1980

Kenneth Solomon and Norman Levy (eds.), *Men in Transition: Changing Male Roles, Theory, and Therapy,* Plenum, 1981

Life-Cycle Development and Change

Peter Chew, *The Inner World of the Middle-Aged Man,* Houghton Mifflin, 1977

Henry Still, *Surviving the Male Mid-Life Crisis,* Crowell, 1977

George Vaillant, *Adaptation to Life,* Little Brown, 1977

Derek Bowskill and Anthea Linane, *The Male Menopause,* Brooke House, 1978

Roger Gould, *Transformations,* Simon and Schuster, 1978

Daniel Levinson et al., *The Seasons of a Man's Life,* Knopf, 1978

Nancy Mayer, *The Male Mid-Life Crisis,* Doubleday, 1978

Robert Robertiello, *A Man in the Making: Grandfathers, Fathers and Sons,* Marek, 1979

Peter Filene (ed.), *Men in the Middle: Work and Family in the Lives of Middle-Aged Men,* Prentice-Hall, 1980

Education

Patricia Cayo Sexton, *The Feminized Male: Classrooms, White Collars, and the Decline of Manliness,* Vintage, 1969

David A. Sadker, *Being a Man: A Unit of Instructional Activities on Male Role Stereotyping,* U.S. Govt. Printing Office, 1977, stock number 017-080-01777-7, $2.10

History

Peter Filene, *Him/Her/Self,* Harcourt Brace, 1975

Alan M. Kirshner (ed.), *Masculinity in an Historical Perspective,* University Press of America, 1977

Joe L. Dubbert, *A Man's Place: Masculinity in Transition,* Prentice-Hall, 1979

Elizabeth H. Pleck and Joseph H. Pleck (eds.), *The American Male,* Prentice-Hall, 1980

Peter Stearns, *Be a Man! Males in Modern Society,* Holmes and Meier, 1980

Literature

Martin Duberman, *Male Armor: Selected Plays, 1968–1974,* Dutton, 1975

Ross Firestone (ed.), *A Book of Men: Visions of the Male Experience,* Stonehill, 1975

Peter Weltner, *Myth and Masculinity,* Harper, 1975

Leonard Kriegel (ed.), *The Myth of American Manhood,* Dell, 1978

"Men's Lives in America," curriculum guide, single copies free from National Humanities Institute, 53 Wall St., New Haven, CT 06520

Art and Media

Margaret Walters, *The Nude Male: A New Perspective,* Paddington, 1974; Penguin, 1979

Joan Mellen, *Big Bad Wolves: Masculinity in the American Film,* Pantheon, 1978

Donald Spoto, *Camerado: Hollywood and the American Man,* New American Library, 1978

Media Resources

A Man, 22 mins., b/w, from the About Men Workshop, 45-14 39th Ave., Long Island City, NY 11104, rental $30

A Man's Place, 30 mins., color, from the Institute for Research and Development in Occupational Education, CUNY Graduate Center, 33 W. 42 St., New York, NY 10036

Between Men (masculinity and the military), from United Documentary Films, P.O. Box 315, Franklin Lakes, NJ 07417

Caution: Men Working, 140 slides and 18 min.-cassette, from C.S. Productions, 400 Sibley St., St. Paul, MN 55101

Masculinity: Fact or Act?, 78 slides and 20-min cassette, from Men's Resource Center, 3534 S.E. Main, Portland, OR 97214, rental $5, sale $30

Men's Lives, 44 mins., color, from New Day Films, P.O. Box 315, Franklin Lakes, NJ 07417, rental $56 +$3 handling, sale $500

Walls to Roses: Songs of Changing Men, Folkways FTS 37587, available from record stores and Walls to Roses, 20 Highland Ave. #3, Cambridge, MA 02139

Major Publications

Achilles Heel: A Magazine of Men's Politics, Men's Free Press, 7 St. Mark's Rise, London E8 2NJ, U.K., single copy $1.50 U.S. or Canadian check

Changing Men, Men's Resource Center, 3534 S.E. Main, Portland, OR 97214, subscriptions $5 individual

M: Gentle Men for Gender Justice, P.O. Box 313, 306 N. Brooks St., Madison, WI 53715, subscriptions $8.00 individual

Bibliography and Information Resources

Bibliography of the Men's Studies Collection, MIT Humanities Library, 4th ed., January 1980, 63 pages, approx. 1,400 entries, with author index, $4.00, pre-paid. Write Human Studies Collection, MIT Humanities Library, Cambridge, MA 02139. Checks payable to MIT Libraries. This is the most complete available bibliography on male roles and men's liberation

Kathleen E. Grady, Robert Brannon, and Joseph H. Pleck, *The Male Sex Role: A Selected and Annotated Bibliography,* single copies available (while supply lasts) free from National Clearinghouse for Mental Health Information, NIMH, 5600 Fishers Lane, Rockville, MD 20857

Notes

Chapter 2

1. Miller and Swanson (1960, pp. 88–92), Biller and Borstelman (1967), and Lynn (1969, chapters 3–6) come closest to a comprehensive presentation. Odenwald (1965) and Winick (1968) present ideas of the identity paradigm in popular form.

Chapter 3

1. There are also variations in which the figure is in an envelope (the "concealed It") or the child is shown a blank card.

2. On the third task, the ranking of response from most masculine to most feminine is boy, girl dressed as a boy, boy dressed as a girl, and girl. The relative ranking that should be given the middle two responses presents interesting conceptual issues. It should also be noted that the scoring of the test (not described in detail here) is such that the child's response on the second task is weighted much more strongly than the two; it contributes almost 75% of the total score.

3. Other useful critiques of m-f scales (on which my own analysis is based in part) appear in Kohlberg (1966, pp. 91–92, 109–111), Herzog and Sudia (1971, pp. 42–50), Constantinople (1973), and Harrison (1975).

4. LaTorre and Piper's (1978) replication of the AIAT examined its internal reliability but unfortunately assessed it only by split-half correlations. They explicitly consider and then reject the possibility of using Cronbach's *coefficient alpha* (which they mistakenly call the alpha correlation), a much more sophisticated statistic and the one most widely used at present. They reject using coefficient alpha on the grounds that it would not be comparable to Terman and Miles's split-half correlations, and that the difference between the alpha coefficient and the split-half correlation is negligible. The latter statement is false, and the former is an argument for evaluating split-half reliability in addition to, rather than instead of, a more sophisticated reliability statistic.

5. Brannon's (1978) critique of the misuses and misinterpretations of factor analysis in research on sex role attitudes contains many points applying equally well to factor-analytic research on sex typing.

6. Sears, Rau, and Alpert also included in this analysis a measure of a child's willingness to play a member of the other sex in a game and several masculinity-femininity scores deriving from a doll-play game. These other variables also had quite mixed relationships to the five core m-f measures.

Chapter 4

1. Hartley (1959), in a much earlier review, cites several studies showing that father-son similarity is lower than mother-daughter, but this view has not been supported by more recent studies. Also, Ward (1973), in a study too recent to be included in either Lynn's or Maccoby and Jacklin's reviews, finds that sons are no more similar to their own fathers than they are to other fathers picked at random from the sample.

2. See also a briefer and updated version in Herzog and Sudia (1973). This review, so strongly contradicting the conventional wisdom about paternal absence, has been ignored by other reviewers of this literature such as Biller (1972, 1974) and Lynn (1974). Biller (1972), for example, cites their report only once, as the source of a statistic about the number of boys living in fatherless families, but he nowhere notes that this review contradicts one of the major theses of his own book.

3. Lynn's (1974, pp. 153–158) review, which is concerned solely with fathers, comes to the same conclusion. But a more recent study by Duncan and Duncan (1978, p. 271), using a community probability sample, suggests that fathers are more concerned about a son's sex typing in childhood but a daughter's sex typing in adolescence.

4. Block (1978) also gives data on students' perceptions of their parents' behavior toward them. We shall not consider these here since they are indirect report and because students rated their fathers in only one of the student samples.

5. Sears, Rau, and Alpert do find, however, that masculinity of interests is moderately related for both sexes to parental permissiveness regarding sex play and mild socialization generally (weak demands for good table manners, toilet training, and light physical punishment for aggression). It should be noted, however, that it is difficult to relate these findings to what is known about differences between the sexes. For example, parents are not less permissive with boys' sex play than girls', yet boys nonetheless are more masculine than girls; boys are punished more than girls, yet boys are not more feminine. Further, it is also hard to square these results with what is known about social class differences. Since boys from a lower SES experience less parental permissiveness for sex play and greater punishment, they should be less masculine than boys from a higher SES if Sears, Rau, and Alpert's relationship holds across social classes. But boys from a lower SES are in fact more masculine.

Chapter 5

1. The term excludes individuals who have various biological syndromes in which the different indicators of biological sex (chromosomal pattern, hormonal balance, internal genital organs, external genital organs) are inconsistent and whose biological sex is therefore ambiguous. Transsexuality is quite distinct from transvestism. It is also distinct, of course, from homosexuality. For more information on transsexuality, see Money and Ehrhardt (1972), Stoller (1968), and Green (1974).

2. It might seem that Biller's (1968) finding of a high correlation in boys between the sex of the figure drawn first on the DAP and their sex typing on the It scale establishes, through convergent validity, that the DAP assesses something deeper. But the It scale has exactly the same interpretive problems as the DAP, and their high correlation in this study may simply show that boys who stereotypically interpret (sex-unspecified) figures or instructions as male on one test do so on another test.

3. One might wonder whether this finding is due to classifying more activities as feminine than masculine. Fagot and Patterson do not appear to present data directly relevant to this point. They do note, however, that the two sexes spend almost exactly the same proportion of time in same-sex activities (38%), suggesting that this is not the case.

4. O'Leary and Donoghue (1978) inaccurately characterize Bem (1974) and Spence, Helmreich, and Stapp (1974, 1975a) as finding equal proportions of sex-typed men and women. They also erroneously include the Heilbrun (1976) study as a relevant analysis.

5. For nonhomophobic reviews of other research on homosexuality, see Weinberg (1973) and Freedman (1971).

6. Bender, Davis, and Glover and also Ward report results on the PAQ m-f scale, a third scale similar to traditional bipolar sex typing measures.

Chapter 6

1. The research literature on the relationship between sex role identity and mental illness shows the same kind of disconfirming and contradictory results. The most thorough critical review of this literature appears in Harrison (1975, chapters 5–11). Studies not included in Harrison's review that do not find predicted relationships are Elfert (1972), Small, Biller, and Prochaska (1975), and Small et al. (1977).

I do not discuss in detail the important contributions to the identity paradigm by Heilbrun (1965, 1968, 1973, 1976; see also Consentino and Heilbrun (1964), Rosenberg and Sutton-Smith (1959, 1960a,b, 1964) and Rosenberg (1971).

2. Spence and Helmreich (1979) also show that in some analyses the androgynous group actually shows lower self-esteem than the masculine group.

3. A methodological interpretation of the anomalous results in the Spence, Helmreich, and Stapp data might concern the nature of the dependent measure, the TSBI. This measure contains items of the fol-

lowing sort: "When I am in disagreement with other people, my opinion usually prevails," "I would describe myself as self-confident," and "Other people look up to me." The reason that the TSBI is associated exclusively with the m subscale of androgyny tests may simply be that the TSBI operationally defines social self-esteem in an exclusively masculine way. This scale raises all the issues discussed in the earlier section on the problems of defining psychological adjustment.

Chapter 7

1. A related line of research not reviewed here concerns the *couvade,* a practice in which men in some societies mimic symptoms of pregnancy and birth. See Munroe and Munroe (1971, 1973) and Munroe, Munroe, and Whiting (1973).

2. Delinquents from female-headed households are rated as significantly more manly by other boys than boys from a fourth family type, father-headed single-parent households. But there are no differences between delinquents from these father-headed households and from other households on the subjects' self-ratings on this variable, nor on the discrepancies between self-ratings and either peer or staff ratings. (The father-headed household group is, of course, quite small, and is omitted from this discussion.)

3. Unlike Miller and Swanson's original studies, this study did examine MFs.

4. Another way to evaluate the domination and identification hypotheses is through cross-cultural comparisons. Presumably, in cultures in which mothers are closer to, or more dominating of, their children men's attitudes toward women should be even more negative. This kind of analysis has not been formally carried out, although Ember (1978) performs a tangentially related cross-cultural analysis relating men's fears of sex with women to parent-child sleeping arrangements.

5. An indirect way of evaluating proposition 7 is to examine the relationship between attitudes toward women and sex typing. Both Ellis and Bentler (1973) and Spence, Helmreich, and Stapp (1974) find that they are unrelated.

Chapter 8

1. Fagot and Patterson do not note this explicitly, but a comparison of the figures they give for the proportion of time each sex spends in sex-appropriate and sex-inappropriate behavior (p. 566) with the data in their table 1 makes it apparent that this is their procedure.

2. Another indication of the way the social sciences reflect their times occurs in the sentence immediately following: "The hazing, sleeplessness, tests of manhood, and painful genital operation, together with promise of high status—that of being a man if the tests are successfully passed— are indeed similar to the brainwashing techniques employed by the Communists" (p. 90). Studies of brainwashing (for example, Lifton, 1957) do not indicate that testing or reinforcing manhood is one of the

techniques used, and Burton and Whiting's interpretation of it in these terms is quite striking.

3. A fascinating application of the historical feminization analysis to German culture is Bednarik's *The Male in Crisis* (1971). Mogey's (1957) "A Century of Declining Paternal Authority" provides another intriguing formulation of the historical feminization hypothesis. See also Odenwald (1965) and Winick (1968).

Chapter 9

1. For my earlier formulations of the SRS paradigm, see Pleck (1976a) and Garnets and Pleck (1979). Previous analyses of sex role strain include Turner (1974, pp. 293–313), Komarovsky (1976, pp. 225–241), and Brannon and David (1976). See also Podell (1966), Kando (1972), and Goode (1960).

2. In spite of this perceptive observation, Spence, Helmreich, and Stapp's (1974) Sex Role Stereotype Questionnaire (SRSQ) is designed in such a way as to yield information only about relative stereotyping.

3. In discussing the perceptions of males with liberal sex role attitudes in this study, Spence, Helmreich, and Stapp (1975b) develop a sex role identity argument: "The profile of this group that emerges is of males who are made uncomfortable by 'femininity' in other males, who react less favorably to competent individuals of either sex than other subjects, who rate incompetents more positively, and who, despite their professed belief in feminism, like competent women who are feminine rather than masculine" (p. 98). The ubiquity and resilience of the MSRI paradigm is once again evident.

4. Filene's *Him/Her/Self: Sex Roles in Modern America*, 1975; Dubbert's *A Man's Place: Masculinity in Transition*, 1979; Byars's "The Making of the Self-Made Man," 1979; Stearns's *Be A Man! Males in Modern Society*, 1979; and Pleck and Pleck's *The American Man*, 1980a, provide useful information on the history of the male role.

Chapter 10

1. Chodorow's (1971, 1974) earlier arguments are embedded, however, in the MSRI paradigm and were treated as such in chapter 7.

Bibliography

Abrahams, R. (1965). *Deep Down in the Jungle.* Hatboro, PA: Folklore Associates.

Abrahamsen, D. (1960). *The Psychology of Crime.* New York: Columbia University Press.

Adams, B. (1968). *Kinship in an Urban Setting.* Chicago: Markham.

Adler, A. (1927). *The Practice and Theory of Individual Psychology.* New York: Harcourt.

Adorno, T. W. (1950). Frenkel-Brunswick, E., Levinson, D. J., and Sanford, R. N. *The Authoritarian Personality.* New York: Wiley.

Allen, D. (1954). Antifemininity in men. *American Sociological Review* 19:581–593.

Allen, J., and Haccoun, D. (1976). Sex differences in emotionality: A multidimensional approach. *Human Relations* 29:711–722.

Allen, J., and Hamsher, J. (1974). The development and validation of a test of emotional styles. *Journal of Consulting and Clinical Psychology* 42:663–668.

Asher, S. R., and Gottman, J. M. (1973). Sex of teacher and student reading achievement. *Journal of Educational Psychology* 65:168–171.

Bacon, M., Child, I., and Barry, H. (1963). A cross-cultural study of the correlates of crime. *Journal of Abnormal and Social Psychology* 66:291–300.

Balswick, J., and Avertt, C. (1977). Differences in expressiveness: Gender, interpersonal orientation, and perceived parental expressiveness as contributing factors. *Journal of Marriage and the Family* 39:121–128.

Baruch, G., and Barnett, R. (1981). Fathers' involvement in the care of their preschool children. *Sex Roles* (in press).

Bass, B. M., Krusell, J., and Alexander, R. (1971). Male managers' attitudes toward working women. *American Behavioral Scientist* 15:221–236.

Bateson, G. (1972). *Steps to an Ecology of Mind.* New York: Ballantine.

Bednarik, K. (1971). *The Male in Crisis.* New York: Knopf.

Bell, A., and Weinberg, M. (1978). *Homosexualities: A Study of Diversity Among Men and Women.* New York: Simon and Schuster.

Bem, S. (1972). Psychology looks at sex roles: Where have all the androgynous people gone? Presented at UCLA Symposium on Sex Differences, May, 1972.

Bem, S. (1974). The measurement of psychological androgyny. *Journal of Clinical and Consulting Psychology* 42:155–162.

Bem, S. (1975). Sex role adaptability: One consequence of psychological androgyny. *Journal of Personality and Social Psychology* 31:634–643.

Bem, S. (1976). Probing the promise of androgyny. In A. Kaplan & J. Bean (eds.), *Beyond Sex Role Stereotypes: Toward a Psychology of Androgyny.* Boston: Little Brown.

Bem, S. (1977). On the utility of alternate procedures for assessing psychological androgyny. *Journal of Consulting and Clinical Psychology* 45:196–205.

Bem, S., Martyna, W., and Watson, C. (1976). Sex typing and androgyny: Further explorations of the expressive domain. *Journal of Personality and Social Psychology* 34:1,016–1,023.

Bender, V., Davis, Y., and Glover, O. (1976). Patterns of self-disclosure in homosexual and heterosexual college students. *Sex Roles* 2:149–160.

Berman, P. (1981). Are women more responsive than men to the young? A review of developmental and situational variables. *Psychological Bulletin* 88:668–695.

Berzins, J., Welling, M., and Wetter, R. (1978). A new measure of psychological androgyny based on the Personality Research Form. *Journal of Consulting and Clinical Psychology* 46:126–138.

Best, D. L., Williams, J. E., and Briggs, S. R. (1980). A further analysis of the affective meanings associated with male and female sex-trait stereotypes. *Sex Roles* 6:735–746.

Bezdek, W., and Strodtbeck, F. (1970). Sex role identity and pragmatic action. *American Sociological Review* 35:481–502.

Biber, H., Miller, L. B., and Dyer, L. L. (1972). Feminization in preschool. *Developmental Psychology* 7:86.

Biedenkamp, M., and Goering, J. (1971). How "masculine" are male elementary teachers? *Phi Delta Kappan* 53:9–13.

Biller, H. (1968). A multiaspect investigation of masculine development in kindergarten age boys. *Genetic Psychology Monographs* 78:89–138.

Biller, H. (1970). Father absence and the personality development of the young child. *Developmental Psychology* 2:181–201.

Biller, H. (1972). *Father, Child, and Sex Role.* Lexington, MA: Heath.

Biller, H. (1973). Paternal and sex-role factors in cognitive functioning. In J. Cole & R. Dienstbier (eds.), *Nebraska Symposium on Motivation,* vol. 21. Lincoln, NE: University of Nebraska Press.

Biller, H. (1974). *Paternal Deprivation: Family, School, Sexuality and Society.* Lexington, MA: Heath.

Biller, H., and Borstelmann, L. (1967). Masculine development: An integrative review. *Merrill-Palmer Quarterly* 13:253–294.

Biller, H., and Meredith, D. (1975). *Father Power.* New York: Doubleday.

Blanchard, W. (1959). The group process in gang rape. *Journal of Social Psychology* 49:259–266.

Block, J. (1973). Conceptions of sex role: Some cross-cultural and longitudinal perspectives. *American Psychologist* 28:512–526.

Block, J. (1978). Another look at sex differentiation in the socialization behaviors of mothers and fathers. In J. Sherman and F. Denmark (eds.), *The Psychology of Women: Future Directions of Research.* New York: Psychological Dimensions.

Blood, R. O., Jr., and Wolfe, D. M. (1960). *Husbands and Wives.* Glencoe, IL: Free Press.

Boehm, F. (1932). The femininity-complex in men. *International Journal of Psychoanalysis* 11:444–469.

Booth, A. (1972). Sex and social participation. *American Sociological Review* 37:183–192.

Boressoff, T. (1977). Male sex roles: Stereotypes and strategies for change in the early childhood classroom. Unpublished paper.

Bowman, G. W., Worthy, N. B., and Greyser, S. A. (1965). Are women executives people? *Harvard Business Review* 43(4):14ff.

Brannon, R. (1978). Measuring attitudes toward women (and otherwise): A methodological critique. In J. Sherman & F. Denmark (eds.), *The Psychology of Women: Future Directions of Research.* New York: Psychological Dimensions.

Brannon, R. (1981). A biological basis for male aggression: Fact or fiction? Unpublished paper.

Brannon, R., and David, D. (1976). The male sex role: Our culture's blueprint for manhood, and what it's done for us lately. In D. David and R. Brannon (eds.), *The Forty-Nine Percent Majority: The Male Sex Role.* Reading, MA: Addison-Wesley.

Brannon, R., Juni, S., and Grady, K. (1982). A scale for measuring attitudes about masculinity. In D. David and R. Brannon (eds.), *The*

Forty-Nine Percent Majority: The Male Sex Role, 2nd ed. Reading, MA: Addison-Wesley.

Bremer, J. (1959). *Asexualization: A Follow-Up Study of 224 Cases.* New York: Macmillan.

Brigham, J. C. (1971). Ethnic stereotypes. *Psychological Bulletin* 76:15–38.

Brophy, J. E., and Laosa, L. M. (1971). The effect of a male teacher on the sex-typing of kindergarten children. *Proceedings of the 79th Annual Meeting of the American Psychological Association* 6:169–170.

Broverman, I. K., Vogel, S. R., Broverman, D. M., Clarkson, E. E., and Rosenkrantz, P. S. (1972). Sex-role stereotypes: A current appraisal. *Journal of Social Issues* 28(2):59–78.

Brown, D. (1956). Sex-role preference in young children. *Psychological Monographs* 70(14):Whole No. 421.

Brown, D. (1957a). Masculinity-femininity development in children. *Journal of Consulting Psychology* 21:197–202.

Brown, D. (1957b). The development of sex-role inversion and homosexuality. *Journal of Pediatrics* 50:613–619.

Brown, D. (1958a). Inversion and homosexuality. *American Journal of Orthopsychiatry* 28: 424–429.

Brown, D. (1958b). Sex-role development in a changing culture. *Psychological Bulletin* 55:232–242.

Brown, D., and Tolor, A. (1957). Human figure drawings as indicators of sexual identification and inversion. *Perceptual and Motor Skills* 7:199–211.

Brown, R. (1965). *Social Psychology.* New York: Free Press.

Browmiller, S. (1975). *Against Our Will: Men, Women, and Rape.* New York: Simon and Schuster.

Burgess, E., and Locke, H. (1945). *The Family: From Institution to Companionship.* New York: American Book Company.

Burton, A. (1947). The use of the masculinity-femininity scale of the Minnesota Multiphasic Personality Inventory as an aid in the diagnosis of sexual inversion. *Journal of Psychology* 24:161–164.

Burton, R., and Whiting, J. (1961). The absent father and cross-sex identity. *Merrill-Palmer Quarterly* 7:85–95.

Byars, R. P. (1978). The making of the self-made man: The development of masculine roles and images in antebellum America. Ph.D. dissertation, Michigan State University, 1979. (*Dissertation Abstracts International* 40(1979):2221A; University Microfilms No. 7921135.)

Caldwell, M., and Peplau, L. (1981). Sex differences in same-sex friendship. *Sex Roles* (in press).

Cascario, E. (1972). The male teacher and reading achievement in first-grade boys and girls. Ed.D. dissertation, Lehigh University, 1971. (*Dissertation Abstracts International* 32 (1972):6185A; University Microfilms No. 72-15, 876.)

Casey, M. D., Blank, C. E., McLean, T. M., Kohn, P., Street, D. K. R., McDougal, J. M., Gordon, J., and Platts, J. (1973). Male patients with chromosome abnormality in two state hospitals. *Journal of Mental Deficiency Research* 16:215–256.

Center for Studies of Crime and Delinquency, NIMH (1970). *Report on the XYY Chromosomal Abnormality.* PHS Publ. 2103, Washington, DC: US Government Printing Office.

Child, I. L., Potter, E. H., and Levine, E. M. (1946). Children's textbooks and personality development: An exploration in the social psychology of education. *Psychological Monographs* 60 (entire).

Chodorow, N. (1971). Being and doing: A cross-cultural examination of the socialization of males and females. In V. Gornick and B. K. Moran (eds.), *Woman in Sexist Society.* New York: Basic Books.

Chodorow, N. (1974). Family structure and feminine personality. In M. S. Rosaldo and L. Lamphere (eds.), *Woman, Culture, and Society.* Stanford: Stanford University Press.

Chodorow, N. (1978). *The Reproduction of Mothering: Psychoanalysis and the Sociology of Gender.* Berkeley: University of California Press.

Cicone, M., and Ruble, D. (1978). Beliefs about males. *Journal of Social Issues* 34(1):5–16.

Clark, K. (1965). *Dark Ghetto.* New York: Harper and Row.

Colley, T. (1959). The nature and origins of psychological sexual identity. *Psychological Review* 66:165–177.

Conner, R. L. (1972). Hormones, biogenic amines, and aggression. In S. Levine (ed.), *Hormones and Behavior.* New York: Academic Press.

Consentino, F., and Heilbrun, A. B. (1964). Anxiety correlates of sex-role identity in college students. *Psychological Reports* 14:729–730.

Constantinople, A. (1973). Masculinity-femininity: An exception to a famous dictum? *Psychological Bulletin* 80:389–407.

Constantinople, A. (1979). Sex-role acquisition: In search of the elephant. *Sex Roles* 5:121–134.

Costrich, N., Feinstein, J., Kidder, L., Maracek, J., and Pascale, L. (1975). When stereotypes hurt: Three studies of penalties for sex-role reversals. *Journal of Experimental Social Psychology* 11:520–530.

Cottle, T. J., Edwards, C. N., and Pleck, J. H. (1970). The relationship of sex identity and social and political attitudes. *Journal of Personality* 38:435–452.

Cozby, P. (1973). Self-disclosure: A literature review. *Psychological Bulletin* 79:73–91.

Cronenwett, L., and Newmark, L. (1974). Fathers' responses to childbirth. *Nursing Research* 23:210–217.

Dahlstrom, W. G., Welsh, G. S., and Dahlstrom, L. E. (1972a). *An MMPI Handbook, Vol. 1: Clinical Interpretation.* Minneapolis: University of Minnesota Press.

Dahlstrom, W. G., Welsh, G. S., and Dahlstrom, L. E. (1972b). *An MMPI Handbook, Vol. 2: Research Applications.* Minneapolis, Minn.: University of Minnesota Press.

De Lucia, L. A. (1963). The toy preference test: A measure of sex role identification. *Child Development* 34:127–139.

Derlega, V., and Chaikin, A. (1976). Norms affecting self-disclosure in men and women. *Journal of Consulting and Clinical Psychology* 44:376–380.

Deutsch, C., and Gilbert, L. (1976). Sex role stereotypes: Effects on perceptions of self and others and on personal adjustment. *A Journal of Counseling Psychology* 23:373–379.

Dinnerstein, D. (1976). *The Mermaid and the Minotaur: Sexual Arrangements and the Human Malaise.* New York: Harper and Row.

Doehring, C. H., Brodie, K. H., Kraemer, H. C., Becker, H., and Hamburg, D. A. (1974a). Plasma testosterone levels and psychologic measures in men over a two-month period. In R. C. Friedman et al., (eds.), *Sex Differences in Behavior.* New York: Wiley.

Doehring, C. H., Kraemer, H. C., Brodie, K. H., and Hamburg, D. A. (1974b). A cycle of plasma testosterone in the human male. *Journal of Clinical Endocrinology and Metabolism* 40:492–500.

Douvan, E., and Adelson, J. (1968). *The Adolescent Experience.* New York: Wiley.

Douvan, E., and Pleck, J. H. (1978). Separation as support in dual-career couples. In R. Rapoport and R. N. Rapoport (eds.), *Working Couples.* New York: Harper and Row.

Doyle, J., and Moore, R. (1978). Attitudes toward the male's role scale (AMR): An objective instrument to measure attitudes toward the male's sex role in contemporary society. *JSAS Catalog of Selected Documents in Society* 8:35–36 (Ms. 1678).

Dubbert, J. (1974). Progressivism and the masculinity crisis. *Psychoanalytic Review* 61:433–455.

Dubbert, J. (1979). *A Man's Place: Masculinity in Transition.* Englewood Cliffs, NJ: Prentice-Hall.

Duncan, B., and Duncan, O. (1978). *Sex Typing and Social Roles: A Research Report.* New York: Academic Press.

Edwards, A. and Abbott, R. (1973). Measurement of personality traits: Theory and technique. *Annual Review of Psychology* 24:241–278.

Ehrenberg, O. (1960). Concepts of masculinity: A study of discrepancies between men's self-concepts and their relationship to mental health. Ph.D. dissertation New York University, 1960. (*Dissertation Abstracts International* 21(1960):1275B; University Microfilms No. 60-3740.)

Ehrhardt, A., and Baker, A. (1974). Fetal androgens, human central nervous system differentiation, and behavior sex differences. In R. Friedman et al. (eds.), *Sex Differences in Behavior*. New York: Wiley.

Elfert, D. (1971). Sex-role identification in ambulatory schizophrenics and neurotics: A comparative study of levels of sexual identity. Ph.D. dissertation, University of Massachusetts, Amherst, 1971. (*Dissertation Abstracts International* 32 (1972):4207B; University Microfilms No. 72-3067.)

Ellis, L. J., and Bentler, P. M. (1973). Traditional sex-determined role standards and sex stereotypes. *Journal of Personality and Social Psychology* 25:28–34.

Elman, J., Press, A., and Rosenkrantz, P. (1970). Sex roles and self-concepts: Real and ideal. *Proceedings of the 78th Annual Convention of the American Psychological Association*: 455–456.

Ember, C. (1978). Men's fear of sex with women: A cross-cultural study. *Sex Roles* 4:657–678.

Endsley, R. C. (1967). Effects of concealing "It" on sex-role preferences of preschool children. *Perceptual and Motor Skills* 24:998.

Erikson, E. (1943). Clinical studies in childhood play. In R. Barker, J. Kounin, and J. Wright (eds.), *Child Behavior and Development*. New York: McGraw-Hill.

Erikson, E. (1964). Womanhood and inner space. In R. Lifton (ed.), *The Woman in America*. Boston: Beacon.

Erikson, E. (1968). Race and the wider identity. In E. Erikson, *Identity: Youth and Crisis*. New York: Norton.

Etaugh, C., Collins, G., and Gerson, A. (1975). Reinforcement of sex-typed behaviors of two-year-old children in a nursery school setting. *Developmental Psychology* 11:255.

Etaugh, C., and Hughes, V. (1975). Teachers' evaluations of sex-typed behaviors in children: The role of teacher sex and school setting. *Developmental Psychology* 11:394–395.

Etheredge, L. (1978). *A World of Men: Private Sources of American Foreign Policy*. Cambridge, MA: MIT Press.

Fagot, B., and Patterson, G. (1969). An *in vivo* analysis of reinforcing contingencies for sex-role behaviors in the preschool child. *Developmental Psychology* 1:563–568.

Farrell, W. (1974). *The Liberated Man.* New York: Random House.

Fasteau, M. (1974). *The Male Machine.* New York: McGraw-Hill.

Fein, R. (1978). Research on fathering: Social policy and an emergent perspective. *Journal of Social Issues* 34(1):122–135.

Feinman, S. (1974). Approval of cross sex-role behavior. *Psychological Reports* 35:643–648.

Fenichel, O. (1945). *The Psychoanalytic Theory of Neurosis.* New York: Norton.

Ferguson, L. R., and Maccoby, E. E. (1966). Interpersonal correlates of differential abilities. *Child Development* 37:549–571.

Filene, P. (1975). *Him/Her/Self: Sex Roles in Modern America.* New York: Harcourt Brace.

Fisher, S. and Fisher, R. (1976). *What We Really Know about Childrearing.* New York: Simon & Schuster.

Fling, S., and Manosevitz, M. (1972). Sex typing in nursery school children's play interests. *Developmental Psychology* 7:146–152.

Forslund, M. A., and Hull, P. E. (1972). Sex-role identification and achievement at preadolescence. *Rocky Mountain Social Science Journal* 9:105–110.

Franck, K., and Rosen, E. (1949). A projective test of masculinity-femininity. *Journal of Consulting Psychology* 13:247–256.

Frass, L. (1970). Sex of figure drawing in identifying practicing male homosexuals. *Psychological Reports* 27:172–174.

Freedman, M. (1971). *Homosexuality and Psychological Functioning.* Belmont, CA: Brooks/Cole.

Freund, K., Nagler, E., Langevin, R., Zajac, A., and Steiner, B. (1974). Measuring feminine gender identity in homosexual males. *Archives of Sexual Behavior* 3:249–260.

Friedan, B. (1963). *The Feminine Mystique.* New York: Norton.

Friedman, M., and Rosenman, R. (1974). *Type A Behavior and Your Heart.* Greenwich, CT: Fawcett.

Frodi, A., Macaulay, J., and Thome, P. (1977). Are women always less aggressive than men? A review of the experimental literature. *Psychological Bulletin* 84:634–660.

Gagnon, J., and Simon, W. (1975). *Sexual Conduct.* Chicago: Aldine.

Garnets, L. (1978). Sex role strain analysis: Effects of sex role discrepancy and sex role salience on adjustment. Ph.D. dissertation, University of Michigan, 1978. (*Dissertation Abstracts International* 39 (1979):5064B; University Microfilms No. 7907078.)

Garnets, L., and Pleck, J. (1979). Sex role identity, androgyny, and sex role transcendence: A sex role strain analysis. *Psychology of Women Quarterly* 3:270–283.

Gaudreau, R. (1977). Factor analysis of the Bem Sex Role Inventory. *Journal of Consulting and Clinical Psychology* 45:299–302.

Gilbert, L., Deutsch, C., and Strahan, R. (1978). Feminine and masculine dimensions of the typical, desirable, and ideal woman and man. *Sex Roles* 4:767–778.

Goffman, E. (1963). *Stigma: Notes on the Management of Spoiled Identity*. Englewood Cliffs, NJ: Prentice-Hall.

Goldberg, H. (1973). Men's lib. *Human Behavior* (April):37–77.

Goldberg, H. (1976). *The Hazards of Being Male: Surviving the Myth of Masculine Privilege*. New York: Nash.

Goldberg, S. (1975). *The Inevitability of Patriarchy*. New York: Morrow.

Gonen, J., and Lanksy, L. (1968). Masculinity, femininity, and masculinity-femininity A phenomenological study of the Mf scale of the MMPI. *Psychological Reports* 23:183–194.

Goode, W. J. (1960). A theory of role strain. *American Sociological Review* 25:483–496.

Goodenough, E. (1957). Interest in persons as an aspect of sex differences in the early years. *Genetic Psychology Monographs* 55:287–323.

Gough, H. (1952). Identifying psychological femininity. *Educational and Psychological Measurement* 12:427–439.

Gough, H. (1964). An interpreter's syllabus for the CPI. In P. McReynolds (ed.), *Advances in Psychological Assessment*, vol. 1. Palo Alto: Science and Behavior Publications.

Grady, K., Brannon, R., and Pleck, J. H. (1979). *The Male Sex Role: An Annotated Research Bibliography*. Rockville, MD: National Institute of Mental Health.

Gray, S. (1957). Masculinity-femininity in relation to anxiety and social acceptance. *Child Development* 28: 203–214.

Green, R. (1974). *Sexual Identity Conflict in Children and Adults*. New York: Basic Books.

Greenberg, M., and Morris, N. (1974). Engrossment: The newborn's impact upon the father. *American Journal of Orthopsychiatry* 44:520–531.

Greenstein, J. M. (1966). Father characteristics and sex typing. *Journal of Personality and Social Psychology* 3:271–277.

Greven, P. (1977). *The Protestant Temperament: Patterns of Child-Rearing, Religious Experience, and the Self in Early America*. New York: Knopf.

Grier, W., and Cobbs, W. (1968). *Black Rage*, New York: Basic Books.

Griffiths, A. W., Richards, B. W., Zaremba, J., Abramowicz, T., and

Stewart, D. (1970). Psychological and sociological investigation of XYY prisoners. *Nature* 227:290–292.

Gross, N., Mason, W., and McEachern, W. (1958). *Explorations in Role Analysis: Studies of the School Superintendency Role.* New York: Wiley.

Grygier, T. (1957). Psychometric aspects of homosexuality. *Journal of Mental Science* 103:514–526.

Hacker, H. (1957). The new burdens of masculinity. *Marriage and Family Living* 3:227–233.

Hall, M., and Keith, R. (1964). Sex-role preference among children of upper- and lower-class. *Journal of Social Psychology* 62:101–110.

Halverson, C., and Waldrop, M. (1973). The relation of mechanically-recorded activity level to varieties of preschool play behavior. *Child Development* 44:678–681.

Hamburg, D. A. (1971). Recent research on hormonal factors relevant to human aggressiveness. *International Social Science Journal* 23:36–47.

Hannerz, U. (1971). *Soulside.* New York: Columbia University Press.

Hantover, J. (1978). The Boy Scouts and the validation of masculinity. *Journal of Social Issues* 34(1):184–195.

Hare, N. (1971). The frustrated masculinity of the Negro male. In R. Staples (ed.), *The Black Family: Essays and Studies.* Belmont, CA: Brooks/Cole.

Harford, T., Willis, C., and Deabler, H. (1967). Personality correlates of masculinity-femininity. *Psychological Reports* 21:881–884.

Harlow, R. (1951). Masculine inadequacy and the compensatory development of physique. *Journal of Personality* 19:312–333.

Harrington, C. (1970). *Errors in Sex-role Behavior in Teen-age Boys.* New York: Teachers College Press.

Harrison, J. (1975). A critical evaluation of research on "masculinity-femininity" and a proposal for an alternative paradigm for research on psychological differences and similarities between the sexes. Ph.D. dissertation, New York University, 1975. (*Dissertation Abstracts International* 36(1975):1903B; University Microfilms No. 75-22, 890.)

Harrison, J. (1978). Warning: The male sex role may be hazardous to your health. *Journal of Social Issues* 34(1):65–86.

Hartley, R. L. (1959). Sex-role pressures in the socialization of the male child. *Psychological Reports* 5:459–468.

Hartley, R. L. (1970). American core culture: Continuity and change. In G. Seward and R. Williamson (eds.), *Sex Roles in Changing Society.* New York: Random House.

Hawke, C. C. (1950). Castration and sex crimes. *American Journal of Mental Deficiency* 55:220–226.

Heilbrun, A. B. (1965). Sex differences in identification learning. *Journal of Genetic Psychology* 106:185–193.

Heilbrun, A. B. (1968). Sex role identity in adolescent females: A theoretical paradox. *Adolescence* 3:78–88.

Heilbrun, A. B. (1973). Parent identification and filial sex-role behavior: The importance of biological context. In J. Cole and R. Dienstbier (eds.), *Nebraska Symposium on Motivation,* vol. 21. Lincoln, NE: University of Nebraska Press.

Heilbrun, A. B. (1976). Measurement of masculine and feminine sex role identities as independent dimensions. *Journal of Consulting and Clinical Psychology* 44:183–190.

Heilbrun, A. B., and Thompson, N. (1977). Sex-role identity and male and female homosexuality. *Sex Roles* 3:65–79.

Herman, J., and Gyllstrom, K. (1977). Working men and women: Inter- and intra-role conflict. *Psychology of Women Quarterly* 1:319–333.

Hershey, M. (1978). Racial differences in sex-role identities and sex stereotyping: Evidence against a common assumption. *Social Science Quarterly* 58:584–596.

Herzog, E., and Sudia, C. (1971). *Boys in Fatherless Families.* DHEW Publ. No. (OCD) 72-33. Washington, DC: US Government Printing Office.

Herzog, E., and Sudia, C. (1973). Children in fatherless families. In E. M. Hetherington and P. Riccinuti (eds.), *Review of Child Development and Research*, vol. 5. Chicago: University of Chicago Press.

Hoffman, M. (1977). Sex differences in empathy and related behaviors. *Psychological Bulletin* 84:712–722.

Holmes, D. (1967). Male-female differences in MMPI ego strength: An artifact. *Journal of Consulting Psychology* 31:408–410.

Horney, K. (1932). The dread of women. *International Journal of Psychoanalysis.* 13:348–360.

Howells, J. (1971). Fathering. In J. Howells (ed.), *Modern Perspectives in International Child Psychiatry.* New York: Brunner-Mazel.

Humez, A., and Stavely, K. (1978). *Family Man: What Men Feel about Their Wives, Their Children, Their Parents and Themselves.* Chicago: Contemporary Books.

Jacklin, C., and Mischel, H. (1973). As the twig is bent: Sex role stereotyping in early readers. *School Psychology Digest* 2:30–37.

Jacobs, P. A., Brunton, M., Melville, M. M., Brittain, R. P., and McClemont, W. F. (1965). Aggressive behavior, mental subnormality, and the XYY male. *Nature* 208:1,351–1,352.

Jencks, C., Smith, M., Acland, H., Bane, M., Cohen, D., Gintis, H., Heyns, H., and Michelson, S. (1972). *Inequality: A Reassessment of the Effect of Family and Schooling in America.* New York: Basic Books.

Jenkin, N., and Vroegh, K. (1969). Contemporary concepts of masculinity and femininity. *Psychological Reports* 25:679–697.

Johnson, M. M. (1963). Sex role learning in the nuclear family. *Child Development* 34:319–333.

Jourard, S. (1964a). Lethal aspects of the male role. In S. Jourard, *The Transparent Self: Self-Disclosure and Well-Being*. Princeton: Van Nostrand.

Jourard, S. (1964b). A technical appendix for psychologists. In S. Jourard, *The Transparent Self: Self-Disclosure and Well-Being*. Princeton: Van Nostrand.

Kagan, J. (1964a). Acquisition and significance of sex typing and sex-role identity. In M. L. Hoffman and L. W. Hoffman (eds.), *Review of Child Development Research*, vol. 1. New York: Russell Sage Foundation.

Kagan, J. (1964b). The child's sex role classification of school objects. *Child Development* 35:1,051–1,056.

Kagan, J., and Moss, H. (1962). *Birth to Maturity: A Study in Psychological Development*. New York: Wiley.

Kando, T. M. (1970). Role strain: A comparison of males, females, and transsexuals. *Journal of Marriage and the Family* 34:459–464.

Kanin, E. (1967). An examination of sexual aggression as a response to sexual frustration. *Journal of Marriage and the Family* 29:428–433.

Kanin, E. (1970). Sex aggression by college men. *Medical Aspects of Human Sexuality* (Sept.):28ff.

Kaplan, A. (ed.) (1979). Psychological androgyny: Further considerations. *Psychology of Women Quarterly* 3(3):221–315.

Katz, J. (1976). *Gay American History: Lesbians and Gay Men in the U.S.A.* New York: Crowell.

Kellogg, R. L. (1969). A direct approach to sex role identification of school objects. *Psychological Reports* 24:839–841.

Kelly, J., Furman, W., and Young, V. (1978). Problems associated with the typological measurement of sex roles and androgyny. *Journal of Consulting and Clinical Psychology* 46:1,574–1,576.

Kelly, J., and Worell, J. (1977). New formulations of sex roles and androgyny: A critical review. *Journal of Consulting and Clinical Psychology*, 45:1101–1115.

Kelly, R. (1979). *Employment and Families in Mecklenburg County, North Carolina*. Durham, NC: Center for the Study of the Family and the State, Duke University.

Kessler, S., and Moos, R. (1970). The XYY karyotype and criminality: A review. *Journal of Psychiatric Research* 7:153–170.

Kinsey, A., Pomeroy, W., and Martin, C. (1948). *Sexual Behavior in the Human Male*. Philadelphia: Saunders.

Kinsey, A., Pomeroy, W., Martin, C., and Gebhard, P. (1953). *Sexual Behavior in the Human Female*. Philadelphia: Saunders.

Kirkpatrick, C. (1963). *The Family as Process and Institution*, 2nd ed.. New York: Ronald Press (1st ed. 1955).

Kitagawa, E., and Hauser, P. (1973). *Differential Mortality in the United States: A Study in Socioeconomic Epidemiology*. Cambridge, MA: Harvard University Press.

Knox, W., and Kupferer, H. (1971). A discontinuity in the socialization of males in the United States. *Merrill-Palmer Quarterly* 17:251–261.

Kobliska, J. (1974). Growing up male. *New Schools Exchange Newsletter* 109 (Jan. 15):10.

Kohlberg, L. (1966). A cognitive-developmental analysis of children's sex-role concepts and attitudes. In E. E. Maccoby (ed.), *The Development of Sex Differences*. Stanford: Stanford University Press.

Kohlberg, L., and Zigler, E. (1967). The impact of cognitive maturity on the development of sex-role attitudes in the years 4 to 8. *Genetic Psychology Monographs* 75:84–165.

Kolodny, R., and Masters, W. (1974). Depression of plasma testosterone levels after chronic intensive marijuana use. *New England Journal of Medicine* 290:872–874.

Komarovsky, M. (1946). Cultural contradictions and sex roles. *American Journal of Sociology* 52:182–189.

Komarovsky, M. (1953). *Women in the Modern World, Their Education and Their Dilemmas*. Boston: Little Brown.

Komarovsky, M. (1964). *Blue Collar Marriage*. New York: Vintage.

Komarovsky, M. (1973). Presidential address: Some problems in role analysis. *American Sociological Review* 38:649–662.

Komarovsky, M. (1976). *Dilemmas of Masculinity: A Study of College Youth*. New York: Norton.

Komisar, L. (1976). Violence and the masculine mystique. In D. David and R. Brannon (eds.), *The Forty-Nine Percent Majority: The Male Sex Role*. Reading, MA: Addison-Wesley.

Kreuz, L. E., and Rose, R. J. (1972). Assessment of aggressive behavior and plasma testosterone in a young criminal population. *Psychosomatic Medicine* 34:321–332.

Kristal, J., Sanders, D., Spence, J., and Helmreich, R. (1975). Inferences about femininity of competent women and their implications for likeability. *Sex Roles* 1:33–40.

Kuhn, T. (1962). *The Structure of Scientific Revolutions*. Chicago: University of Chicago Press.

Lansky, L. M. (1967). The family structure also affects the model: Sex-role attitudes in parents of preschool children. *Merrill-Palmer Quarterly* 13:139–150.

Lansky, L. M., and McKay, G. (1963). Sex-role preferences of kindergarten boys and girls: Some contradictory results. *Psychological Reports* 13:415–421.

LaTorre, R., and Piper, W. (1978). The Terman-Miles M-F test: An examination of exercises 1, 2, and 3 forty years later. *Sex Roles* 4:141–154.

Lederer, W. (1968). *The Fear of Women*. New York: Grune and Stratton.

Lee, P. (1973). Male and female teachers in elementary schools: An ecological analysis. *Teachers College Record* 75:79–98.

Lee, P., and Wolinsky, A. (1973). Male teachers of young children: A preliminary empirical study. *Young Children* 28:342–352.

Lee, R., and Schneider, R. (1958). Hypertension and arteriosclerosis in executive and nonexecutive personnel. *Journal of the American Medical Association* 167:1,447–1,450.

LeMasters, E. (1975). *Blue Collar Aristocrats*. Madison: University of Wisconsin Press.

Lenney, E. (1979a). Androgyny: Some audacious assertions toward its coming of age. *Sex Roles* 5:703–719.

Lenney, E. (ed.) (1979b). Androgyny. *Sex Roles* 5(6):703–840.

Levine, J. (1976). *Who Will Raise the Children? New Options for Fathers (and Mothers)*. Philadelphia: Lippincott.

Levitin, T. E., and Chananie, J. D. (1972). Responses of female primary school teachers to sex-typed behaviors in male and female children. *Child Development* 43:1,309–1,316.

Lewis, R. A., (1978). Emotional intimacy among men. *Journal of Social Issues* 34(1):108–121.

Lewis, R. A., and Pleck, J. H. (eds.) (1979). Men's roles in the family. *The Family Coordinator* 28(4):429–626.

Lidz, T. (1968). *The Person: His Development through the Life Cycle*. New York: Basic Books.

Lifton, R. (1957). *Thought Reform and the Psychology of Totalism*. New York: Vintage.

Lipsitt, P., and Strodtbeck, F. (1967). Defensiveness in decision-making as a function of sex-role identification. *Journal of Personality and Social Psychology* 6:10–15.

Lynn, D. B. (1961). Sex differences in identification development. *Sociometry* 24:373–383.

Lynn, D. B. (1966). The process of learning parental and sex-role identification. *Journal of Marriage and the Family* 28:466–470.

Lynn, D. B. (1969). *Parental and Sex Role Identification: A Theoretical Formulation.* Berkeley: McCutchan.

Lynn, D. B. (1974). *The Father: His Role in Child Development.* Belmont, CA: Wadsworth.

Lynn, D. B. (1976). Fathers and sex role development. *Family Coordinator* 25:403–410.

Maccoby, E. E., and Jacklin, C. N. (1974). *The Psychology of Sex Differences.* Stanford: Stanford University Press.

Mackey, W., and Day, R. (1979). Some indicators of fathering behaviors in the United States: A crosscultural examination of adult male-child interaction. *Journal of Marriage and the Family* 41:287–299.

Madigan, F. (1957). Are sex mortality differentials biologically caused? *Millbank Memorial Fund Quarterly* 35:202–223.

Madigan, F., and Vance, R. (1957). Differential sex mortality: A research design. *Social Forces* 35:193–199.

Manosevitz, M. (1970). Item analyses of the MMPI Mf scale using homosexual and heterosexual samples. *Journal of Consulting and Clinical Psychology* 35:395–399.

Manosevitz, M. (1971). Education and MMPI Mf scores in homosexual and heterosexual males. *Journal of Clinical and Consulting Psychology* 36:395–399.

Masih, L. (1967). Career saliency and its relation to certain needs, interests, and job values. *Personnel and Guidance Journal* 45:653–658.

Mason, K., and Bumpass, L. (1975). U.S. women's sex-role ideology, 1970. *American Sociological Review* 40:1,212–1,219.

Matteson, D. (1975). *Adolescence Today: Sex Roles and the Search for Identity.* Homewood, IL: Dorsey.

McArthur, L., and Eisen, S. (1976a). Achievement of male and female storybook characters as determinants of achievement behavior by boys and girls. *Journal of Personality and Social Psychology* 33:467–473.

McArthur, L., and Eisen, S. (1976b). Television and sex-role stereotyping. *Journal of Applied Social Psychology* 6:329–351.

McFarland, W. J. (1969). Are girls really smarter? *Elementary School Journal* 70:14–19.

McGovern, J. (1966). David Graham Phillips and the virility impulse of the Progressives. *New England Quarterly* 39:334–355.

McKee, J. P., and Sherriffs, A. C. (1975). The differential evaluation of males and females. *Journal of Personality* 25:356–371.

McKee, J. P., and Sherriffs, A. C. (1959). Men's and women's beliefs, ideals, and self-concepts. *American Journal of Sociology* 64:356–363.

Mead, M. (1935). *Sex and Temperament in Three Primitive Societies.* New York: Morrow.

Mead, M. (1949). *Male and Female*. New York: Morrow.

Megargee, E. (1972). *The California Psychological Inventory Handbook*. San Francisco: Jossey-Bass.

Meier, H. C. (1972). Mother-centeredness and college youths' attitude toward social equality for women: Some empirical findings. *Journal of Marriage and the Family* 34:115–121.

Metropolitan Life Insurance Company (1974). Longevity of corporate executives. *Metropolitan Life Statistical Bulletin* (Feb.):3–7.

Meyer-Bahlburg, H. F. L. (1974). Aggression, androgens, and the XYY syndrome. In R. C. Friedman et al. (eds.), *Sex Differences in Behavior*. New York: Wiley.

Meyer-Bahlburg, H. F. L., Boon, D., Sharma, M., and Edwards, J. (1974). Aggressiveness and testosterone measures in man. *Psychosomatic Medicine* 36:269–274.

Milgram, J., and Sciarra, D. (1974). Male preschool teachers: The realities of acceptance. *Educational Forum* 38:244–247.

Miller, D., and Swanson, G. (1960). *Inner Conflict and Defense*. New York: Holt.

Miller, W. (1958). Lower-class culture as a generating milieu for gang delinquency. *Journal of Social Issues* 14:5–19.

Mills, C. (1956). *White Collar: The American Middle Classes*. New York: Oxford University Press.

Mischel, W. (1966). A social-learning view of sex differences in behavior. In E. Maccoby (ed.), *The Development of Sex Differences*. Stanford: Stanford University Press.

Mischel, W. (1969). Sex-typing and socialization. In P. Mussen (ed.), *Carmichael's Manual of Child Psychology* 3rd ed., vol. 2. New York: Wiley.

Mitchell, G. (1969). Paternalistic behavior in primates. *Psychological Bulletin* 71:339–417.

Mitchell, G., Redican, W., and Gomber, J. (1974). Lesson from a primate: Males can raise babies. *Psychology Today* (April):23–28.

Mogey, J. (1957). A century of declining paternal authority. *Marriage and Family Living* 19:234–239.

Money, J., and Ehrhardt, A. (1972). *Man and Woman, Boy and Girl*. Baltimore: Johns Hopkins University Press.

Moore, D., and Nutall, J. (1981). Perceptions of the male sex role. *Personality and Social Psychology Bulletin* (in press).

Moreland, J., Gulanick, N., Montague, E., and Harren, V. (1978). Some psychometric properties of the Bem Sex Role Inventory. *Applied Psychological Measurement* 2:249–256.

Moreland, J. and Van Tuinen, M. (1978). The attitudes toward masculinity transcendence scale. Unpublished, Department of Psychology, Ohio State University.

Morgan, B. (1976). Intimacy of disclosure topics and sex differences in self-disclosure. *Sex Roles* 2:161–165.

Mowrer, O. (1950). *Learning Theory and Personality Dynamics*. New York: Ronald.

Moyer, K. E. (1974). Sex differences in aggression. In R. C. Friedman et al. (eds.), *Sex Differences in Behavior*. New York: Wiley.

Moynihan, D. (1967). The Negro family: The case for national action. In L. Rainwater and W. Yancey (eds.), *The Moynihan Report and the Politics of Controversy*. Cambridge, MA: MIT Press.

Munroe, R. L., and Munroe, R. H. (1971). Male pregnancy symptoms and cross-sex identity symptoms. *Journal of Social Psychology* 84:11–25.

Munroe, R. L., and Munroe, R. H. (1973). Psychological interpretation of male initiation rites: The case of male pregnancy symptoms. *Ethos* 1:490–498.

Munroe, R. L., Munroe, R. L. and Whiting, J. W. M. (1973). The couvade: A psychological analysis. *Ethos* 1:30–74.

Mussen, P. (1961). Some antecedents and consequents of masculine sex-typing in adolescent boys. *Psychological Monographs* 75(2):1–24.

Mussen, P. (1962). Long-term consequents of masculinity of interests in adolescence. *Journal of Consulting Psychology* 26:435–440.

Mussen, P. (1969). Early sex-role development. In D. Goslin (ed.), *Handbook of Socialization Theory and Research*. New York: Rand McNally.

Mussen, P., and Rutherford E. (1963). Parent-child relations and parental personality in relation to young children's sex-role preferences. *Child Development* 34:589–607.

Nance, R. (1949). Masculinity-femininity in prospective teachers. *Journal of Educational Research* 42:658–666.

National Center for Health Statistics, USDHEW (1976), *Vital Statistics of the United States, 1975*, vol. 2. Washington, D.C.: US Government Printing Office.

Nichols, R. (1962). Subtle, obvious, and stereotype measures of masculinity-femininity. *Educational and Psychological Measurement* 22:449–461.

Norbeck, E., Walker, D., and Cohen, M. (1962). The interpretation of puberty rites. *American Anthropologist* 64:463–485.

Oakley, A. (1974). *Sex, Gender, and Society*. New York: Harper and Row.

Odenwald, R. (1965). *The Disappearing Sexes*. New York: Random House.

O'Leary, V., and Donoghue, J. (1978). Latitudes of masculinity: Reactions to sex role deviance in men. *Journal of Social Issues* 34(1):17–28.

Owen, D. R. (1972). The 47,XYY male: A review. *Psychological Bulletin* 78:209–233.

Parke, R. D., and O'Leary, S. (1975). Father-mother-infant interaction in the newborn period: Some findings, some observations, and some unresolved issues. In K. Riegel & J. Meacham (eds.), *The Developing Individual in a Changing World, Vol. 2: Social and Environmental Issues.* The Hague: Mouton.

Parke, R. D., and Sawin, D. (1976). The father's role in infancy: A re-evaluation. *Family Coordinator* 25:365–372.

Parsons, T. (1947). Certain primary sources and patterns of aggression in the social structure of the Western World. *Psychiatry* 10:167–181.

Parsons, T. (1954). Age and sex in the social structure of the United States. In T. Parsons, *Essays in Sociological Theory* rev. ed. New York: Free Press.

Parsons, T. (1959). The social structure of the family. In R. Anshen (ed.), *The Family: Its Function and Destiny.* New York: Harper and Row.

Parsons, T., and Bales, R. F. (1955). *Family Socialization and Interaction Process.* Glencoe, IL: Free Press.

Persky, H., Smith, K. D., and Basu, G. R. (1971). Relation of psychologic measures of aggression and hostility to testosterone production in men. *Psychosomatic Medicine* 33:265–277.

Pettigrew, T. (1964). *A Profile of the Negro American.* Princeton, NJ: Van Nostrand.

Pleck, E. H. (1976). Two worlds in one: Work and family. *Journal of Social History* 10(2):178–195.

Pleck, E. H., and Pleck, J. H. (eds.) (1980a). *The American Man.* Englewood Cliffs, NJ: Prentice-Hall (Spectrum Books).

Pleck, E. H., and Pleck, J. H. (1980b). U.S. men's history: An introduction. In Pleck and Pleck (eds.), *The American Man.* Englewood Cliffs, NJ: Prentice-Hall (Spectrum Books).

Pleck, E. H., Pleck, J. H., Grossman, M., and Bart, P. B. (1977/1978). The battered data syndrome: Reply to Steinmetz. *Victimology* 2:680–683.

Pleck, J. H. (1973a). *Male threat from female competence: An experimental study in college dating couples.* Doctoral dissertation, Harvard University, 1973. (*Dissertation Abstracts International* 34(1974):6221B; University Microfilms, No. 74-11, 721.)

Pleck, J. H. (1973b). Psychological frontiers for men. *Rough Times* 3(6) (June-July):14–15. (Reprinted in S. Gordon and R. Libby (eds.), *Sexuality Today and Beyond.* N. Scituate, MA: Duxbury Press, 1976.)

Pleck, J. H. (1974). My male sex role—and ours. *WIN Magazine* (April 11):8–12. (Reprinted in D. David and R. Brannon (eds.), *The Forty-Nine Percent Majority: Readings on the Male Role.* Reading, MA: Addison-Wesley, 1976.)

Pleck, J. H. (1975a). Masculinity-femininity: Current and alternate paradigms. *Sex Roles* 1:161–178.

Pleck, J. H. (1975b). Man to man: Is brotherhood possible? In N. G. Malbin (ed.), *Old Family/New Family: Interpersonal Relationships.* New York: Van Nostrand Reinhold.

Pleck, J. H. (1975c). Men's reactions to the changing consciousness of women. In E. L. Zuckerman (ed.), *Women and Men: Roles, Attitudes, and Power Relationships.* New York: Radcliffe Club of New York.

Pleck, J. H. (1975d). Issues for the men's movement. *Changing Men: A Newsletter for Men against Sexism (Portland, OR)* 20 (Nov.); 21 (Dec.); 23 (March 1976).

Pleck, J. H. (1976a). The male sex role: Definitions, problems, and sources of change. *Journal of Social Issues* 32(3):155–164.

Pleck, J. H. (1976b). Male threat from female competence. *Journal of Consulting and Clinical Psychology* 44:608–613.

Pleck, J. H. (1976c). The psychology of sex roles: Traditional and new views. In L. A. Cater and A. F. Scott (eds.), *Women and Men: Changing Roles, Attitudes, and Perceptions.* Stanford: Aspen Institute for Humanistic Studies. (Republished by Praeger Publishers, Inc., 1977).

Pleck, J. H. (1976d). Male sex role behaviors in a representative national sample, 1973. In Dorothy G. McGuigan (ed.), *New Research on Women and Sex Roles.* Ann Arbor, MI: Center for Continuing Education of Women.

Pleck, J. H. (1976e). *Men's new roles in the family: Housework and childcare.* Wellesley, MA: Working Papers, Wellesley College Center for Research on Women.

Pleck, J. H. (1977a). The work-family role system. *Social Problems* 24:417–427.

Pleck, J. H. (1977b). Men's power with women, other men, and society: A men's movement analysis. In D. Hiller and R. Sheets (eds.), *Women and Men: The Consequences of Power.* Cincinnati: Office of Women's Studies, University of Cincinnati.

Pleck, J. H. (1977c). Developmental stages in men's lives: How do they differ from women's? Paper presented to the National Vocational Guidance Association Conference on "Resocialization of Sex Roles: Challenge for the 1970's."

Pleck, J. H. (1978a). Men's traditional attitudes toward women: Correlates of adjustment or maladjustment? *Psychological Reports* 42:975–983.

Pleck, J. H. (1978b). Males' traditional attitudes toward women: Conceptual issues in research. In J. Sherman and F. Denmark (eds.), *The Psychology of Women: Future Directions of Research.* New York: Psychological Dimensions.

Pleck, J. H. (1979). Men's family work: Three perspectives and some new data. *Family Coordinator* 29(4):94–101.

Pleck, J. H. (1981). The work-family problem: Overloading the system.

In B. Forisha and B. Goldman (eds.), *Outsiders on the Inside: Women in Organizations*. Englewood Cliffs, NJ: Prentice-Hall.

Pleck, J. H. (1982). Husbands' paid work and family roles: Current research issues. In H. Lopata (ed.), *Research in the Interweave of Social Roles: Women and Men*, vol. 3. Greenwich, CT: JAI Press.

Pleck, J. H., and Brannon, R. (eds.) (1978a). Male roles and the male experience. *Journal of Social Issues* 34(1):1–199.

Pleck, J. H., and Brannon, R. (1978b). Male roles and the male experience: An introduction. *Journal of Social Issues* 34(1):1–4.

Pleck, J. H., and Lang, L. (1978). *Men's family role: Its nature and consequences*. Wellesley, MA: Working Paper, Wellesley College for Research on Women.

Pleck, J. H., and Rustad, M. (1980). Husbands' and wives' time in family work and paid work in the 1975-76 Study of Time Use. Wellesley, MA: Working Paper, Wellesley College Center for Research on Women.

Pleck, J. H., and Sawyer, J. (eds.) (1974). *Men and Masculinity*. Englewood Cliffs, NJ: Prentice-Hall (Spectrum Books).

Pleck, J. H., Staines, G., and Lang, L. (1980). Conflict between work and family life. *Monthly Labor Review* (March):29–32.

Plog, S. (1965). The disclosure of self in the United States and Germany. *Journal of Social Psychology* 65:193–203.

Podell, L. (1966). Sex role conflict. *Journal of Marriage and the Family* 28:163–165.

Preston, R. (1962). Reading achievement of German and American children. *School and Society* 90:350–354.

Price, W. H., and Whatmore, P. B. (1967a). Behavior disorders and patterns of crime among XYY males identified at a maximum security hospital. *British Medical Journal* 1:533–536.

Price, W. H., and Whatmore, P. B. (1967b). Criminal behavior and the XYY males. *Nature* 213:815.

Pulaski, M. (1970). Play as a function of toy structure and fantasy dispositions. *Child Development* 41:531–537.

Quadagno, D., Briscoe, R., and Quadagno, J. (1977). Effect of prenatal gonadal hormones on selected nonsexual behavior patterns: A critical assessment of the nonhuman and human literature. *Psychological Bulletin* 84:62–80.

Quinn, R., and Staines, G. (1978). *The 1977 Quality of Employment Survey*. Ann Arbor, Michigan: Institute for Social Research.

Rabban, M. (1950). Sex-role identification in young children in two diverse social groups. *Genetic Psychology Monographs* 42:81–158.

Radin, N. (1976). The role of the father in cognitive, academic, and intellectual development. In M. Lamb (ed.), *The Role of the Father in Child Development.* New York: Wiley.

Rapoport, R., and Rapoport R. N. (1971). *Dual-career Families.* London: Penguin.

Rebecca, M., Hefner, R., and Oleshansky, B. (1976). A model of sex-role transcendence. *Journal of Social Issues* 33: 197–206.

Redican, W., and Mitchell, G. (1973). A longitudinal study of paternal behavior in adult male rhesus monkeys: I. Observations on the first dyad. *Developmental Psychology* 8:135–136.

Reece, M. M. (1964). Masculinity and femininity: A factor analytic study. *Psychological Reports* 4:123–139.

Reich, C. (1970). *The Greening of America.* New York: Random House.

Renaud, H. (1950). *Clinical correlates of the masculinity-femininity scale of the Minnesota Multiphasic Personality Inventory.* Ph.D. dissertation, University of California, Berkeley. (Summarized in Sanford, 1964)

Retherford, R. (1975). *The Changing Sex Differential in Mortality.* Westport, CT: Greenwood Press.

Rieff, P. (1966). *The Triumph of the Therapeutic: Uses of Faith After Freud.* New York: Harper and Row.

Robinson, B., and Canaday, H. (1978). Sex-role behaviors and personality traits of male day care teachers. *Sex Roles* 4:853–865.

Robinson, J. P. (1977). *How Americans Use Time: A Social-Psychological Analysis of Everyday Behavior.* New York: Praeger.

Rohrer, J., and Edmonson, M. (1960). *The Eighth Generation.* New York: Harper.

Roper Organization. (1974). *The Virginia Slims American Women's Opinion Poll,* vol. III. New York: Roper Organization, Inc.

Rose, R. M., Holaday, J. W., and Bernstein, I. S. (1971). Plasma testosterone, dominance rank, and aggressive behavior in rhesus monkeys. *Nature* 231:366–368.

Rose, R. M., Gordon, T. P., and Bernstein, I. S. (1971). Plasma testosterone levels in the male rhesus: Influences of sexual and social stimuli. *Science* 178:643–645.

Rose, R. M., Gordon, T. P., and Bernstein, I. S. (1972). Sexual and social influences on testosterone secretion in the rhesus. *Psychosomatic Medicine* 34:473.

Rosen, L. (1969). Matriarchy and lower class Negro male delinquency. *Social Problems* 17:175–189.

Rosen, L. (1970). The broken home and male delinquency. In M. Wolfgang, L. Savitz, and N. Johnston (eds.), *The Sociology of Crime and Delinquency,* 2nd ed. New York: Wiley.

Rosenberg, B. (1971). Social roles and social control: Changing concepts of masculinity-femininity. In J. P. Scott and S. F. Scott (eds.), *Social Control and Social Change*. Chicago: University of Chicago Press.

Rosenberg, B., and Sutton-Smith, B. (1959). The measurement of masculinity and femininity in children. *Child Development* 30:373–380.

Rosenberg, B., and Sutton-Smith, B. (1960a). The measurement of masculine-feminine differences in play activities. *Journal of Genetic Psychology* 96:165–170.

Rosenberg, B., and Sutton-Smith, B. (1960b). A revised conception of masculine-feminine differences in play activities. *Journal of Genetic Psychology* 96:165–170.

Rosenberg, B., and Sutton-Smith, B. (1964). Ordinal position and sex-role identification. *Genetic Psychology Monographs* 70:297–328.

Rosenberg, B., Sutton-Smith, B., and Morgan, E. (1961). The use of opposite-sex scales as a measure of psychosexual deviancy. *Journal of Consulting Psychology* 25: 221–225.

Rosenfeld, H. (1969). Delinquent acting-out in adolescent males and the task of sexual identification. *Smith College Studies in Social Work* 40:1–29.

Rosenkrantz, P., Vogel, S., Bee, H., and Broverman, I. (1968). Sex-role stereotypes and self-concepts among college students. *Journal of Consulting and Clinical Psychology* 32:287–295.

Ross, D., and Ross, S. (1972). Resistance by preschool boys to sex-inappropriate behavior. *Journal of Educational Psychology* 63:342–346.

Ross, S. (1971). A test of generality of the effects of deviant preschool models. *Developmental Psychology* 4:262–267.

Rossi, A. (1977). A biosocial perspective on parenting. *Daedalus* 106(2):1–32.

Rothbart, M. K., and Maccoby, E. E. (1966). Parents' differential reactions to sons and daughters. *Journal of Personality and Social Psychology* 4:237–243.

Rudy, A. J., and Peller, R. (1972). Men's liberation. *Medical Aspects of Human Sexuality* 6 (September):84–85.

Ruitenbeek, H. (1967). *The Male Myth*. New York: Dell.

Russell, D. (1973). Rape and the masculine mystique. Paper presented to the American Sociological Association, New York, August.

Ryan, W. (1966). *Blaming the Victim*. New York: Vintage.

Rychlak, J., and Legerski, A. (1967). A sociocultural theory of appropriate sexual role identification and level of personality adjustment. *Journal of Personality* 35:31–49.

Rypma, C. (1976). The biological bases of the paternal response. *Family Coordinator* 25:335–340.

Sadker, D. A. (1977). *Being a Man: A Unit of Instructional Activities on Male Role Stereotyping*. Washington: US Government Printing Office.

Sanford, [R.] N. (1966). Masculinity-femininity in the structure of personality. In R. Sanford, *Self and Society*. New York: Atherton.

Sciarra, D. J. (1970). A study of the effects of male role models on children's behavior in a day care center. Ed.D. dissertation, University of Cincinnati, 1970. (*Dissertation Abstracts International* 3 (1971):4391–4392A; University Microfilms No. 71-6771.)

Sears, R., Maccoby, E., and Levin, H. (1957). *Patterns of Child Rearing*. New York: Harper and Row.

Sears, R., Rau, L., and Alpert, R. (1965). *Identification and Child Rearing*. Stanford: Stanford University Press.

Seeley, J., Sim, R., and Loosey, E. (1956). *Crestwood Heights*. New York: Simon and Schuster.

Segall, M. (1977). *Human Behavior and Public Policy: A Political Psychology*. New York: Pergamon.

Seifert, K. (1973). Some problems of men in child care center work. *Child Welfare* 102:167–171.

Sennett, R., and Cobb, J. (1972). *The Hidden Injuries of Class*. New York: Random House.

Sexton, P. C. (1970). *The Feminized Male: Classrooms, White Collars, and the Decline of Manliness*. New York: Vintage Books.

Seyfried, B., and Hendrick, C. (1973). When do opposites attract? When they are opposite in sex and sex-role attitudes. *Journal of Personality and Social Psychology* 25:15–20.

Sherriffs, A. C., and McKee, J. P. (1957). Qualitative aspects of beliefs about men and women. *Journal of Personality* 25:451–464.

Silverman, I. J., and Dinitz, S. (1974). Compulsive masculinity and delinquency. *Criminology* 11:499–515.

Silvern, L. (1977). Children's sex-role preferences: Stronger among girls than boys. *Sex Roles* 3:159–171.

Silvern, L., and Ryan, V. (1979). Self-rated adjustment and sex-typing on the Bem Sex-Role Inventory: Is masculinity the primary predictor of adjustment? *Sex Roles* 5:739–763.

Slater, P. (1963). Toward a dualistic theory of identification. *Merrill-Palmer Quarterly* 7:113–126.

Small, A., Biller, H., Gross, R., and Prochaska, J. (1977). Congruency of sex-role identification in normal and disturbed adolescent males. *Psychological Reports* 41:39–46.

Small, A., Biller, H., and Prochaska, J. (1975). Sex-role development and parental expectations among disturbed adolescent males. *Adolescence* 40:609–615.

Spence, J. T., and Helmreich, R. (1972a). The attitude toward women scale: An objective instrument to measure attitudes toward the rights and roles of women in contemporary society. *JSAS Catalog of Selected Documents in Psychology* 2:66.

Spence, J. T., and Helmreich, R. (1972b). Who likes competent women? Competence, sex-role congruence of interests, and subjects' attitudes toward women as determinants of interpersonal attraction. *Journal of Applied Social Psychology* 2:197–213.

Spence, J. T., and Helmreich, R. (1978). *Masculinity and Femininity: Their Psychological Dimensions, Correlates, and Antecedents.* Austin: University of Texas Press.

Spence, J. T., and Helmreich, R. (1979). On assessing "androgyny." *Sex Roles* 5:721–738.

Spence, J. T., Helmreich, R., and Stapp, J. (1973). A short version of the attitudes to women scale (AWS). *Bulletin of the Psychonomic Society* 2:21–220.

Spence, J. T., Helmreich, R., and Stapp, J. (1974). The personal attributes questionnaire: A measure of sex role stereotypes and masculinity-femininity. *JSAS Catalog of Selected Documents in Psychology* 4:43.

Spence, J. T., Helmreich, R., and Stapp, J. (1975a). Ratings of self and peers on sex role attributes and their relation to self-esteem and conceptions of masculinity and femininity. *Journal of Personality and Social Psychology* 32:29–39.

Spence, J. T., Helmreich, R., and Stapp, J. (1975b). Likability, sex-role congruence of interest, and competence: It all depends on how you ask. *Journal of Applied Social Psychology* 5:93–109.

Stacey, J., Bereaud, S., and Daniels, J. (1974). *And Jill Came Tumbling After: Sexism in American Education.* New York: Dell.

Staines, G. L., Pleck, J. H., Shepard, L. J., and O'Connor, P. (1978). Wives' employment status and marital adjustment: Yet another look. *Psychology of Women Quarterly* 3:90–120.

Staines, G. L., Seashore, S. E., and Pleck, J. H. (1979). Evaluating the quality of employment. *Economic Outlook USA* (Spring): 34–39.

Staples, R. (1971). The myth of the impotent black male. *Black Scholar* 2(10):2–9.

Staples, R. (1978). Masculinity and race: The dual dilemma of Black men. *Journal of Social Issues* 34(1):169–183.

Stearns, P. (1979). *Be a Man! Males in Modern Society.* New York: Holmes and Meier.

Stein, A., and Bailey, M. (1970). The socialization of achievement orientation in females. *Psychological Bulletin* 80:345–366.

Steinem, G. (1974). The myth of masculine mystique. In J. Pleck and J. Sawyer (eds.), *Men and Masculinity.* Englewood Cliffs, NJ: Prentice-Hall.

Steinmann, A., and Fox, D. J. (1966). Male-female perceptions of the female role in the United States. *Journal of Psychology* 64:265–276.

Steinmann, A., and Fox, D. J. (1974). *The Male Dilemma: How to Survive the Sexual Revolution.* New York: Jason Aronson.

Stockard, J., and Johnson, M. (1979). The social origins of male dominance. *Sex Roles* 5:199–218.

Stoller, R. (1968). *Sex and Gender: On the Development of Masculinity and Femininity.* New York: Science House.

Stone, I. F. (1974). Machismo in Washington. In J. Pleck and J. Sawyer (eds.), *Men and Masculinity.* Englewood Cliffs, NJ: Prentice-Hall.

Strodtbeck, F., Bezdek, W., and Goldhammer, W. (1970). Male sex role and response to a community problem. *Sociological Quarterly* 11:291–306.

Strodtbeck, F. and Creelan, P. (1968). Interaction linkage between family size, intelligence, and sex-role identity. *Journal of Marriage and the Family* 30:301–307.

Sturup, G. K. (1961). Castration of sex offenders. *Canadian Journal of Corrections* 3:250–258.

Sullerot, E. (1971). *Women, Society, and Change.* New York: McGraw-Hill.

Sutton-Smith, N., and Rosenberg, B. (1961). Sixty years of historical change in the game preferences of American children. *Journal of American Folklore* 74:17–46.

Tavris, C. (1973). Woman and man: Results of a survey. In C. Tavris (ed.), *The Female Experience.* Del Mar, CA: CRM Books.

Tavris, C. (1977). Masculinity. *Psychology Today* 10(8): (Jan.)35ff.

Terman, L. and Miles, C. (1936). *Sex and Personality.* New York: McGraw-Hill.

Thomas, E., and Biddle, B. (1966). The nature and history of role theory. In B. Biddle and E. Thomas (eds.), *Role Theory: Concepts and Research.* New York: Wiley.

Thompson, N., Schwartz, D., McCandless, B. and Edwards, D. (1973). Parent-child relationships and sexual identity in male and female homosexuals and heterosexuals. *Journal of Consulting and Clinical Psychology* 41:120–127.

Thune, J. (1949). Personality of weightlifters. *Research Quarterly* 20:296–306.

Tiger, L. (1969). *Men in Groups.* New York: Random House.

Tiller, P. (1958). Father absence and personality development in children of sailor families. *Nordisk Psykologi's Monographs* Series 9.

Toby, J. (1966). Violence and the masculine mystique: Some qualitative data. *Annals of the American Academy of Political and Social Science* 36(4):19–27.

Triplett, L. (1968). Elementary education—a man's world? *The Instructor* 78:50–52.

Trivers, R. (1972). Parental investment and sexual selection. In B. Cambell (ed.), *Sexual Selection and the Descent of Man 1871–1971*. Chicago: Aldine.

Turner, R. (1970). *Family Interaction*. New York: Wiley.

Tyler, L. (1968). Individual differences: Sex differences. In D. Sills (ed.), *International Encyclopedia of the Social Sciences*. New York: Macmillan.

Vincent, C. (1966). Implications of changes in male-female role expectations for interpreting M/F scores. *Journal of Marriage and the Family* 28:196–199.

Vontress, C. (1971). The black male personality. *Black Scholar* 2(10):10–17.

Wakefield, J., Sasek, J., Friedman, A., and Bowden, J. (1976). Androgyny and other measures of masculinity-femininity. *Journal of Consulting and Clinical Psychology* 44:766–770.

Waldron, I. (1976). Why do women live longer than men? *Journal of Human Stress* 2:1–13.

Ward, W. P. (1968). Variance of sex-role preference among boys and girls. *Psychological Reports* 23:467–470.

Ward, W. P. (1969). Process of sex role development. *Developmental Psychology* 9:163–168.

Ward, W. P. (1973). Patterns of culturally defined sex-role preference and parental imitation. *Journal of Genetic Psychology* 122:337–343.

Webb, A. P. (1963). Sex-role preferences and adjustment in early adolescents. *Child Development* 34:609–618.

Weinberg, G. (1973). *Society and the Healthy Homosexual*. New York: Anchor.

West, D. J. (1960). *Homosexuality*. Harmondsworth: Penguin.

West, D. J. (1977). *Homosexuality Re-examined*. Minneapolis: University of Minnesota Press.

West, D. J., Roy, C., and Nichols, F. (1978). *Understanding Sexual Attacks*. London: Heinemann.

Wetter, R. (1975). Levels of self-esteem associated with four sex role categories. In R. Bender (Chair), *Sex Roles: Masculine, Feminine, Androgynous, or None of the Above?* Symposium presented at the American Psychological Association, Chicago, 1975.

Wheeler, K., and Wheeler, M. (1974). The lack of male teachers—Does it hurt boys? *The Instructor* 83:24–25.

Whiting, B. B. (1965). Sex identity conflict and physical violence: A comparative study. *American Anthropologist* 67:123–146.

Whiting, J., W. M., Kluckhohn, C., and Anthony, A. (1958). The function of male initiation ceremonies at puberty. In E. Maccoby, T. Newcomb, and E. Hartley (eds.), *Readings in Social Psychology.* New York: Holt.

Whyte, W. F. (1943). *Street Corner Society.* Chicago: University of Chicago Press.

Whyte, W. H. (1956). *The Organization Man.* New York: Simon and Schuster.

Wilensky, H. (1961). Life cycle, work situation, and participation in formal associations. In R. Kleemeier (ed.), *Aging and Leisure.* New York: Oxford University Press.

Wilkinson, D. and Taylor, R. (eds.) (1977). *The Black Male.* Chicago: Nelson-Hall.

Williams, J. (1973). Sexual role identification and personality functioning in girls: A theory revisited. *Journal of Personality* 41:1–9.

Wilson, E. (1978). *On Human Nature.* Cambridge, MA: Harvard University Press.

Winick, C. (1968). *The New People: Desexualization in American Life.* New York: Pegasus.

Wolf, T. M. (1973). Effects of live modeled sex-inappropriate behavior in a naturalistic setting. *Developmental Psychology* 9:120–123.

Wolf, T. M. (1975). Response consequences to televised modeled sex-inappropriate play behavior. *Journal of Genetic Psychology* 127:35–44.

Woodbridge, D. (1973). Male teacher in the elementary school: Image-breaker or super-stereotype? *California Journal of Teacher Education* 1:42–47.

Woolfolk, R. and Richardson, F. (1978). *Sanity, Stress, and Survival.* New York: Signet.

Worell, J., and Worell, L. (1971). Supporters and opponents of women's liberation: Some personality correlates. Paper presented to the American Psychological Association, Washington, August.

Woronoff, I. (1962). Negro male identification problems. *Journal of Educational Sociology* 36:30–32.

Wylie, R. (1968). The present status of self theory. In E. Borgatta and W. Lambert (eds.), *Personality Theory and Research.* Chicago: Rand McNally.

Yalom, E., Green, R., and Fisk, N. (1973). Prenatal exposure to female hormones: Effect on psychosexual development in boys. *Archives of General Psychiatry* 28:554–561.

Yankelovich, D. (1974). *The New Morality: A Profile of American Youth in the '70's.* New York: McGraw-Hill.

Young, F. (1962). The function of male initiation ceremonies: A cross-cultural test of an alternative hypothesis. *American Journal of Sociology* 67:379–391.

Young, F. (1965). *Initiation Ceremonies: A Cross-Cultural Study of Status Dramatization.* Indianapolis, IN: Bobbs-Merrill.

Name Index